U.S Air Force Historical Study No. 107
(Formerly Army Air Forces Reference History No 7)
(Short Title - AAFRH-7)

THE ANTISUBMARINE COMMAND

=====Prepared by=====
ASSISTANT CHIEF OF AIR STAFF
INTELLIGENCE
HISTORICAL DIVISION

REFERENCE HISTORY

THE AAF ANTISUBMARINE COMMAND

(Short Title: AAFRH-7)

Prepared by
Assistant Chief of Air Staff, Intelligence
Historical Division
April 1945

CONTENTS

I	THE BACKGROUND	1
	U. S. preparations for antisubmarine defense . . .	1
	Army and Navy relations	11
	The origins of the Antisubmarine Command	17
II	THE ANTISUBMARINE CONTROVERSY	41
	The issues remain unsolved	41
	The strategic issue.	46
	The administrative issue	56
	The crisis of March 1943	62
	The problem before the Joint Chiefs of Staff . . .	68
	The Arnold-McNarney-McCain Agreement and the dissolution of the AAFAC	77
III	OPERATIONS	86
	The Battle of the Atlantic	86
	Operations in the Eastern Atlantic	94
	The Bay of Biscay	94
	The Moroccan Sea Frontier	114
	Operations in the Western Atlantic	130
	The Eastern and Gulf Sea Frontiers	130
	The Caribbean and South Atlantic areas	136
	The North Atlantic convoy route	146
	Antisubmarine Tactics and Attack Narratives	155
	Summary and Result of Antisubmarine Command Operations	188
IV	PROBLEMS OF LOGISTICS, RESEARCH COORDINATION, AND TRAINING	195
	Logistical problems	195
	Research coordination	205
	Training	215
V	CONCLUSION	225
	GLOSSARY	229
	NOTES	230

BIBLIOGRAPHICAL STATEMENT 263

APPENDIX

    1. Memorandum by Gen. George C. Marshall 264
    2. Attacks on U-boats by Antisubmarine
       Command aircraft 268
    3. Encounters with enemy aircraft 283
    4. Action status reports 292
    5. Station lists 300
    6. Key personnel, Hq AAFAC, 1 May 1943 304
    7. Order of Battle, Antisubmarine aircraft,
       for final week of August 1943 306

INDEX 308

ILLUSTRATIONS

	following
Map: Western Atlantic defense areas, 1 August 1942	3
Chart: Location of aircraft attacks on U-boats, 1 January-4 September 1942. From ASWORG Memo #20	35
Chart: Disposition and strength of 1st Bomber Command and AAFAC squadrons. From 7 MIR 43.	40
Chart: Summary of U-boat warfare, January-September 1943. From 8 MIR 43	86
Charts: Merchant vessels sunk in the Atlantic, September 1941-August 1943. From charts published at intervals in AAFAC Monthly Intelligence Reports, 1943	93
Activity in the Moroccan Sea Frontier Area	123
Location of Antisubmarine Command airfields	130
Mission, 480th Group, Port Lyautey	157
Operational diagrams	164
B-24, modified for antisubmarine operations	213

The AAF Antisubmarine Command

Chapter I
THE BACKGROUND

In the days immediately following the attack on Pearl Harbor, the armed forces of the United States had to face the threat of a similar catastrophe on their eastern defenses. The Germans fully appreciated the advantages of swift offensive action in the Atlantic. They knew that American participation in the war would depend on the free and rapid movement of supply. Consequently, with the entry of the United States into active warfare, the Battle of the Atlantic became a key point in German strategy. And the Germans possessed in their submarine fleet, already used with devastating effect in the eastern Atlantic, the means of prosecuting this "trade war" to the utmost. It is not yet clear why the U-boats took nearly a month to become operative in American waters, but it appears that a detachment of the German submarine fleet was sent to the western Atlantic as soon as practicable after the formal entry of the United States into the war.

On 31 December a Coast Guard cutter reported a periscope in Portland Channel, and on 7 January an Army plane sighted a submarine off the coast of New Jersey. On that same day the Navy reported the presence of a fleet of U-boats in the waters south of Newfoundland. The SS *Cyclops* was sunk off Nova Scotia on 11 January; three days later the tanker *Norness* went down southeast of Montauk Point, Long Island. These sinkings merely head the tragically long list of similar losses which served almost more than the disaster of Pearl Harbor to bring home to the American public the grim realities of total war. Here was not only a drain on supply lines of our war effort, perilously thin at best, but an attack virtually on our Atlantic seaboard. In the remaining 17 days of January, 13 more ships sank in the North Atlantic Naval Coastal Frontier.[1]

The situation rapidly became desperate. During the 76 days following the sinking of the *Norness*, 53 ships amounting to over 300,000 gross tons had gone down. With March sinkings at an annual rate of over 2,000,000 tons, the morale of merchant crews showed signs of rapid deterioration, and insurance companies had ceased writing marine insurance.[2] Worst of all was the fact that, prior to May 1942, the enemy submarines operated with relative impunity in American coastal waters.

The question thus arose: what sort of antisubmarine defense could be brought to bear against this threat to the entire U. S. strategy in the Atlantic? According to general defense plans, which will be discussed in some detail a little later, the Navy had assumed responsibility for operations beyond the coast line, leaving to Army aircraft only a supporting, emergency role in coastal defense. Steps had been taken to provide the means of cooperation between the services, resulting in the completion of a joint control and information center at New York 4 days after war was declared.[3] Nevertheless, the shock of Pearl Harbor found the Navy quite unable to carry on the offshore patrol necessary to the fulfillment of its mission. The

Commander of the North Atlantic Naval Coastal Frontier[1] (later, Eastern Sea Frontier), on whom fell naturally the initial responsibility for countering the submarine menace, had at his disposal on 7 December 1941 approximately 20 surface vessels, including 4 PY boats, 4 SC boats, one 165-foot Coast Guard cutter, six 125-foot Coast Guard cutters, 2 PG boats, and 3 Eagle boats to patrol the 1,200-mile coast line from Maine to Key West. Of this force he wrote to COMINCH on 22 December: "There is not a single vessel available that an enemy submarine could not out-distance when operating on the surface. In most cases the guns of these vessels would be out-ranged by those of the submarine."[5] Nor was it possible to augment the surface forces rapidly enough to make antisubmarine patrol, even convoy, practicable.[6] The only destroyers available were those which happened to be in the ESF on fleet duties. In actual practice an average of only two destroyers per day was available for use. Repeated requests made to COMINCH for reinforcements apparently could not be met. For example, on 30 March 1942 the Commander, ESF sent a message in which he requested additional destroyers because four submarines had been sighted off Cape Hatteras and two more were believed to be operating there, while all except one of the four destroyers in the area were searching for survivors of a lost ship or were refueling or were under repair. COMINCH replied on 31 March briefly: "Your knowledge of other demands for DD's as imperative as your own is not given sufficient credit in your [message] 302218."[7]

If the surface forces were wholly inadequate, the naval air arm was little stronger. In December, the naval planes at the disposal of the Commander, ESF totaled 103. Of these, however, the majority were trainers or utility ships; only one was listed as a bomber, although 9 were classified as patrol or torpedo bombers.[8] A month later the picture appeared little if at all brighter. Of the 63 aircraft available for duty between Salem and Elizabeth City (including four lighter-than-air ships at Lakehurst), only 49 were actually in commission. Of these, the majority could carry only one depth bomb.[9] Adm. Adolphus Andrews, Commander, ESF summed up the air situation in words reminiscent of those he used to describe the paucity of surface vessels. He wrote to COMINCH on 14 January 1942: "There are no effective planes attached to the frontier, First, Third, Fourth, or Fifth Naval District capable of maintaining long-range seaward patrols."[10] Nor did he receive much more comfort from higher headquarters on this topic than on that of the extra destroyers. In reply to his urgent request for air reinforcement he received the reply that allocation of additional air forces was "dependent on future production."[11] Here, as elsewhere in the early days of 1942, the demands for men and equipment were great but the supply small.

So the burden for antisubmarine patrol fell mainly on the Army Air Forces whose units had been neither trained nor equipped for that specific task, but were nevertheless better able than the Navy's air arm to present a menacing front to the enemy. As soon as the news of Pearl Harbor arrived, the Commander of the North Atlantic

Naval Coastal Frontier requested the Commanding General of the Eastern Defense Command to undertake offshore patrols with all available aircraft. On the afternoon of 8 December 1941, units of the I Bomber Command began overwater patrols,[12] and for nearly 10 months that command bore the brunt of the air war against the U-boats. But it was a motley array of aircraft that the Bomber Command assembled in December and January to meet the submarine threat. Almost on the same day on which it was called upon to undertake overwater patrol duties it was stripped of the best trained of its tactical units for missions on the West Coast and for overseas assignment.[13] Every available Army plane in the First Air Force capable of carrying a bomb load was drafted to augment what was left of I Bomber Command.* As a result of these frantic efforts approximately 100 two-engine aircraft of various sizes and types were assembled and placed at the disposal of the naval commander. To this force, likened by one observer to the taxicab army by means of which the French attempted, in 1914, to stem the German advance, the I Air Support Command* added substantial aid in the way of reconnaissance.[14] Admiral Andrews described the operation of these Army air units, on 14 January 1942, as follows:[15]

> The Army Air Support Command is operating during daylight hours patrols in single-motored land observation planes extending about forty miles offshore from Portland, Maine, to Wilmington, N. C. These planes are not armed and carry only sufficient fuel for flights of between two or three hours. The pilots are inexperienced in the type of work they are endeavoring to do. Not more than ten of these observation planes are in the air along the Coastal Frontier at any one time.

* The designation "1st" was used prior to September 18, 1942.

The First Bomber Command has been maintaining, since the week of 7 December 1941, patrols from Westover Field, Mass.; Mitchel Field, N. Y.; and Langley Field, Va.; and as of 11 January 1942 are commencing patrols from Bangor, Maine. These patrols, averaging three planes each, have extended, weather permitting and according to the type of plane, to a maximum distance of six hundred miles to sea. Two flights each day are being made from the aforementioned fields. The First Bomber Command has been utilizing approximately half of its available equipment in order to maintain these patrols, at the expense of a striking force which could be called upon in case of enemy attack.

It was a creditable effort, all things considered, but the Army forces were themselves pitifully inadequate. By 31 January 1942, the I Air Support Command reported 114 planes, of which 93 were in commission; the I Bomber Command numbered 119 planes of which only 46 were carried as in commission.[16]

If the forces available during December and January for antisubmarine activity were too small for the job, they were even weaker in equipment and organization. Hunting submarines is a highly specialized business, as all those concerned found out during the next few months. Yet little had been done prior to the outbreak of hostilities to develop the specialized technique and materials required to carry it on successfully. Except for the establishment of a Joint Control and Information Center little had been done to set up the system of communication and intelligence necessary to cope adequately with such a highly mobile, not to say illusive, enemy. Fortunately, the U-boats did not begin operations in U. S. waters for nearly a month, which gave the I Bomber Command time to organize some sort of wire communication to all its bases, to establish an intelligence system through which information could be relayed from Bomber Command headquarters to the squadron operations room, and from Bomber Command airplanes to headquarters.[17] By the end of January, however, the problem of transmitting intelligence remained a vexing one.

The Army suffered also from poorly equipped planes and inadequately trained personnel. Charges to this effect were frequently made and were well justified. Most of the units involved in the antisubmarine war were, at this early date, still in a training status, and those best trained had been taken away for service in the West.[18] In addition, prewar agreements had assigned overwater operations to the Navy and had placed restrictions on Army overwater flying.[19] So it is scarcely surprising that the Army planes entered on their adopted task with demolition bombs instead of depth charges and with crews who were ill-trained in naval identification or in the best method of attacking submarines. The aircraft used against the U-boats were generally unsuited to that kind of work. All, with the exception of a squadron of B-17's, were of relatively short range and limited carrying capacity. And all, of course, as yet lacked special detection equipment. The old B-18, though obsolescent, proved to be the most useful in the early months, but even they were at first scarce.[20]

Those in charge of the antisubmarine war attacked these problems wholeheartedly. They revived the training program to convert crews, hitherto accustomed only to high-altitude bombings, to the intricacies of low-level attack on submerged targets. They adapted the aircraft as fast as the materials became available and the necessary research could bear fruit. As operations continued and experience was collected, it became evident that successful warfare against U-boats demanded improved methods of joint control in order to dispatch both air and surface forces to the scene of a sighting as rapidly as the situation required. Here the British, who had accumulated a good deal of experience in this sort of work, contributed vitally to the improvement of the joint control system. With the help of several experienced liaison officers, sent to America for the purpose, a new "control room" was projected which led to more effective cooperation between Army and Navy forces. The original control room permitted "joint" operations, but the two services worked independently in different parts of the same building, each maintaining its own situation plot and receiving intelligence from different sources. There was little interchange of information or methods.[21]

By the end of March it is possible to notice very real improvement in the situation. Though the U-boats continued in increasing numbers to exact an increasing toll of merchant shipping, they also met increasing opposition in the coastal waters. Operational hours flown by AAF planes in March were well over double those flown in January.[22] Relatively few attacks were made even yet, and their quality left much to be desired.[23] But the submarines were being forced more and more to submerge, which prevented as free hunting on their part as they had formerly enjoyed. A very few Army planes were beginning to be equipped with radar, another step, though a small one, in the right direction. In March, too, the first offshore patrol missions were flown by the Civil Air Patrol. Although totally unsuited in both training and equipment to antisubmarine warfare, these auxiliary units were able to assume some of the burden of reconnaissance flying.[24]

Many difficulties of course remained. More and better-trained personnel, more and better-equipped aircraft, a better communications system--these were only the more obvious requirements in the Army antisubmarine force. Much more deeply rooted was the problem of jurisdiction which arose out of the anomalous position of the AAF units engaged in antisubmarine operations. The I Bomber Command was, in fact, waging full-scale antisubmarine war, yet it enjoyed no correspondingly adequate legal position. It was still theoretically acting in an emergency capacity, in support of Naval forces, and might at any time be withdrawn to its normal duties of bombardment. Indeed, training had to be conducted literally on two levels, both for low-level antisubmarine attacks and for high-level bombing in connection with coastal defense.[25] Worse still, no system of unified command had been set up specifically for that type of joint operations peculiar to antisubmarine warfare. Prior to 26 March 1942, in fact, even the command relationship existing between Bomber Command and the Eastern Sea Frontier remained indefinite, the former serving without specific directives under the "operational control" of the latter.[26] Any decision on these questions of jurisdiction would necessarily have involved a radical review of the existing relationship between the services, especially in their relation to the air arm. And some decision was obviously necessary if antisubmarine operations were not to founder hopelessly in a maze of overlapping jurisdictional boundaries and tortuous command channels. It was a kind of fighting that demanded extreme mobility on the part of the antisubmarine forces and almost instantaneous transmission of intelligence if the enemy, itself extremely mobile and under closely integrated command, were to be successfully engaged.

Almost from the beginning it began to appear that, if the Army Air Forces were to continue in the antisubmarine business, their units engaged in that work would have to be organized into a specially trained and equipped command with antisubmarine operations as its sole duty. Such a prospect at once raised a family of problems. In the first place, who, Army or Navy, should control this command? Secondly, should it be deployed defensively, in support of the fleet, primarily for the protection of the shipping lanes, or as a highly mobile force capable of carrying the battle aggressively to the enemy wherever the latter might be located? On these two grounds, the jurisdictional and the strategic, there arose a long and intensive controversy, a debate which centered on the creation, organization, and deployment of an AAF antisubmarine command, but which involved issues of much broader scope. In order, therefore, to understand these issues and to explain the confusion as a result of which the Army Air Forces found itself engaged in the submarine hunt, it will be necessary to review in some detail the evolution of policy governing the use of the air arm in overwater operations.

Ever since the advent of air power the Army and the Navy had argued over its control. Each service took a logical enough position. To the Army, control of land-based aircraft whether operating over land or water should be its responsibility. To the Navy, it seemed equally natural that operations over water, against seaborne targets, should be a naval responsibility. It all depended on where the respective arguments started: if it was a question of the primary mission of land-based aircraft, as a result of which they had been developed as such, the Army had a strong position; if it became a question of where the actual operations took place, whether as a result of the primary mission of the forces or merely ancillary to it, the Navy was well able to claim control over seaward aviation. No one disputed the Navy's control over seaplanes and carrier-based aircraft which operated clearly as an arm of the fleet. Actually, logic had very little to do with the problem. Since the air was a medium which extended over both land and water, arguments concerning its control could drift more or less at will. So it all became a question which would have to be answered either arbitrarily, by some competent authority, or with reference to some factors contingent upon the tactical or strategic situation. As things turned out, it was answered by both.

As early as 1920 it had been recognized that, in providing an air arm for both services, there lay a serious danger of duplicating installations and equipment. In that year Congress had enacted that Army aviation should control all aerial operations from land bases and that naval aviation should control all such activity attached to the Fleet, including the maintenance of such shore installations as were necessary for operation, experimentation, and training connected with the Fleet.[27]

Joint Action of the Army and Navy, 1935 (FTP-155) did much to clarify the relationship between the services.[28] The Navy not only retained control of aviation connected with the Fleet, but was given responsibility for all inshore and offshore patrol for the purpose of protecting shipping and defending the coastal frontier.[29] It was further stated that Army aircraft might temporarily execute Navy functions in support of, or in lieu of, Navy forces, and, conversely, that Navy aircraft might be called upon to support land operations.[30] In neither case should any restriction be placed by one service on the freedom of the other to use its power against the enemy should the need arise.[31] Each service was declared responsible for providing the aircraft needed for the proper performance of its primary function: in the Army's case, the conduct of air operations over land and such air operations over the sea as were incident to the accomplishment of Army functions; in the case of the Navy, conduct of operations over the sea and such air operations over the land as were incident to the accomplishment of Navy functions.[32]

All of which left the responsibility for the conduct of seaward patrols and the protection of shipping pretty definitely up to the Navy. But no formal agreement could be expected to end discussion on the matter, especially since the particular tactical situation was likely to change frequently. It was still, for example, an open question whether the Navy should control all air operations in frontier defense or whether it should control only those operations specifically in support of the Fleet. Naval spokesmen claimed that unity of command should be vested in whichever service held paramount importance in a given situation. Then, assuming that naval preeminence existed over land and air forces in all coastal defense, they claimed that unity of command in such operations should rest with the Navy. The Army, sensing a train of logic which might prove ruinous to its control of air forces, raised its voice in protest. The assumption of naval preeminence in coastal defense it declared unsound, witness the case of Alaska where land-based bombers were likely to be the principal arm employed. Furthermore, since most situations in which the Navy would be called upon for defensive operations would be ones in which the air forces would also be present, owing to their mobility and striking power, the Navy would, according to this argument, gain control of Army air forces, wherever the latter were most likely to be used in a tactical situation. This, the Army felt, would lead ultimately to complete naval control of the Army air forces.[33] In short, the Army felt that the primary mission of its air arm was not support of the Navy, however likely such support might be in frontier defense.

When it came time to implement plans for frontier defense, it was clear that the Navy held the responsibility for protection of coastwise shipping and for the conduct of offshore patrols. And this province was guarded jealously.[34] Units of the GHQ Air Force had been effectively discouraged from undertaking practice reconnaissance flights over water beyond the 100-mile limit, and their part in joint Army-Navy exercises had been strictly limited to a supporting role against a carrier-borne or shore attack;[35] this despite the fact that plans explicitly made the GHQ Air Force responsible for whatever reconnaissance was essential to its combat efficiency in operations along the coast, regardless of whether or not the Fleet were present. Without an air arm trained in long- or even medium- range reconnaissance over water, the seaboard would clearly become vulnerable to submarine attack. Yet the Navy had done very little to prepare for antisubmarine air patrol by any type of aircraft, much less by long-range types. Joint Action had not only implied that this function belonged to the Navy, but had stated that it was up to the Navy to provide and maintain the equipment and installations necessary to the fulfillment of that function. Yet 7 December 1941 found the North Atlantic Naval Coastal Frontier practically without effective planes capable of conducting long-range seaward patrols, and with pathetically few surface craft capable of chasing a submarine.

Fortunately, some preparations had been made for joint operations. A "joint" control room had almost been completed and provision had been made for I Bomber Command and I Air Support Command to operate on seaward patrol missions wherever requested to do so by the naval authority.[36] It was in fulfillment of these plans that the I Bomber Command undertook seaward patrol duty promptly on 8 December. But even this meager air force had been equipped not for antisubmarine activity but for normal bombardment action, and had been systematically discouraged from increasing its knowledge of overwater flying.

Every contingency, including enemy submarine activity in the coastal shipping lanes, had been considered in <u>Joint Action</u>.[37] Yet nothing had been planned specifically to counter a campaign by enemy submarine forces. Training exercises off the Atlantic coast had apparently envisaged a surface task force, supported by carrier-based aircraft, as the only likely form of enemy action.[38] The British had also failed at first to take the U-boat threat seriously, feeling that it should not be relatively as great in this as in the last war. After the Germans had built submarine bases on the west coast of France, however, the British answered this increased menace by creating the Coastal Command, a separate RAF agency under the operational control of the Admiralty. No such plan had been laid or agencies established in the United States.

By the time the German submarines began to appear in American waters, the idea had become pretty well fixed that long- and medium-range land-based bombers would be, if not the backbone of the anti-submarine campaign, at least an indispensible part of its composition, especially in view of the fact that operations from ice-bound north Atlantic bases would be limited virtually to aircraft of that type.[39] In a very natural effort to implement the Navy's responsibility for offshore patrol, Admiral King at once requested that 200 B-24's and 400 B-25's be allocated from future production of Army-type planes for Navy use, the total number to be made available by 1 July 1943.[40] This request did little to improve relations between the services, coming as it did on top of a long discussion of the problem of jurisdiction over coastal defense operations, and at a time when the Army was confronted by urgent obligations in half a dozen theaters, all demanding heavy-and medium-bombardment planes. The Navy received part, though not all, of the Army-type allocations asked for, but had to be content for the time being with the forces supplied mainly by the I Bomber Command and related units. Considerable effort was made to increase the number of aircraft allocated by the Army to antisubmarine activity, but it was felt in the War Department that diversion beyond that already made would seriously jeopardize other equally important projects.[41]

And so, from the very first, the Army's participation in the antisubmarine campaign became involved in, and at times overshadowed by, the issues of jurisdiction and organization which it had raised. The Navy request for Army-type planes raised again, or rather reinvigorated, the standing controversy concerning control of the air arm. To Admiral King's request, General Arnold replied that for the Navy to build up a force of land-based aircraft would lead to a duplication of equipment, maintenance, and supply that would eventually "deny the essential differences between armies and navies."[42] Some felt that, if Army aircraft were so vital a part of coastal defense, unity of command over joint operations in the coastal frontiers should be vested in the Army.[43] This notion, of course, ran counter to the established policy as outlined in Joint Action, and would in any case have lacked the support of the Navy. General Arnold proposed to settle the question in a practical compromise. In a letter to Admiral King, 9 May 1942, he wrote: "to meet the present situation, I propose to recommend the establishment of a Coastal Command, within the Army Air Corps which will have for its purpose operations similar to the Coastal Command, RAF," operating "when necessary under the control of the proper Naval authority."[44] The virtues of such an organization would, he felt, be many: it would not only do the job, it would also have the flexibility necessary for antisubmarine action, and could readily be decreased as the need decreased, the units then simply reverting to normal bombardment duty without becoming stranded wastefully in a naval program which left no place for them. In this proposal General Arnold pointed the way to the settlement finally adopted in the creation of the AAF Antisubmarine Command.

Many other influences were tending in the same direction by May of 1942. Above all, of course, was the ugly fact that in that month sinkings in the sea frontiers had risen to a new and terrifying point. Something had obviously to be done to improve the organization of the antisubmarine campaign. Closely related was the fact that the enemy had shifted his strategy and had once more caught the U. S. defenses badly prepared. Most of the May sinkings had occurred in the Gulf and Caribbean areas. Scarcely adequate to protect shipping in the ESF, the existing organization of antisubmarine operations proved quite inadequate to cope with a greatly extended area of activity.

In answer to a request for reinforcement from the Commander, Gulf Sea Frontier, a few B-18's were sent south, and shortly after, on 26 May, Maj. Gen. Follett Bradley, Commanding General of the First Air Force, created the Gulf Task Force.[45] This unit was to control all aircraft of the First Air Force which were operating, according to the agreement of the Joint Chiefs of Staff for such situations,[46] under the operational control of the Gulf Sea Frontier. For a time located at Charleston, S. C., the new headquarters was finally set up at Miami.

The situation in the Gulf and Caribbean areas had, however, become so serious that General Arnold requested the Third Air Force to use certain of its units for antisubmarine patrol during their regular overwater training missions.[47] General Frank responded by advising the placing of the appropriate units under the operational control of the Gulf Task Force and the routing of training missions over sea and Gulf shipping lanes. This plan was approved on 1 July, and steps were at once taken to put it into effect.[48] Meanwhile, arrangements were made to establish a combined operations center at Miami, to be built on the general pattern being laid down for similar purposes in New York City. This project was initiated early in June.[49]

Considerable progress was made in relocating units to meet the expanded and fluid nature of the campaign. Beginning in January with operations from four states only, from Bangor, Maine, to Langley Field, Va., the I Bomber Command by September 1942 was operating in seven states, from Westover Field, Mass., to Galveston, Tex.[50]

Despite this energetic effort to meet a rapidly changing situation with complicated machinery constructed essentially on static principles, the extension of AAF antisubmarine operations emphasized the need for reform in the existing system of joint command. Only recently had any attempt been made to clarify even this existing system. Prior to 26 March 1942, units of the I Bomber Command and the I Air Support Command had been operating under the control of the Commander, Eastern Sea Frontier, but the system rested only on very general definitions set forth in <u>Joint Action</u>. And there had been some talk of "mutual cooperation" rather than "unity of command."[51] On that date the Joint Chiefs of Staff sent a message to the commanding generals of the defense commands which read, in extract, as follows:[52]

> Pending the reaching of agreements as to terms under which unity of command will be exercised . . . unity of command as set forth in . . . Joint Action of the Army and Navy, 1935, is hereby vested in sea Frontier Commands over all Navy forces duly allocated thereto and over all Army air units allocated by defense commanders over the sea for the protection of shipping and for antisubmarine and other operations . . . Defense commanders will allocate Army air units on full time basis but may rotate them in not less than two week periods as requisite for essential training. . . .

This seemed a convenient temporary arrangement, but in reality it did nothing to meet the administrative and tactical problems. It merely made more definite what had hitherto been left studiously vague.

The fact was that the two services were not organized for this type of joint control. Command boundaries overlapped: the areas assigned to the First Air Force and the I Bomber Command extended beyond the Eastern Sea Frontier into the territory of the Gulf Sea

Frontier, and the Third Air Force had to share the operational control of the Commander, Gulf Sea Frontier with the First Air Force. Worse than that, joint operations involved two complete sets of headquarters through which orders must be filtered before reaching the combat unit.

General McNarney described the command situation in April as follows:[53]

> At present the Bomber Command is allocated to the Eastern Sea Frontier for operational control. The Civil Air Patrol is under the Air Support Command for operational control. The Air Support Command is under the Bomber Command for operational control. The Bomber Command is operating under a directive from the Navy, which was a two page, seven paragraph letter, which was very verbose.

He might have added that the Bomber Command was under the First Air Force and the Eastern Defense Command for administration, if any further complication were desired.

Desired or not, further complication did enter the picture when in May it became necessary to extend operations into the Gulf and Caribbean areas. The I Bomber Command was still the only agency equipped and situated to provide the Army air coverage necessary for successful antisubmarine activity. It was therefore essential to extend its operation southward to include the entire EDC and that part of the Southern Defense Command which borders on the Gulf of Mexico. In this area I Bomber Command operated under the control of the Gulf Sea Frontier. To augment this over-extended force, some aircraft had been loaned by the Third Air Force to the ESF and GSF commanders for patrol purposes. These units, however, operated under the direct control of the Bomber Command, which retained responsibility for Army antisubmarine patrol in the coastal frontiers. The plight of these few pilots, who were connected administratively or operationally with two defense commands, two sea frontiers, two air forces, and an antisubmarine bomber command, simply represents the reductio ad absurdum of the command situation.[54]

The trouble was obvious. A multiplicity of headquarters would have slowed up the functioning of any dependent organization. It was all the more serious in its effects on antisubmarine operations which depended above all else on rapid coordination and extreme mobility. The division of the sea frontiers into districts and subdistricts had been enough of a handicap especially in view of the habit of thinking in terms of rigid boundaries or "chop lines" which seemed to be an ingrained part of the naval administrative mind. Yet local arrangement had been made to mitigate this handicap. Army air units were apparently not attached to district naval commanders, a practice which, if adopted, would have ruined the effectiveness of the Army antisubmarine forces. The real trouble came when aircraft were required in other sea frontiers, all of which were under COMINCH, but without liaison or means of rapid inter-communication.[55] Yet the antisubmarine campaign depended on the ability of air striking units to follow the submarines wherever they might go and to change stations rapidly.

Unity of command, then, became the first prerequisite for improved operations. The antisubmarine campaign needed other things:

better equipment, a better training program, a better communication system, and an organization devoted completely to the task of hunting U-boats, unimpeded by competing claims on its services.[56] Above all, it required mobility of forces. But all these needs were subordinate to, and in one way or another dependent upon, the attaining of unity of command.

With these needs in mind, and impelled by the desperate shipping situation, the War Department began, in May, to take concerted action to improve the situation. On the 20th of that month, Maj. Gen. Dwight D. Eisenhower, then Assistant Chief of Staff, OPD, directed the commanding generals of the AAF and the EDC to do everything in their power to improve the antisubmarine activity being undertaken by the First Air Force. Specifically he directed that all available planes on the eastern seaboard be fitted with bomb racks and all B-18 aircraft be equipped with radar, even at the expense of prior allocations. All necessary bases were to be made available, and the EDC was to cooperate with the First Air Force in the solution of problems of supply, maintenance, and communications for the antisubmarine squadrons. An organization was to be established "with the least possible delay" for the purpose of engaging in the development of antisubmarine weapons, tactics, and techniques in cooperation with all agencies working toward a similar end. A training unit was also authorized in order to make available crews trained in the use of these devices and techniques.

Finally, General Arnold was requested to reorganize the I Bomber Command in such a way as to "fulfill the special requirements of antisubmarine and allied air operations, in consonance with the Army responsibility in operating in support of, or in lieu of naval forces for protection of shipping."[57]

This action on the part of the War Department General Staff marks the beginning of plans for a separate, mobile air striking force, organized within the Army for the sole purpose of hunting submarines. In taking this action the Army in effect accepted the responsibility for a job not generally considered part of its function. No longer considered simply as an emergency, short-term measure, the participation of AAF units in the antisubmarine war now became admittedly part of the Army program. And, in the circumstances, the Army found itself in a relatively strong position. Its air force had the weapons, and had already taken part in antisubmarine activity for nearly 5 months during which time it had developed some sort of organization, some special techniques, and many ambitious plans.

Plans of a more or less specific nature soon followed. General Eisenhower had stated in his directive that "although unity of command is vested in the Navy, it is felt that the Army must be prepared to submit recommendations and to take every action to make antisubmarine warfare fully effective." He had requested that General Bradley and Brig. Gen. Westside T. Larson, Commanding General, I Bomber Command, confer with the Assistant Chief of Staff and present plans for future development.[58]

Plans had for some weeks been evolving in the minds of the AAF officials concerned. In general they had been shaped along the lines suggested in General Eisenhower's directive: a separate organization was to be created for the purpose of waging antisubmarine warfare, with mobility and striking power as its chief characteristic, and with an experimental agency acting as an auxiliary for developing new techniques and for training personnel in their use. But they were naturally more specific and somewhat more radical in their color than that directive called for. Through all this initial planning can be seen the strong influence of the British Coastal Command. And naturally so, because that command had pioneered since the beginning of the war in antisubmarine warfare under circumstances roughly analogous to those in which the American forces found themselves in 1942. A few officers from the British Coastal Command had been detailed to advise the I Bomber Command in its early efforts to combat the U-boats, and their influence was in many respects decisive.[59] In February, Wing Commander P. F. Canning, RAF, had outlined the Coastal Command system of operational control as a pattern for a similar organization modified to suit the situation in the western Atlantic. Admittedly far from perfect, this system bore the authority of 4 years' experience in joint action for the specific purpose of antisubmarine warfare.[60] In March, Wing Commander S. R. Libles, RAF, submitted a report on his observations of antisubmarine activity in which he stressed the need for a clearer allocation of responsibility between Army and Navy, for closer cooperation between the headquarters involved, and for a decreased emphasis on rigid command boundaries. All these factors pointed toward the ultimate solution in the form of a separate command, presumably shaped on lines similar to those of the British Coastal Command.[61]

General Eisenhower had suggested that a conference on antisubmarine measures be held in Washington. In preparation for this meeting, Generals Bradley and Larson drew up and discussed various plans. Although a detailed critique of these proposals is unnecessary, some of the points highlighted in them clarify the train of thought that led to the establishment of the Antisubmarine Command. A précis of the principal plans follows:

1. The basic principle upon which successful antisubmarine warfare must rest is unity of command. The submarine possesses great mobility; successful action against it necessitates elimination of overlapping jurisdiction in order that prompt action may be facilitated. Command channels must be direct, and the "maddening and intolerable" system of verbal orders from one office and written orders from another must be eliminated. Mobility is essential. A successful antisubmarine force must be able to move units from point to point to meet the requirements of a shifting strategic situation.

2. A "Coastal Air Force" should be organized with the I Bomber Command as its nucleus. The chain of command then would be from Commanding General, AAF, to Commanding General, Coastal Air Force, to Coastal Air Force Controller to Squadron Commander. An operations control room would be set up at each base, and steps would be taken

to establish adequate coordination of intelligence with the Navy. The Navy would, however, no longer exercise direct operational control over Army planes, because all orders would pass through Headquarters, Coastal Air Force.

3. In the Coastal Air Force, the area of operation would be unlimited and not confined by existing boundaries of commands having other missions to perform.

4. A chain of bases should be set up on the Atlantic coast to operate directly under the Coastal Air Force. Weather, intelligence, communications, maintenance and housing and all housekeeping facilities would be provided by the bases, leaving the striking forces to consist of combat and key personnel only. The combat squadrons would therefore be "in reality mobile."[62]

Another plan, evidently prepared by General Bradley for use in the conference with General Eisenhower, proposed that the I Bomber Command, or similar organization, be charged with the protection of all coastal shipping, the operation to be under the direct control of the Commanding General of the First Air Force. Not only would all Army aircraft thus be placed under an Army officer, but all Navy and Marine heavier-than-air aircraft allocated to antisubmarine activity would also be under the I Bomber Command for operational control, only dirigibles (a waning force) remaining under the Navy.

> All other coordinations between Army and Navy to be by cooperation rather than by unity of command, as is now the case between Eastern Defense Command and Eastern Sea Frontier. If operational control by Navy must be continued, a single Navy commander, not three, should be responsible for the entire East and Gulf Coasts and Bermuda, and exercise operational control or unity of command over those Army Air Forces which are allotted to him.[63]

In short, the Navy had been relegated to a position of remote and shadowy authority. But they left no doubt on certain other points: the need for unity of command, a more direct chain of command, greater potential mobility, and a continued and increased participation of Army air forces in the "trade war," all of which depended in some way on the creation of a separate command, organized, trained, and equipped for the purpose.

Running through this entire discussion there may be discerned an already well-defined strategic doctrine, namely, that, in anti-submarine warfare, defensive measures, though essential, can never destroy the U-boat menace, but must be supplemented by a vigorous offensive campaign. The authors of the plans outlined above considered the protection of convoys by aircraft "a last ditch defense." Such purely defensive tactics were, and should be, the first priority, but they were "the smaller part of the total effort necessary to force the enemy from our coastal waters." A well-coordinated offensive by aircraft and surface vessels could drive the enemy craft a considerable distance from the coast or restrict their operations to such an extent that their results would become negligible. Admittedly the airplane as it was then equipped failed to possess the necessary killing power to destroy the U-boat; but it did have great searching power, and was quite able to keep a submarine submerged so long that its effectiveness decreased.[64] Whenever a sinking occurred or the presence of a submarine was detected, long-range planes should be sent to that area for intensive search. Constant patrol should be conducted within 300 miles of the coastline.[65] Even if these measures failed to sink a single submarine, it was argued, they would keep the enemy submerged and so require him to use so much time going to and from his bases that his operating period would materially be shortened. Moreover, the submarines could thus be prevented from concentrating rapidly and effectively on convoys, and the morale of their crews would be seriously impaired.[66]

Here again the example of the RAF Coastal Command exercised a profound influence. Although it had apparently taken the Admiralty some time to revise its doctrines to such an extent that it could incorporate within them an air striking force organized for an aggressive antisubmarine campaign,[67] still that was the end finally attained. Two of the cardinal principles governing the British antisubmarine warfare were stated by Air Marshal Joubert:[68] first, close cooperation between sea and air forces, between Admiralty and Coastal Command; and secondly, constant offensive action. He advised that

> while a certain amount of close escort of convoys, particularly when threatened, is a necessary feature of air operations, the main method of defeating the U-boat is to seek and strike. The greater portion of the air available should always be engaged in the direct attack of U-boats and the smallest possible number in direct protection of shipping. Our experience is that a purely defensive policy only leads to heavy loss in merchant shipping.

Ideas such as these may seem natural enough to those unacquainted with the conflict of policies between Army and Navy. There would, for instance, seem to be little objection on any score to action which, while preserving the existing convoy system and routine patrol, would carry the war to the enemy as well. But to organize an offensive would mean to reorganize the entire antisubmarine campaign. Specifically it would require the creation of just such a semi-independent and mobile command as the AAF planners had in mind. For, at the time, only such a body could carry out a strategic policy that reached beyond the Navy's defensive doctrine of convoy and offshore patrol, and be able to attack the U-boats at their point of greatest concentration. Moreover, the long-range Army-type bombers alone combined the range and striking power necessary for such offensive action, and as yet the AAF was better able than the Navy to equip such a force. In short, under existing conditions, an offensive strategy simply would not fit into the Navy scheme of things. Not only did it run counter to the Navy's preference for a defensive antisubmarine war, but it also would tend to weaken naval control over the Army elements engaged in the antisubmarine campaign.

By the summer of 1942, therefore, it is possible to see the outlines of those two related controversies, the jurisdictional and the strategic, which determined the history of the AAF antisubmarine effort. The AAF plans, as shaped in May, could lead only in one direction. Unchecked they would eventually have placed the entire responsibility for the air antisubmarine campaign in the hands of those who held the aggressive strategic doctrine and who were in immediate possession of the organization and the weapons necessary to carry out that doctrine. But the Army plans did not remain unchecked. They met the consistent opposition of the Navy, energetic in this defensive action as in its defensive Battle of the Atlantic.

In view of all this discussion it is surprising to find formal action taking a much slower and more compromising course. For the rest of the summer little was done in a radical way to reorganize the antisubmarine campaign. In immediate response to General Eisenhower's directive of 20 May, General McNarney, Assistant Chief of Staff, WDGS, informed Admiral King that 10 B-18's, ASV-equipped, together with 10 additional medium bombers without ASV, had been sent to the bedeviled Gulf area where they would work under the operational control of the Gulf Sea Frontier commander. He also outlined a proposed reorganization of the Army antisubmarine program. The I Bomber Command was to be organized as a unit to wage antisubmarine "and related operations" on the East and Gulf coasts. Air bases were to be established at strategic locations in order to take maximum advantage of the mobility of land-based aircraft. As soon as available, ASV-equipped aircraft would be welded into units "particularly suited for hunting down and destroying enemy submarines by methods developed by our experimental units which have been operating off Cape Hatteras." Mobility was to be the keynote of this reorganized force. When a unit moved to an area outside the EDC, it would operate under the control of the particular sea frontier commander concerned, but it would still remain assigned to the I Bomber Command. "Movement to and operation in areas beyond the jurisdiction of the latter will be viewed as a temporary detachment therefrom."[69]

Admiral King's reaction to these cautious proposals was expressed with equal caution. They were, he felt, satisfactory but he planned to place the control of aircraft assigned to each sea frontier in the hands of the commander of that frontier. Moreover, in providing air coverage for convoys it would not be necessary for planes attached to one frontier to operate in another "unless exceptional conditions make it necessary." In a note to the sea frontier commanders, concerning General McNarney's letter, he said, further: "It will be noted that the division of aircraft, both Army and Navy, as between the sea frontiers, will be a matter under the cognizance of the Commander in Chief, and that the air operations within the sea frontiers will be under the direction of the Commander Sea Frontier concerned."[70] In other words, rigid geographic lines were to be retained in the use of Army planes, and such use was to be dictated unequivocally by naval authorities.

While these plans were under discussion, the heavy shipping losses continued at such an alarming rate that on 19 June 1942 General Marshall expressed to Admiral King his fear that "another month or two" of similar losses would "so cripple our means of transport that we will be unable to bring sufficient men and planes against the enemy in critical theaters to exercise a determining influence on the war."[71] This note of alarm elicited a definite statement of the Navy's strategic doctrine in its campaign against the U-boat. Admiral King had already made it clear that the system of Navy regional control would remain a part of the united command that the Navy was to exercise. Now he set himself clearly in opposition to the Army's offensive doctrine. If that doctrine had not been emphasized officially, it had certainly been given enough informal currency to have established it as a basic point of difference between the services. And Admiral King apparently took General Marshall's memo as an implied criticism of the Navy's antisubmarine strategy. The Navy had, he said in reply, employed, and would continue to employ, all available forces in the antisubmarine war and that "not only the Navy itself but also all other agencies concerned must continue to intensify the antisubmarine effort." But that intensified effort to him meant intensified convoy protection. "Escort," he declared, "is not just _one_ way of handling the submarine menace; it is the only way that gives any promise of success. . . . We must get every ship that sails the seas under constant close protection." The work of the I Bomber Command had been valuable in this respect, and after 15 May the coastal waters of the United States had been quite safe for coastwise shipping under convoy. The convoy system was being extended, as rapidly as possible, but the Army should supply at least 500 medium bombers for use in the four sea frontiers-- Eastern, Gulf, Caribbean, and Panama--to augment the force of 850 planes the Navy hoped to operate in those areas.[72]

The Army was thus exhorted to bend every effort in the common cause. It had, however, been far from idle. The I Bomber Command had been useful, if not determinative, in making the Atlantic seaboard unhealthy for U-boats. Lack of proper equipment and training continued to keep the quality of attacks on a comparatively low level. But, from July on, improvement in materiel and a half year of experience in actual submarine hunting had made it possible for the Army antisubmarine units to contribute impressively to the campaign which made the

Germans reconsider the value of operations in U. S. coastal waters.

The figures themselves are misleading.[73] In 59,343 operational hours flown between January and October 1942, not many more than 200 sightings were reported, of which several were no doubt mistaken identification by inexperienced crews. In 81 instances attacks followed which resulted in one U-boat definitely destroyed, six seriously damaged, and seven damaged to some extent.[74] The aircraft made their contribution rather in forcing submarines to submerge so frequently that their targets were lost and their activity slowed up to the point where the returns became marginal or submarginal.

The quality of the patrols and especially of the attacks improved steadily as suitable equipment became available and crews gained in experience. The first attack that was assessed as in any degree damaging in the U-boat did not occur until 2 April 1942. During the next 4 months the bulk of the damaging attacks were made. The frequency of attacks roughly paralleled the density of U-boats in the area and also the sinking of merchant vessels. It is estimated that, during May and June, when the U-boats were thickest and their work most deadly, each was attacked on an average of twice each month by aircraft of the I Bomber Command.[75]

After June, enemy activity fell off rapidly in the coastal waters. Here again a look at the figures alone would convey a false impression.[76] It is clear from them, and perfectly true, that in August the enemy began to withdraw to other areas, and by October had virtually abandoned the Eastern and Gulf Sea Frontiers. After 4

September no more bombings occurred in 1942 as a result of enemy submarine action in those waters. The Germans had shifted their area of activity steadily farther south in approximately direct proportion to the intensity of the aerial defense.[77] June 1942 saw the pattern of sinkings moving toward the Caribbean area. By August the Gulf was practically free of sinkings which were by that time concentrated around Cuba and in the Trinidad area. By September the enemy had given up attacks around Cuba, Haiti and Puerto Rico, but continued in the Trinidad area until November when a certain amount of coordination, previously lacking, was achieved between air and surface defenses.

This progressive withdrawal of the enemy submarines does not, however, mean that the I Bomber Command had by itself made the Eastern and Gulf Sea Frontiers untenable. Its activity was a contributing, perhaps a determining factor, but it was not the only one. It appears that in the late summer of 1942 the U-boat fleet had been forced to abandon to some extent its original strategic mission of striking at Allied shipping wherever it might be found in most profitable quantities, and to have adopted a more defensive strategy dictated by Allied plans in Russia and North Africa. This shift in strategy involved greater concentrations in the northern and eastern Atlantic waters at the expense of operations in the American shipping lanes. The convoy system also did much to discourage attacks, although convoys without adequate air coverage were extremely vulnerable. And an increasingly large share of this coverage, as well as of routine patrol, was being provided by Navy planes, which accounted for 75

out of the total of 125 attacks made in the western Atlantic prior to 5 September 1942.[78] The AAF 1st Sea-Search Attack Group, operating primarily as an experimental unit from Langley Field, under the operational control of the Bomber Command, also made five successful attacks during the period from July to October.[79] At any rate, the constant air patrol maintained by the various agencies in the antisubmarine campaign undoubtedly exercised a determining influence in the enemy's strategic withdrawal.[80] However, the enemy had not been defeated, scarcely even embarrassed; he merely concentrated his efforts in other areas, and so effectively that in November, 2 months after he had virtually abandoned the U. S. coastline, total Allied shipping losses reached a new high.[81]

Steps had been taken by the Army Air Forces to increase the efficiency of its antisubmarine units. An effort had been made to increase the number of medium bombers deployed in the campaign, and to equip as many of them as possible with ASV. Above all, the Army Air Forces had established in June the Sea Search Attack Development Unit (SADU) for the purpose of research in antisubmarine techniques and devices.[82] By August this agency was in full operation. It was through the medium of this technical development that Dr. Edward L. Bowles, Expert Consultant to the Secretary of War, hoped to revitalize the antisubmarine campaign. Considerable attention had been given to the problem of equipment, especially radar, by the Joint Committee on New Weapons and Equipment (JNW) and it was becoming pretty evident that, if the submarines were to be defeated, some aid must be sought from these technical sources.

Unfortunately, a research unit could not win the "trade war" by itself. It was one thing to develop the weapons and quite another to use them effectively. The latter demanded a correspondingly streamlined organization of the entire program, which meant in this instance the creation of a new command committed to an aggressive, closely knit campaign of U-boat destruction. Again the whole basic controversy was opened. It was, Dr. Bowles insisted, no longer so much a question of over-all unity of command between Army and Navy. That could well be conceded to the Navy. It was rather a question of organization within the Army itself, and for a frankly offensive campaign reaching beyond coastal patrol into the deeper waters of the mid-ocean.

He therefore proposed that an "Air Antisubmarine Force" be organized under the command of a general officer who would control the entire land-based air component of the antisubmarine forces, including the Navy land-based inshore patrol aircraft, and the research and training unit. In this way, without disturbing the ultimate unity of command, the vexing question concerning the allocation of land-based aircraft, which was tending dangerously toward the creation of two separate air forces with duplicated function, would be solved. This entire force would be placed under the Commanding General, Army Air Forces, in order to relieve it from dependency on any local command. It would confine its operations to U. S. coastal waters, but would be free to send "detachments or task forces to other parts of the world."[83]

The last of the major arguments that led to the establishment of the Army Air Forces Antisubmarine Command had now been presented in this penetrating document. The problem of aircraft allocations to the Army and Navy, the evident tactical need for unity of command and mobility of organization, and the Army's strategic doctrine of the coordinated offensive were all leading in an intricate and overlapping pattern of influences to the creation of a separate command. Now the requirements dictated by the employment of new devices added one more telling item to this list which, together with the continuing grave situation in the Atlantic, made action essential.

None of the plans prepared and discussed in the summer of 1942 was used as the final pattern--none, that is, in its entirety. The ideas developed in the plans, however, determined the nature of the new command. Allowance naturally had to be made for the views of the Navy which had not been favorable to the establishment of such an organization. So the solution finally adopted was a modest one, retaining most of the reforms proposed by Army planners except those specifically reducing the authority of the Navy.

The first formal step in setting up the new command was taken by General Marshall. On 14 September, he wrote to Admiral King:

> Experience with the First Bomber Command in antisubmarine operations since March indicates that the effective employment of air forces against the submarine demands rapid communications, mobility, and freedom from the restrictions inherent in command systems based upon area responsibility.

Accordingly, he proposed to create the "First Antisubmarine Army Air Command," which would absorb those portions of the I Bomber Command engaged in antisubmarine work. Control of the new unit would be centralized in the War Department in order that it might "be promptly dispatched" to successive zones of submarine activity. It would begin operation in Atlantic coastal waters, the Gulf and the Caribbean; its expansion to other areas "will depend upon the planes available." Operations "naturally will be under the operational control of the sea frontier concerned." The closest cooperation with the Navy, especially in the transmission of intelligence which could only be compiled through naval sources, would be essential to the proper functioning of this antisubmarine command. Provision would therefore have to be made for liaison between "our immediate headquarters."[84]

Admiral King replied at once, concurring in general, but expressing his belief that "the preferable method" was allocation of air units to sea frontiers, changing the allocations from time to time and from frontier to frontier as the exigencies of the war dictated. He would, he said, continue to exercise control over Army planes through the commander of the various sea frontiers. To provide the close liaison suggested by General Marshall, he had designated Adm. P. N. L. Bellinger, Deputy Chief of Staff of the U. S. Fleet, as liaison officer.[85]

On 22 September, General McNarney instructed General Arnold to organize the First Antisubmarine Army Air Command, using the I Bomber Command as cadre. The principal mission of the command was to be "the location and destruction of hostile submarines." As a necessary

means to this end it had the secondary mission of training crews and developing devices and techniques. The command was to be directly under the CG AAF, although operations were to be conducted under naval control. It was not to be limited by the boundaries of defense areas, and its operations in areas other than the EDC or SDC were to be coordinated with OPD, WDGS.[86] It was activated 15 October 1942[87] under the designation, Army Air Forces Antisubmarine Command.

The mission of the command was elaborated in subsequent orders which gave considerable latitude to its activities. It was to attack hostile submarines "wherever they may be operating." Although operations on the Eastern and Gulf Sea Frontiers were to be conducted under the tactical control of Navy officials, direct control over the command was vested in the office of the Commanding General, AAF; and provision was made for future transfer of units to extra-continental areas on a detached service base. General Larson, as Commanding General, was responsible for operations under the Director of Military Requirements, through the Director of Bombardment, but matters of "policy, broad plans, and the development of new weapons and equipment" remained with the Commanding General, AAF.[88]

Such were the plans and orders under which the Antisubmarine Command was organized and under which it operated during the short course of its restless career.

Chapter II

THE ANTISUBMARINE CONTROVERSY

The AAF Antisubmarine Command began operations at once, and with essentially the same units and equipment as had been employed against the U-boats by its predecessor, the I Bomber Command. These squadrons were, on 20 November 1942, organized in two wings, the 25th and the 26th, with headquarters at New York and Miami, and operating in the Eastern and Gulf Sea Frontiers, respectively. Provision was made for redesignating several observation squadrons and re-equipping them for antisubmarine operations. Equipment of the I Bomber Command available for the new assignment, although including several types of aircraft, was seriously limited in the critical category of long-range bombardment.[1] Eventually the Antisubmarine Command was to consist of 25 squadrons, most of which were equipped with B-24's, especially adapted for anti-U-boat warfare. Command headquarters remained at 90 Church St., New York City.

The command faced a large and varied problem of build-up. Not only did it have to increase its effective strength as rapidly as possible, but to meet its new obligations it had also to inaugurate an entirely new training program, new supply procedures, and new administrative machinery for coordinating research in the tactics and techniques of antisubmarine warfare. The Bomber Command had been constantly handicapped by the officially temporary nature of its assignment. The new command was able to attack its problems with all the ingenuity and energy it possessed, because it was officially committed to antisubmarine duty and had no legal reason to anticipate that at any time it might be returned to normal bombardment duties.

The command also faced the immediate necessity of extending the range of its activities beyond the western Atlantic. In November 1942, two of its squadrons, completely equipped with B-24's, were ordered to England. Later, other units were dispatched overseas, in all six squadrons doing service in the eastern Atlantic--to be specific, in the Bay of Biscay and in the Moroccan Sea Frontier. Still other units served, during 1943, in Newfoundland and in the Caribbean.

These movements were dictated by a fundamental change in German strategy for the deployment of the U-boat fleet. Indeed, the activation of the Antisubmarine Command coincided with this shift of enemy forces. Since May 1942, the Germans had been gradually withdrawing their submarine forces from the U. S. coastal waters. By September they had apparently abandoned the policy of attacking merchant shipping wherever it might be found in profitable quantities, and had begun to concentrate their forces defensively against the military shipping which the Allies were sending to the British Isles and to Africa in preparation for offensive action in those areas. Specifically, this meant deployment in the North Atlantic and in the approaches toward North Africa. Little activity remained in the western Atlantic except in the poorly defended Trinidad area, and except for a few nuisance raiders sent to keep large antisubmarine forces tied down to patrol off the U. S. coast. This shift of enemy strategy called for a similar shift in U. S. strategy; and, since it was on the enemy's part essentially a shift from offense to defense, it pointed toward a corresponding change in American policy from defense to a vigorous offense. Even if this natural logic were ignored, the new situation made a greatly expanded antisubmarine campaign absolutely essential.

The new submarine situation thus necessitated a review of antisubmarine measures. Old questions regarding the strategy and organization of the antisubmarine campaign, never satisfactorily settled, began again to render unstable the relationship between the services and to imperil a vital sector of the Allied war effort. It again became a crucial question whether the extended antisubmarine war should proceed on essentially offensive lines, carrying the battle to the enemy as briskly as resources would permit, or whether it should consist primarily of extended convoy coverage. And it again became a subject for the most heated debate whether the long-range, land-based aviation engaged in the campaign should be controlled ultimately by the Army or by the Navy.

The creation of the Antisubmarine Command, then, settled nothing. It had the effect of substantially legalizing the Army's antisubmarine mission, hitherto considered exclusively a naval one, entrusted to the Army only as a temporary emergency measure. But it reconciled none of those differences of opinion which had harassed the antisubmarine campaign from the very beginning. On both the strategic and the administrative level, the newly aggravated debate led inevitably toward a crisis in the summer of 1943 which, in turn, affected the entire system of joint action and, incidentally, removed the Antisubmarine Command entirely from the scene.

Although the command had been conceived originally as a unit whose permanent field of operations should be the U. S. Atlantic coast, the Gulf, and the Caribbean, it did not take the War Department long to recognize the need for extending its activities beyond the western Atlantic. General Marshall had, in fact, hinted at the possibility of extending the scope of the Army's antisubmarine forces in his letter of 14 September.[2] Dr. Bowles had urged the possibility of extracontinental expansion in his memo of 7 August,[3] and apparently he had the support of General Eisenhower, General Arnold, and Secretary Stimson in this point of view.[4] As conceived by General Arnold and presented to the Joint Chiefs of Staff in JCS 93/1 (dated 19 October 1942), "The unit /the newly activated command/ has freedom of action in that it may be moved to where it is most needed, and operate in conjunction with but not under the command of the local sector commander." And in December the scope of its operations was officially widened to include the destruction of submarines "whereover they may be operating in opposition to our war effort."[5] Plans had matured, by October, to send two squadrons to England to operate with the Coastal Command, and, on 2 November the first unit left

Langley Field. The Joint Chiefs of Staff had approved a plan for considerably extended antisubmarine operation, in which 416 AAF bombardment aircraft (288 heavy and 128 medium) were set as the forces to be made available for this task.[6]

These figures, though representing a greatly enlarged program, failed to satisfy General Larson whose ideas were shaped on an even broader pattern. To be sure, the forces immediately at hand were, as he put it on 6 January 1943, still too small to allow him to fulfill the mission with which he was officially charged. They consisted of 19 squadrons operating 209 planes, of which only 20 were B-24's, the type already recognized as the best available weapon for the purpose.[6a] Interpreting his mission literally, General Larson on that date presented to General Arnold a plan providing for the creation of antisubmarine wings to operate in the North Atlantic, the United Kingdom, Northwest Africa, the Mediterranean, Central West Africa, South Africa, Natal, the Antilles, the Pacific Coast, the Northwest Pacific, the Southwest Pacific, India, Asia, Hawaii, and Russia. Owing to the relative mobility of antisubmarine units, he felt that "for initial planning" the mission could be accomplished by expanding the Antisubmarine Command to a strength less than half that required to maintain squadrons in all possible areas. He therefore requested that the AAF Antisubmarine Command be authorized a total strength of six wings composing a total number of 42 squadrons. In order to equip these units, a total of 544 B-24D aircraft, fully equipped for antisubmarine activity, would be required.[7] He further requested that the recommendations be approved in principle regardless of whether the means of implementing them were available.⁷ᵃ

AAF Headquarters approved this plan in principle with, among others, one major exception. The Antisubmarine Command was intended to be "a highly mobile striking force" which at no time would "become confined to a stabilized effort" but would operate "where operation is most profitable." With this in mind it had been limited to 20 heavy and 4 medium squadrons, not including such as might be transferred to the command and be redesignated as antisubmarine squadrons.⁸ Immediate requirements were placed at 228 B-24's, 12 for each of the existing 19 squadrons.⁹ In the absence of fully adequate forces, those that were available had to be utilized to the utmost, which involved rapid movement from one threatened area to another. In other words, mobility was considered essential not only to the tactical and strategic situations, but to the logistical as well.

This plan for expansion implied a doctrine of the strategic offensive. It was based on the notion that the job of the Antisubmarine Command was not mere protection of shipping but an organized U-boat hunt, aiming ultimately at destroying the submarine at sea. The Antisubmarine Command was not alone in this crusade for the offensive. In January, Dr. P. M. Morse, of the Antisubmarine Warfare Operations Research Group (ASWORG), analyzed the situation in the following terms:¹⁰

> . . . a major change in the antisubmarine battle requires that we pass from the defensive to the offensive. The plane is primarily an offensive weapon against U-boats; being preeminent, by reason of its speed, in its ability to seek out the enemy. The surface vessel is, at present, less than one tenth as efficient at finding submarines as is the plane and

is no more efficient at killing the submarine, once found. Its major advantage over the plane is its staying power, essentially a defensive property: the surface vessel will always be the backbone of the convoy escort. The plane is also useful as an escort; but it is a most inefficient use of the plane's offensive capabilities to hold it down to protecting convoys which are not specifically threatened.

Moreover, like General Larson, Dr. Morse looked to a vastly increased aerial campaign, going so far as to say that 1,000 to 2,000 long-range aircraft would be necessary in the total antisubmarine war if that effort were to result in eliminating the U-boat.[11] The Bay of Biscay and the North African coast had, he said, at the time (5 January 1943), the highest submarine density of any portion of the North Atlantic. He therefore strongly urged the Antisubmarine Command to provide enough planes to carry on offensive operations in these areas.[12]

A similar attitude was taken about the same time by the Joint U. S. Committee on New Weapons and Equipment. This agency complained of the naval policy which employed AAF antisubmarine aircraft chiefly in convoy escort and in patrol of waters that had been practically free of submarines for months. For, although two units (ultimately organized as the 480th Antisubmarine Group) had been allowed to operate under the RAF Coastal Command in a campaign of search and attack in areas of high submarine density, the bulk of the AAFAC squadrons remained in the U. S. coastal frontiers from which the enemy had long since withdrawn the bulk of his forces. It advocated extending the idea of "special groups with the specific task of killing submarines." These, it claimed, "might well reduce substantially the number of enemy submarines operating." The AAFAC was, it continued, such a group, and it recommended that the command be provided with an adequate supply of long-range planes and sent out in an offensive U-boat hunt.[13]

From other sources, however, came certain qualifications to these somewhat enthusiastic statements of the offensive concept. Brig. Gen. C. W. Russell, Army liaison officer for antisubmarine warfare, had, in November, made an analysis of the situation in the Atlantic and had come up with a modified faith in the "killer-hunt" idea.[14] Certain points rose obtrusively to the surface in his report. One was that the number of U-boats would have to be reduced before shipping losses would permanently decline. However carefully the convoys might be protected, he said, "the inescapable fact is that the more submarines there are operating, the more merchant vessels will be sunk."[15] The second fact was that present defensive operations against the U-boat had failed to hold shipping losses "within tolerable limits." It seemed therefore that "persistent offensive measures" would have to be adopted, aimed at destroying the U-boat fleet. But General Russell was not at all sure that action in the open sea was the type of offensive required. Although, he complained, many attacks were being made on the enemy craft at sea, both by air and surface craft, few had met with success. Equipment fell short of the lethal requirements to kill many U-boats and the latter had the advantage of a highly protective element. Accordingly, while not scorning the part played by long-range bombers operating at sea, he placed in first priority the yards at which the submarines were built.

In January he repeated his recommendation, citing what he believed to be the effective bombing by Eighth Air Force units of French Coast submarine bases. He added, however, that the North Atlantic convoy route indicated the crying need for long-range, land-based aircraft, losses having "invariably" occurred in sections of the convoy route not provided with air coverage. And he advised that the AAFAC be equipped with long-range aircraft at the earliest possible moment.[16] In short, bombing of submarine yards should be given first priority, and long-range air coverage for the North Atlantic convoy route a close second.

A summary of the official AAF policy, formulated 6 February 1943, reflected General Russell's point of view, if anything reducing the emphasis he had placed on long-range air coverage:[17]

> In considering the entire antisubmarine problem [General Stratemeyer wrote], it is desired to emphasize that use of aircraft and surface forces against submarines at sea can never be expected to effectively reduce the total number of operational submarines. The only way to destroy the submarines is to destroy them at their source by destruction of crucial materials, assembly plants, yards and operating bases. Any diversion of a large force of our air effort for the purpose of hunting down the submarines at sea, would be reducing the effective number which can be used against the submarines at their source and is an improper employment of available forces; however, it must also be borne in mind that unless we do protect our shipping, we will be unable to feed and supply forces now committed to the theaters. . . . We must, therefore, divert a certain amount of our effort to protection of our lines of communication. The amount so diverted should be sufficient only to fill the need of protecting our shipping and not sufficient to attempt to destroy the submarine at sea.

It would appear that AAF headquarters was admittedly groping in its effort to assign an unquestionable priority to any one type of air antisubmarine operation. A study had been requested which would indicate, in the light of recent experience, the relative effectiveness of attacking submarine production, repair and maintenance installations, parts manufacturing plants, and the operating submarines themselves.[18] Early in March an exhaustive, if still necessarily tentative, study was submitted by AC/AS, Intelligence. By that time merchant vessel sinkings had taken a sharp upward turn, and emphasis was being placed on immediate results. This report concluded (1) that air patrols, either by land or carrier-based planes, can materially reduce shipping losses, even without a high rate of submarines "killed"; (2) that improved weapons may be expected to raise the lethal rate of aircraft attacks; (3) that bombing of submarine bases and construction yards, though still unproved, should be pressed--the bombing of component parts plants could not, however, be expected to yield large results.[19] This report, then, while not destroying faith in the offensive of the Eighth Air Force against the submarines at their source, renewed somewhat the official confidence in an aggressive sea-search-attack policy. It pointed to the belief that the effect of air patrol could not be measured entirely in terms of U-boats sunk. It was, in fact, quite possible to limit submarine action simply by such harrying tactics as had recently been employed in the Bay of Biscay where antisubmarine forces, although sinking relatively few of the U-boats attacked, had managed to give the enemy craft such a bad time, both in going from and returning to their bases, that their effectiveness in convoy areas was sharply reduced. This report also highlighted what had frequently been mentioned as a major criticism of the over-all U. S. antisubmarine policy, namely that a large proportion of the Antisubmarine Command strength was left tied to a coastal patrol area, flying thousand of hours where few if any submarines were operating, while only limited forces were being moved to those areas, the Bay of Biscay for example, where the submarines abounded.[20]

In general, the Army Air Forces advocated an increased air effort in which bombing of submarine bases, air coverage for convoys, and an independent air offensive where the U-boats were thickest, each had its peculiar function, not to be overrated. Perhaps the Antisubmarine Command stressed the last policy because it was its own; but even it was satisfied with any strategic policy which carried the war as directly and as rapidly as possible to the enemy, considering, of course, commitments of equal or higher priority. Its planners were apparently quite agreed that continued emphasis should be placed on striking the U-boats in their construction yards and operating bases.[21] Yet it was on the question of independent offensive action in areas of enemy concentration that one of the decisive controversies became focused.

Early in 1943, during February, German submarines began their spring offensive. Merchant vessel sinkings, after having decreased rapidly during December and January, suddenly increased, especially along the North Atlantic convoy route. This renewed activity called for drastic measures, but there was considerable room for disagreement as to what those measures should be. Given unlimited supplies of trained men and specialized equipment, both sides might easily have justified their respective measures, each as part of a many-sided, coordinated campaign. But, as usual, the plans were numerous and the equipment meager. Naval authorities, continuing to invest their hopes in an extended system of convoy coverage, stressed the need for more Army B-24's operating from Newfoundland in order to cover that hitherto especially dangerous leg of the journey from U. S. ports to Europe. The AAFAC, without doubting for a moment the need for this activity from Newfoundland--even, in fact, planning experimental operations from Greenland as well--[32] nevertheless felt that a considerable portion of its available strength in VLR aircraft should be devoted to an independent offensive.

Since November 1942, the Coastal Command, RAF had been carrying on just such an offensive against the U-boat in its transit area in the Bay of Biscay. The Bay was a focal area through which virtually all the enemy operating in the Atlantic had to pass as they left or approached their bases on the west coast of France. This campaign, therefore, became not only the pivot on which the RAF turned its anti-submarine war, but the archetype of a VLR air killer offensive. In November two AAFAC squadrons had been sent to England, with the original mission of protecting TORCH convoys. After consultation with the British, the Commanding General, ETO decided to employ these squadrons in the Bay of Biscay to augment the Coastal Command's effort, because that organization had a very limited supply of ASV-10 equipment (the sine qua non for effective U-boat hunting).[23] These two squadrons accordingly took an active part in the "Gondola" campaign, 6-15 February 1943, which marked one of the high points of the Biscay offensive.[24]

The Biscay campaign failed, however, to impress Admiral King who felt that, although "excellent in concept," it had been pushed with a vigor unwarranted by "diminishing returns," and which might better have been expended on the Newfoundland area. Submarine sightings had, he complained, become steadily fewer in the Bay of Biscay, by February no more than one for each 250 hours of flying, while German submarines had been allowed to concentrate and flourish with little interference off the Newfoundland banks "for several months." He appreciated the fact that the AAFAC had "the Newfoundland matter" now in hand. What gave him concern was "the length of time it took to make the picture clear."[25] To this criticism, the AAFAC replied that the Biscay offensive was one which would require continual air effort to restrict U-boat operations; that an increase in the number of hours per sighting was a favorable sign since it indicated that the enemy submarines, which were evidently increasing in number, were having to traverse the Biscay transit area under conditions which could only reduce their efficiency. Furthermore, the recent U-boat concentrations in the North Atlantic were being reported beyond effective range from the Newfoundland air bases. They could be reached from Greenland, and plans were being laid to operate from there with at least one VLR squadron; but operating conditions were so bad in that area that little could be expected from such action. In fine, "Our conception of this problem is that the protection of the sea lanes is basically a Navy problem," and AAFAC units are better employed in the specialized work for which they were specially trained and equipped--specifically, such operations as those in the Bay of Biscay.[26]

And so the discussion developed. Mainly it was a case of emphasis, rather than of mutually exclusive views. As an Eighth Air Force report put it, "The air war against the U-boats should not be regarded as either wholly defensive, nor wholly offensive. It can probably best be termed a counter-offensive."[27] It was also very difficult to prove, conclusively, either argument. It was against this operational and doctrinal background that the Atlantic Convoy Conference met in Washington, from 1 to 12 March 1943, comprising representatives from British, Canadian, and U. S. agencies concerned in the Battle of the Atlantic. Among several other topics, this of the proper deployment of VLR land-based aircraft rose stubbornly to the surface during the deliberations of the conference.

By this time it had become generally recognized that antisubmarine warfare was a problem for air power just as much as for surface forces, if not considerably more. Much time was still being spent in documenting this point and the operational statistics regarding attacks and sinkings of enemy submarines tended to move steadily in favor of aircraft.[23] And it was equally evident that too few aircraft, especially VLR, were being employed in this kind of warfare. Admiral Noble, R.N., struck this note early in the conference:[29]

> The submarine menace, to my mind, is becoming every day more and more an air problem. We haven't had enough aircraft during the last two years. We are just reaching a point where we can see ahead of us the chance of getting enough, and I am sure this conference will come to some agreements and decisions as to how to best use these aircraft when we got them and when they get to their proper operational theaters.

The Atlantic Convoy Conference, however, dealt only with the problem of air coverage for convoys, insofar as air operations were included in its recommendations at all. The problem of an air offensive was ignored, no doubt, for the very good reason that it bore only indirectly on the problem of convoy. Admiral King, however, took pains in his opening address as chairman to make his position on this subject very clear:[30]

> I take upon myself the privilege of offering some advice as to how you should go at the matters in hand. . . . the High Command recognizes that the antisubmarine war is a matter of first importance; but we must also recognize that the defeat of the U-boat is not of itself the goal we seek, however much it is an essential step in reaching the goal. May I add the observation that your immediate task is to protect our shipping by what may be called defensive antisubmarine warfare. . . . We have got to devote our somewhat limited overall resources only in part to fighting the submarines. This makes it necessary that we use what we have to the very best advantage. . . . I have heard something about "killer groups" which may be of great use when we can get enough means, provided they are used directly in connection with the convoy routes, for that is where the "bait" is. I see no profit in searching the ocean, or even any but a limited area, such as a focal area--all else puts to shame the proverbial "search for a needle in a haystack.". . .antisubmarine warfare for the remainder of 1943, at least, must concern itself primarily with the escort of convoys.

In these words, Admiral King recommitted himself, if not the entire U. S. Navy, to a policy of defense in the U-boat war, at least for the rest of the year. Yet at the same time he left the way open for the future development of an offensive strategy.

Concurrently with this debate regarding strategic doctrine ran a parallel debate concerning organization. The controversy over strategy suggested that some reorganization of command would alone be likely to remedy a basic disagreement over the deployment of forces. The nature of the antisubmarine war remained such as to demand as nearly absolute cooperation between the commands and services involved as was humanly possible. And there were other problems which pointed in the same direction. All boil down in the final analysis to the constant need for economy and for mobility in the use of those resources available.

It was the old story over again, reminiscent of the days before the AAFAC was activated. The German submarine fleet, under a single commander, and deployed within a large strategic plan, possessed the great advantage of flexibility; and being flexible it was able to retain the initiative in the Atlantic even after it had been forced by strategic considerations beyond its control to concentrate its efforts defensively against the "invasion" convoys. In contrast, the antisubmarine forces, especially those of the United States, suffered from complicated and divided command and from a wasteful duplication of effort. Little attempt had been made to standardize communications, intelligence dissemination, training, or tactical doctrine, either among the nations concerned or between the U. S.

Army and the U. S. Navy. As a consequence, each agency felt that, in order to discharge its obligation, it would have to plan a much larger program than would have been required in a strictly integrated plan. Finally, no single commander existed, either among the Allies or within the U. S. forces, whose sole responsibility it was to prosecute antisubmarine warfare, and to move antisubmarine forces as the tactical situation indicated.

Although it was a problem involving the entire campaign and each of the Atlantic Allies, it was a particularly vexing one for the United States, where each of the above-mentioned difficulties existed in peculiarly aggravated form. Basic disagreement existed concerning the nature of the antisubmarine mission. Each service seems to have planned with the entire campaign in mind--AAF authorities had observed with some misgivings that the Navy was including in its allocation plans a force sufficient to do the whole job without the aid of the AAFAC.[31] This duplication, or threat thereof, involved training facilities and bases as well as planes. Though the Navy exercised operational control over all U. S. antisubmarine operations, it had as yet no integrated system for exercising that control. The job was left to the various sea frontier commanders who had other responsibilities, under the coordinating authority of the Commander in Chief, U. S. Fleet, whose office had also many other things to do.[32] And the AAFAC, organized, equipped, and trained under the administration of the AAF, actually failed to fit into this inflexible system of naval control.

The result was that the AAFAC flyers had frequently to work with naval commanders who did not understand their training, equipment or tactical doctrine. Still worse, units of valuable antisubmarine aircraft were left frozen to naval frontier commands where practically no submarines existed or to the protection of "unthreatened" convoys, while certain overseas waters teemed with the enemy.[33] It was alleged that the Navy not only failed to act upon over-all intelligence reports concerning U-boat concentrations, but failed also to provide the AAFAC units with enough basic intelligence data upon which to operate effective patrols.[34] The position of the overseas squadrons (the two sent to England in November of 1942 and moved to Africa in March 1943) was especially anomalous. Without wing organization in which they might have found some degree of autonomy, these squadrons were forced to operate under a foreign (although basically congenial) system while in England, and while in Africa under a bitterly disputed area command.[35] Any attempt to move the AAFAC squadrons involved ponderous procedures within War and Navy department channels, possibly even unavoidably slow liaison with other Allied commands. The result was that movements were likely to be too slow to cope with the extreme mobility of the U-boat fleet.[36]

Most agencies concerned recognized the need for reorganization of the antisubmarine effort. Admiral King, himself no friend of radical change, experienced impatience at the slowness with which the antisubmarine forces were being moved to counter the shifting U-boat concentrations.[37] And he had agreed, a little grudgingly, to General Marshall's proposal that a study be undertaken to improve coordination in the campaign.[38] The problem was accordingly entrusted to a subcommittee of the Combined Staff Planners (created 5 January 1943) for study and recommendation.[39]

Preliminary discussions in the subcommittee seem to have been promising. The flaws in existing organization, especially the lack of unified command, were too obvious to excite much disagreement in the abstract. According to the AAF members, however, it appears that on second thought the U. S. Navy members "interposed strenuous objections" to any plan which amounted to a change in their existing organization or policies. The result was a paper which the AAF members felt "intimates much but specifically says nothing."[40]

What this report (CPS 56/3, dated 1 March 1943) did was to present the problem formally and collect considerable reference data on the problem of countering the submarine menace. Little exception could be taken by anyone to the general recommendations concerning organization. It recommended that the national antisubmarine effort in each Allied nation be integrated under one naval commander who "should be able to concentrate entirely on that task." Forces should be allocated to antisubmarine operations exclusively and areas of operation clearly defined, especially for the air forces of the two services. To permit flexibility in control and operation, "an ideal to be aimed at" would be the creation of a system of bases, communications, and weather-forecasting facilities within which the forces might be moved rapidly from one area to another. Although a single authority for the total United Nations antisubmarine effort would be very desirable, that would have to wait until the national organizations became more uniform with each other, a process which would take time. Meanwhile, with increased flexibility and augmented forces, it would be reasonable to expect the antisubmarine machine to be set to work on both offensive and defensive projects in which air and surface forces would operate in close cooperation.

Innocuous as this report appears, it aroused vigorous protest on the part of the AAF members. After much discussion, during which the recommendations had been considerably diluted, they had agreed to sign it rather than to submit a split paper. Colonel Williamson did, however, turn in a minority report in which he objected that the subcommittee had given too little attention to reducing the number of U-boats at sea. He recommended that first priority be given to implementing plans for organizational and technical developments which would increase the effectiveness of action against the submarines at sea, including the use of killer groups composed of radar- and DF-equipped destroyers to break up submarine concentrations. There should, he maintained, be no diversion from offensive operations to defensive convoy coverage.[41]

The AAF members further clarified their position in a plan of their own for reorganizing the antisubmarine machinery, which they submitted to General Arnold.[42] They proposed specifically that each of the major Allied nations concerned should create a task force under a single commander who should control all national anti-U-boat operations; that all national air and surface forces (the latter including carriers) be placed under an air and a surface commander respectively; that all Allied antisubmarine forces in the Atlantic be placed under one commander who would have no other responsibility; and that this over-all commander should be given a deputy for air and one for surface forces operating in the Atlantic. This statement represented the AAFAC position in general, and was in substantial agreement with the British and Canadian opinion. An earlier plan from AAFAC sources had made no objection to leaving supreme control in naval hands "since the responsibility for securing trade routes is the responsibility of the Commander-in-Chief of the Navy."[43] The official AAFAC position was thus less radical than some earlier recommendations, such as that submitted in January 1943 by the Joint U. S. Committee on New Weapons and Equipment which would have removed the AAFAC entirely from the control of the Navy, and made it into a specialized force for locating and destroying U-boats wherever the latter might be found.[44]

The report of the CPS subcommittee (CPS 56/3) continued to be discussed. In general it was felt to be a useful report, lacking, however, in recommendations of a sufficiently specific nature to be of much value in actual planning. As CCS 203, it was submitted to the Joint Chiefs of Staff and the Combined Chiefs of Staff, and on 30 April 1943, after almost 4 months of discussion, it was decided that this document should be approved in principle and sent to the agencies concerned for "guidance" and "appropriate action." Action in any greater detail had been forestalled by Admiral King who feared that, if the CCS approved the paper in its entirety, the result would be to restrict rather than to improve antisubmarine operations.⁴⁵ Throughout these deliberations, Admiral King seems to have been especially concerned to avoid any sort of agreement which would limit the autonomy of the U. S. Navy, by taking from it the right to reorganize the forces under its responsibility according to its own plans.

This same attitude had been apparent when, in the meantime, the Atlantic Convoy Conference met early in March, to ponder the extremely critical situation in the North Atlantic. Short of making clearer the areas of national responsibility in the convoy routes, the conference avoided the ticklish question of organization. Admiral King, its chairman, had warned against what he felt would be an unnecessarily unsettling discussion on that point. He appealed to the conference for "unification of effort," but added:⁴⁶

> May I caution you not to think that unity of command is a panacea for all military difficulties or that it is the *sine qua non* of unity of effort. Unity of Command in appropriate circumstances does unify the effort, but unappropriate centralization of command produces only the form and not the substance of unified effort.

He warned especially of "mixed forces," a comment which surprised Air Marshal Durston, who spoke very favorably of the cooperation achieved by the RAF Coastal Command and the AAFAC squadrons sent to the United Kingdom.⁴⁷

During the spring of 1943, then, the problem of organization was being weighed without more result than an uneasy agreement that some reform, in the direction of closer integration of authority, would be highly desirable. Meanwhile the rugged logic of events was fast outrunning the more academic thinking that prevailed in the official conferences. By March the situation in the North Atlantic had become so grave that President Roosevelt, on the 18th, wrote as follows to the Chief of Staff, U. S. Army and the Commander in Chief, U. S. Fleet:[48]

> Since the rate of sinking of our merchant ships in the North Atlantic during the past week has increased at a rate that threatens seriously the security of Great Britain, and therefore both "Husky" and "Bolero," it seems evident that every available weapon must be used at once to counteract the enemy submarine campaign.

Both Army and Navy high commands had come to about the same conclusion, and every effort was being made to strengthen the antisubmarine striking force. The AAFAC squadrons formerly operating from England were moved, in March, to Pt. Lyautey in North Africa to help cover the vital approaches to that theater. In accordance with the recommendations of the Atlantic Convoy Conference, additional squadrons were made available for Newfoundland to help cover that critical leg of the northern convoy route.[49] General Arnold had declared himself especially anxious to implement the ACC recommendations recommendations in these two areas as quickly as possible.[50] In order to supply the necessary VLR aircraft for this increased ocean coverage, the Combined Chiefs of Staff committed their respective nations to provide, by 1 July 1943, planes of this type according to the following schedule:[51]

                    US AAF   75
                    US Naval AF   60
                    RAF   105
                    RCAF   15

                                    255

General Arnold left no doubt about the "firmness" of this commitment.[52] Fortunately, it was estimated that it could be met without changing planned commitments to other theaters.[53]

What remained to be done was to make the antisubmarine machinery, thus fueled, to operate both effectively and economically. Reorganization would raise basic issues, many of which had proved chronically insoluble. But something had to be done to remedy what was now recognized as the bottleneck of the Allied war effort in the West. In this spirit, General Marshall wrote to Admiral King on 16 April:[54]

> I wish to state now that I feel the air operations against submarines can be greatly improved and that complete reorganization of method, particularly as applies to very long range aircraft, is plainly indicated. . . . We [Generals Marshall, Arnold, and McNarney] are all firmly of the opinion that the present procedure is largely ineffective and makes poor use of a valuable instrument.

And it was in this spirit that he brought the matter before the Joint Chiefs of Staff 3 days later.[55]

War Department experts had meanwhile been at work on plans for reorganizing the antisubmarine effort, insofar as it involved the use of VLR and LR aircraft. It had become evident that this was the crux of the entire problem, overshadowing, in its immediacy, the loftier issue of unified Allied control. It was on the basis of these studies that General Marshall was prepared to take action in the Joint Chiefs of Staff.

Early in March, Dr. Bowles, who had remained throughout its history the sage of the antisubmarine program, and had worked in the closest relationship with Secretary Stimson, submitted an exhaustive report to the Secretary of War covering the entire submarine situation. In it he set forth what may be termed the logical Army policy with regard to the control of the AAFAC. His recommendations arose from certain fundamental assumptions: (1) that the problem of antisubmarine warfare, since on it depended the Army mission in Europe, was essentially an Army problem; (2) that offensive tactics, both against the submarines' breeding grounds and on the open sea, could alone reduce the submarine fleet and therefore the mounting menace to vital Allied shipping; (3) that the long range land-based bomber is the most useful weapon in this offensive strategy; and (4) that an effective use of this weapon depended on a closely coordinated and independent antisubmarine command. Together, these assumptions led to certain inescapable conclusions concerning organization. First of all, antisubmarine forces, whether surface-craft or aircraft, Army or Navy, should be consolidated under one head, who should have the freedom of action and the status of a theater commander. The man to whom the responsibility would be entrusted for the safety of supply to the overseas troops should naturally be an Army man. "The U-boat is primarily a weapon against supply, not against naval fleets."

Since "past difficulties have in no small measure stemmed from a failure to realize the effectiveness of air attack on the U-boat," the new commander and the new organization should be such that the air arm would enjoy the greatest possible mobility and freedom of initiative. Although effective enough in the past, new weapons and navigational aids should, if used intelligently, make future operations against the submarine decisively successful. In order to eliminate the necessity of routing commands through AAF channels—coordination of the Army antisubmarine program was then being accomplished through the Director of Bombardment—Dr. Bowles suggested placing the AAFAC under the direct control of Operations Division, WD General Staff, with theater status.[56]

Dr. Bowles expressed some concern that such a large proportion of B-24 production was being allocated to the Navy, since most of these precious "heavies" would become a part of the Navy's own antisubmarine force on the Atlantic Coast. "Could we not," he urged, "make more efficient use of them in our own Command?" and, moreover, "should not a duplication of effort be discouraged?"[57]

Secretary Stimson gave Dr. Bowles' study his hearty approval. He was especially pleased with the prospect that under the proposed plan the Army could have an attacking system in operation by midsummer rather than by the end of the year, which was the best the Navy could offer under its current plans. He foresaw difficulties in coordinating with the Navy, and he was prepared to take the matter to the President if that service proved "too obdurate in respect to cooperation." In any event he was opposed to a compromise treatment of these plans in the Joint Chiefs of Staff which would "not allow full operational freedom to the Army in the command of killer planes."

Such a compromise /he wrote on 14 March 1943/ might stultify the vigor and initiative available through the faith and initiative of our air command. There is a very good precedent for such freedom in the British relation between the Coastal Command and the British Admiralty. We ought to strike at no less than that.[58]

Planners within the AAFAC followed roughly the lines of policy suggested by Dr. Bowles. Apparently recognizing the fact that, until some final settlement of the command question could be reached, a period of experimental operations would have to be gone through, they proposed two alternate plans to allow units of the command to operate through the AAF chain of command and not "under the operational control of any other headquarters." According to Plan A, the CG, AAFAC would deploy all his units in any required areas, operations to be conducted in cooperation with whatever air and surface antisubmarine forces might be active in those areas, but, presumably, not under the control of any such forces. According to Plan B he would create a task force composed of certain designated units of the Command which would operate on a status similar to that of Plan A, the remainder of the units operating as they were at that date, under operational control of the Navy.[59]

The Secretary of War had, a few days earlier (1 April 1943), made a proposal similar to Plan B. As a temporary stopgap measure he suggested the organization of a small task force within the AAFAC to function "during the experimental period more or less in an independent status." The Secretary of the Navy had given his veto and that of COMINCH to this plan which they felt to be tactically unsound.[60]

With reference to these abortive discussions, and on the basis of plans outlined by War Department experts, General Marshall frankly raised the issue of organization in the Joint Chiefs of Staff. In a memorandum (JCS 268), presented on 19 April 1943, he declared himself strongly of the opinion that the ultimate solution for the employment of the air arm in antisubmarine operations "particularly, and possibly exclusively as applied to VLR aircraft" could only be found in a unified command responsible for that type of operations. If such an authority could be set up, the result would be to override the limiting effect of the system of naval districts and sea frontiers under which the air arm had been forced to operate. If such authority could not be determined, he felt "we will tend to limp along under unavoidable difficulties that always exist when a new procedure has to develop under normal staff routine and operational organization." He therefore proposed that the U. S. shore-based air forces on antisubmarine duty in the Atlantic be organized to provide "highly mobile striking forces" for offensive action in addition to convoy coverage "in certain critical areas," and that this command operate directly under JCS as to policy in a manner similar to that of a theater commander. Moreover, in view of the urgency of the situation, General Marshall added that the Army and Navy should each provide VLR B-24's for this command at the rate of 12 per month during May, June, and July--this in addition to the 75 Army and 60 Navy VLR aircraft currently allocated to the antisubmarine campaign.

In JCS 268, General Marshall hoped to place the joint air force above questions of rival jurisdiction. By vesting the control of his proposed command in the JCS themselves, with COMINCH as their executive,[61] he left the way open for the appointment by JCS of an immediate commander most suitable for the job. It was a solution more in accord with the complex and competing command relationships than Dr. Bowles', though no more logical than the latter's proposal that final authority rest with the War Department. According to policy then in the process of formulation (JCS 263/2/D, dated 20 April 1943), command of any joint force would be settled on the basis of the nature of the mission to be performed, and the single commander would be designated by the Joint Chiefs of Staff. Now it did not take abnormal insight to see that in view of this policy a very strong argument could and would be made for an Army Air Forces officer as commander of the VLR aircraft on antisubmarine duty. For the moment, General Marshall was apparently willing to leave that point unstated, hoping that, as soon as JCS 263/2/D was approved the question would resolve itself.

Navy authorities no doubt arrived at this conclusion themselves, for action on JCS 268 was deferred pending the receipt of a report being prepared by the Navy Department bearing on the same problem.[62] On 1 May, Admiral King presented his alternative plan[63] (JCS 263/1, dated 3 May 1943). He proposed to set up at once in the Navy Department an antisubmarine command to be known as the Tenth Fleet. Headquarters of this command would consist of "all existing antisubmarine activities of the U. S. Fleet." The Commander, Tenth Fleet, would have direct command over all sea frontiers, using frontier commanders as task force commanders; and he would exercise control over all LR and VLR aircraft engaged in the work. In order to avoid duplication, initial training in Army antisubmarine aviation would be given by the AAFAC under guiding directives prepared by the Commander, Tenth Fleet. Maintenance of any antisubmarine aviation would also appropriately remain a function of the Commanding General, AAF. A logistical plan would be evolved to permit the greatest possible mobility on the part of the air units.

The Tenth Fleet proposal provided only a partial answer to the problem. It vested responsibility for antisubmarine operations in a commander who did not have competing claims to his attention. That at least was a step in the right direction. But it did not in any way meet General Marshall's recommendations in JCS 238. It placed shore-based air power under the control of the Navy Department rather than the JCS; and, while it appeared to involve a sweeping reorganization of the Navy Department, it actually did nothing of the sort, for it left the system of sea frontier commands as the basic machinery for the employment of the air arm. Indeed, to AAF observers it seemed that the only real change involved in Admiral King's paper was that COMINCH would emerge with increased control over AAF antisubmarine forces and the right to use Army bases.[64] It also appeared that Admiral King envisaged the possible expansion of the Tenth Fleet's jurisdiction beyond the Atlantic to include the South and Southwest

Pacific.[65] This jurisdiction would actually involve the authority to allocate antisubmarine aircraft and vessels between Atlantic and Pacific areas, a prerogative hitherto resting with the JCS.[66]

Final action on the Tenth Fleet proposal (JCS 268/1) was left to personal discussion between Admiral King, General Marshall, and General Arnold.[67] Although the plan failed to meet his full approval, General Marshall was willing to compromise.[68] He recognized that, according to JCS 263/2/D, the Navy had prior interest in antisubmarine warfare in general. He was therefore willing to accept the Tenth Fleet even at the expense of removing antisubmarine operations from the province of the JCS to that of the Navy Department. And since the air component would be a joint force it should be operated within the Tenth Fleet. But JCS 263/2/D would also govern the command of this joint land-based air force. Not only was the antisubmarine mission of special importance to the Army, but the problems of bases, air transport, maintenance, and supply were all essentially Army problems. And, with some 400 VLR bombers scheduled for this antisubmarine mission by the end of the year, the Army was entitled to some recognition in the command organization.[69] General Marshall therefore requested that an Army air officer be given command of the VLR and LR aircraft engaged in antisubmarine warfare.[70] It is impossible to determine from the available papers how this request was received. It is clear, however, that on 19 May, Admiral King proclaimed the existence of the Tenth Fleet, under the direct command of COMINCH, for the purpose of exercising unity of control over U. S. antisubmarine operations in that part of the Atlantic under U. S. strategic control.[71]

The Tenth Fleet, though a step in the right direction, solved nothing. The situation remained in an acute state of unstable equilibrium. In fact, it may be that, by the latter part of May, a compromise settlement on the antisubmarine situation was no longer possible. By that time, an issue much larger than that of the land-based antisubmarine air force had been raised, and a solution of the lesser problem would have to wait until the larger issue, of which it constituted a part, could be satisfactorily settled. In other words, control of land-based antisubmarine aircraft raised the question of the control of all land-based long-range aircraft employed on overwater missions.

The Navy had steadfastly resisted the notion that land-based aviation constituted a virtually separate arm which no longer fitted into the older pattern of the two primary services. In a perfectly natural effort to make its forces self-contained and to be as free as possible from the cramping necessity of coordinating with forces of another service over which it could exercise only an indirect authority, the Navy had striven to build up an air force of its own. This effort became especially vigorous when the long- and very-long-range land-based bombing plane demonstrated its preeminence in the execution of long-distance offshore patrol. The Navy quickly recognized the value of the B-24 and secured large allocations of these aircraft. By the end of June 1943, the Navy had received almost its full quota of 60 ASV-equipped VLR aircraft specifically designated for antisubmarine operations,[72] and was requesting increased allocations for patrol work in other theaters. According to the Bureau of Aeronautics, this requirement for an increase in land-based aircraft arose in part from a shift of emphasis from seaplanes to long- and medium-range land planes for both antisubmarine operations in the Atlantic, and sea-search, reconnaissance, and patrols in the Pacific.[73] And Admiral King had, in his comments on the unified antisubmarine command, intimated that he hoped such a system could be extended to include operations in the Pacific.

It was a very natural policy on the part of a service which had traditionally maintained a purity of organization impossible in the Army forces. As General Marshall pointed out, the problem of control of long-range aircraft operating with the Navy on antisubmarine patrol bore a marked similarity to the Army problem of divisional organization.[74] A divisional commander knows that he can handle the artillery and engineers more efficiently if they are all organic parts of the division and do not include elements attached only for a particular operation. But, without forces almost unlimited in numbers, such a policy would result in a duplication which, however efficient for the particular project, would be ruinously wasteful to the war effort as a whole. This was a problem which the Army had been forced to face since 1917. But, except for the creation of virtually a second army in the shape of the Marines, the problem had not presented itself to the Navy until the question of air striking forces had arisen. It was a trend which, if carried to its logical conclusion, would mean the eventual consolidation of the Army and Navy, for it would remove the essential distinction between them.

It is clear that the Navy had no such consolidation in mind. But for some time, in fact from the beginning of the allocation of B-24 aircraft to the Navy, Army observers had been concerned about the Navy's plans for controlling these forces. Now, in the summer of 1943, it began to appear that the Navy was bent, not only on building up a large force of long-range land-based bombers for patrol purposes and convoy coverage, but was prepared as well to deploy them on a large-scale strategic offensive, along lines roughly similar to those marked out by the AAFAC. Admiral King had eschewed an offensive for the entire length of the calendar year 1943.[75] For 1944, Navy planners were preparing to deploy antisubmarine forces in a coordinated offensive with the object of destroying the enemy at sea, a policy which the AAFAC had developed from its inception.[76] Signs were apparent by the middle of 1943, however, that indicated the Navy's intention to begin offensive action somewhat earlier. In April the Allied Antisubmarine Survey Board urged employment of support groups, composed of aircraft carriers and destroyers to be given the primary mission of taking offensive action against submarines. It also urged that the "maximum effort" should be put into an offensive in the Bay of Biscay transit areas. All these offensive operations would, however, have to wait until sufficient convoy escort forces had been secured.[77] A few days later Admiral Leahy, in a meeting of the JCS intimated that the only reason for the delay in offensive action was lack of forces.[78] In May the question of an Allied offensive in the Bay of Biscay was again broached by the British Chiefs of Staff.[79] By this time Admiral King offered only initial objections to diverting air units to that project. He maintained that an "irreducible minimum" of antisubmarine forces had to be maintained on the eastern coast of the United States because, while few submarines were currently in those waters, they could change their location more rapidly than aircraft.[80] And he once again declared himself opposed to the mixing of forces in projects of this sort.[81] As soon as it was demonstrated that an excess of VLR aircraft was located in Newfoundland, following the defeat in May of the U-boat packs in the North Atlantic, Admiral King solidly supported a plan for transferring as many as possible of those units to the United Kingdom for the purpose of participating in the Bay of Biscay offensive.[82]

It is not surprising, then, that War Department observers looked on Navy plans relative to land-based aircraft with some apprehension, not unmixed with suspicion. As far as the AAFAC was concerned, it appeared that the Navy was intent either on duplicating its function within its own organization by the increased allocation of B-24's to be deployed on offensive operations, which would be patently wasteful, or on securing complete control of all antisubmarine aircraft, including those of the AAFAC, which would simply remove the danger of duplication to a much higher level and expand it on a much grander scale. The destiny of the AAFAC as a strategic air striking force then became inextricably tied up with the question of strategic air striking forces in general, a question which all but involved the separate existence of the Army Air Forces itself.

So the situation after the establishment of the Tenth Fleet remained extremely acute. Indeed it rapidly deteriorated. For the issues were now clearer, and it had become evident that control of the long-range antisubmarine air force could be disposed of in two ways only: it could be given to the Army Air Forces, with or without the over-all operational supervision of the Navy, or it could be given completely to the naval authroity. The AAFAC, acting merely as the AAF's contribution to the total antisubmarine air force, no longer occupied a tenable position. Logically speaking, there was plenty of middle ground. If, as General Larson himself maintained, the AAFAC were considered the "Strategic" antisubmarine air force and deployed exclusively as a long-range, mobile striking force, then the Navy air arm engaged in antisubmarine patrol could be left the job of close support of the Fleet in the peculiarly naval mission of protecting shipping, and thus become the "Tactical" antisubmarine air force—a division of command into two independent organizations, based on a natural division of function.[83] But the force of circumstances now greatly outweighed the force of logic, and General Larson's conception of his Antisubmarine Command and its place in the military scheme of things bore little relation to the larger conflict of interests in which the Command had become involved.

Pending a final settlement with regard to the control of all air units engaged in antisubmarine warfare, there arose a grave danger that the air campaign itself might suffer. Fortunately, by June, the situation in the North Atlantic no longer threatened the very life line of U. S. forces in the European Theater. But the situation in the Mediterranean depended on the still doubtful ability of ocean convoys to reach African and Mediterranean ports. It was to make safe the passage of those convoys that the Navy urged participation in the British offensive in the Bay of Biscay. The War Department, although well aware of the value of offensive action in this key area, was reluctant to commit U. S. air units to the project until the question of their control could finally be made clear.[84] The project was given War Department and AAF endorsement before any serious delay was experienced.[85] The fact remained, however, that the AAFAC and those agencies having to do with its mission were handicapped by the impossibility of reconciling long term obligations with an immediately precarious status which necessitated planning on a short-term, emergency basis.[86] This momentary hesitation on the part of the War Department helped to force the issue concerning the over-all organization.

Final deliberations had already begun. On 10 June 1943, Rear Adm. McCain met with Generals Arnold and McNarney to draw up an agreement which would settle the question once and for all. From the documents available it is impossible to give a detailed account of the resulting discussions. Suffice it to say that an agreement was reached along the following lines:[87]

    a. The Army is prepared to withdraw Army Air Forces from anti-submarine operations at such time as the Navy is ready to take over those duties completely.

    b. Army anti-submarine airplanes would be continued in that service as long as the Navy has need for them.

    c. Army anti-submarine B-24 airplanes would be turned over to the Navy in such numbers as they could be replaced by Navy combat B-24's.

    d. The Navy is requested to submit a schedule on which the Army can turn over their planes to the Navy and draw Navy replacement B-24's.

    e. The Fleet Air Wings which the Navy proposes to station along the Atlantic and Pacific Coasts will comprise only those types of aircraft whose primary functions are those of offshore patrol and reconnaissance and the protection of shipping.

    f. It is primarily the responsibility of the Army to provide long-range bombing forces (currently called "strategic air forces") for operations from shore bases in defense of the Western Hemisphere and for appropriate operations in other theaters.

    g. Long-range patrol planes assigned to Fleet Air Wings are for the primary purpose of conducting offshore patrol and reconnaissance and the protection of shipping, relieving Army long-range bombing forces from those duties.

    h. Nothing in the foregoing sub-paragraphs is to be so interpreted as to limit or restrict a commander in the field, Army or Navy, in his use of all available aircraft as weapons of opportunity or necessity.

In effect the Arnold-McNarney-McCain agreement constituted a radical division of responsibility in the employment of long-range aircraft. In return for unquestioned control of all forces employed in protection of shipping, reconnaissance, and offshore patrol, the Navy would relinquish all claim to control of long-range striking forces operating from shore bases. The control of these so-called "strategic air forces" would remain, therefore, ineluctably an Army Air Forces responsibility. It was an agreement which affected issues far larger than that of the immediate fate of the AAFAC.

It was one thing to reach an agreement in committee and quite another to secure its approval by those more conservatively attached to the vested interest of their respective services. Neither Admiral King nor Secretary Stimson was willing to give up without a struggle. Admiral King accepted with alacrity the proposal that the Army hand over its antisubmarine responsibility to the Navy. It was, he said, a solution he was himself preparing to propose.[88] He gave no indication, however, of turning over to the Army the quid pro quo by which the concession was to be obtained, apparently preferring to leave unsettled the Army's right to conduct other long-range striking operations by land-based planes.[89]

To Secretary Stimson this failure of Admiral King's to indorse both halves of the Arnold-McNarney-McCain agreement seemed simply to guarantee continuation ad infinitum of trouble between Army and Navy.

Furthermore, he was by no means convinced that the agreement itself promised any improvement in the war effort. He granted the wisdom of clarifying the over-all jurisdiction, provided the result was clear enough to eliminate friction between Army and Navy. But he seriously doubted if the antisubmarine campaign would profit by the elimination of an AAF organization staffed by young, air-minded men, trained in the use of long-range land-based bombers, and possessed of the initiative and inventiveness necessary to develop antisubmarine offensive measures to the utmost. The AAFAC had, he felt, embarked on a policy entirely foreign from anything the Navy had hitherto proposed. And it still possessed the equipment, personnel, and doctrine uniquely adapted to the purpose of destroying the submarines at sea.

Since reorganization was necessary, he had strongly supported the plan originally presented to the JCS by General Marshall, which provided an AAF commander for all land-based VLR planes, who would work under the general operational supervision of the Navy. The plan had an impressive precedent in the relation of the RAF Coastal Command to the Admiralty. To Secretary Stimson, it seemed the only reasonable way of insuring that a concerted offensive would be launched which would clear the Atlantic of submarines in advance of the "enormous stream of our troops which will have to cross that Ocean for the 1944 invasion." In his opinion the organization for antisubmarine warfare proposed by the Navy was deficient in the elements essential to success: namely, free initiative, exercised by men acquainted with modern methods, elasticity in the operation of these methods, and freedom from the limitations imposed by an organization based on coastal frontiers. If these views of Secretary Stimson's did less than justice to the resourcefulness of the U. S. Navy, they full indorsed the potentialities existing in an AAF command for carrying an effective antisubmarine warfare.

In short, Secretary Stimson refused to approve the transfer of any antisubmarine activity to the Navy unless the latter were prepared to accept the entire Arnold-McNarney-McCain agreement, and he stated that he wished to be heard by the President on the subject should it reach the White House.[90]

Faced with a possible impasse in a matter so close to the heart of the war effort, General Marshall issued what General Stratemeyer termed "one of the strongest and most important documents which has been signed by the Chief of Staff thus far during the war".[91],[92]

> The question of responsibility for offensive operations against submarines and that of responsibility for long-range air striking forces are so closely related that a proper solution of one, in my opinion, involves consideration of the other. The tentative Arnold-McNarney-McCain agreement appeared to offer an acceptable solution to both of these issues and solely on that basis I stated to you in my memorandum of June 15 that your proposal to take over anti-submarine air operations appeared to offer a practical solution to a vexing problem which has adversely affected the efficiency of our aerial war effort.
>
> I should state here that in all of these Army and Navy air discussions I have tried very carefully to hold myself to a position from which I could consider the problems from a somewhat detached and I hope, purely logical basis. As I remarked in the meeting of the Joint Chiefs of Staff the other day I feel that the present state of procedure between the Army and Navy is neither economical nor highly efficient and would inevitably meet with public condemnation were all the facts known. I have been hopeful that during the actual war effort we could manage our business in such a manner as to be spared the destructive effects of reorganizational procedure. But I am becoming more and more convinced that we must put our own house in order, and quickly, in order to justify our obligation to the country. I feel this very strongly because it is plain to me, however it may appear to others, that our present procedure is not at all what it should be.
>
> Feeling as I do that the two questions involved are part and parcel of the same problem I believe that the Committee on Missions of the Army and Navy should be given both questions in their entirety for appropriate recommendation, or that we should formalize the entire Arnold-McNarney-McCain agreement. The latter procedure promises earlier, and I believe, more satisfactory results as it appears rather likely that the Committee may reach an impasse in the matter as the result of past strong prejudices and bitter discussions.

General Marshall made it clear that the Arnold-McNarney-McCain agreement did not establish a basis for the duplication of the long-range air striking force now in being in the Army. "Such duplication, if permitted, would be patently uneconomical and would result in an unavoidable drain on our resources." Meanwhile, he assured Admiral King that the AAFAC would continue to function, "insuring that no detriment to the war effort will occur as a result of any delay which may accrue while this matter is being properly settled."

On 9 July 1943, approximately 1 month after the Arnold-McNarney-McCain committee convened, its agreement was accepted by both War and Navy Departments. A schedule was subsequently established whereby 77 Army antisubmarine-equipped B-24's would be transferred with related equipment to the Navy, in return for an equal number of combat-equipped B-24's from Navy allocations. The transfer was to take place gradually from the latter part of July to the end of September.[92] Some difficulty arose over the relief of the squadrons on duty in the United Kingdom and in Northwest Africa. Finally it was decided to keep them in their current duty status until such time as they could be relieved by similarly equipped Navy squadrons. On 6 October 1943, Bombardment Branch, Operations, Commitments, and Requirements, was able to report that the 77 planes in the original agreement had been transferred.[93] In October, also, the Navy Liberators arrived at Dunkeswell, Devonshire, to relieve the 479th Group. By the middle of November, the 480th Group had been relieved and was on its way back to Langley Field from Northwest Africa.

The AAFAC officially passed out of the picture before the complicated mechanism of transfer could be completed. By an order, dated 31 August, from Headquarters, EDC and First Air Force, its headquarters was redesignated Headquarters, I Bomber Command, and assigned to the First Air Force, effective 24 August 1943.[94] The AAFAC wings, the 25th and 26th, were inactivated and their personnel, together with all excess personnel left over from the earlier expansion made necessary by the increase in antisubmarine activity, were made available to AC/AS, Personnel for reassignment. The domestic squadrons, 17 of the 25 separate squadrons of the command, were redesignated as heavy bombardment units and assigned to the Second Air Force. The 18th Squadron, which had operated as an OTU at Langley Field, was assigned to the 1st Sea-Search Attack Group of the First Air Force for the purpose of conducting replacement crew training on radar equipment. The 23d Squadron continued temporarily to serve as a special task unit, on special duty with the Navy in the Caribbean for the purpose of experimenting with 75-mm. armament in B-25 aircraft, after which it went, with the bulk of the other squadrons, to the Second Air Force. The 479th Group, with four squadrons stationed in the United Kingdom, was inactivated and its personnel and equipment (the latter not a part of the 77-plane agreement) assigned to the Eighth Air Force, its personnel to be used as a nucleus in forming a pathfinder group. Similarly, the 480th Group returned intact to the United States, whereupon the bulk of its personnel was assigned to the Second Air Force, a few of the officers remaining on duty with Headquarters, AAF. Its aircraft were made available for use in the American and Pacific theaters.[95] Both the 479th and the 480th Groups continued operations until the latter part of October 1943.

As this slow process neared completion, and the Army Air Forces prepared to bow finally from the stage of antisubmarine operations, the work of its deceased Antisubmarine Command became the subject of several laudatory statements, in which Admirals King and Andrews joined with General Arnold and others, who were in like position to know whereof they spoke, in pronouncing it a job well done.[96]

If there is one fact which stands out above another in this story of the policies and concept surrounding the Army Air Forces' participation in the antisubmarine campaign, it is that the fate of the AAFAC depended not at all on its doctrine of antisubmarine warfare, or on its ability to fulfill the requirements of its mission. Throughout most of the story a sharp cleavage in strategic doctrine had emphasized a cleavage already existing between the services jointly engaged in the work. And there were those who, like Secretary Stimson and General Larson, maintained to the end the value of the Army doctrine and the unique ability of Army air officers to implement it. But, although committed to an organization which scarcely allowed the flexibility considered in air circles essential to the highest efficiency in antisubmarine warfare, and possessed of less adequate experience in the operation of land-based aviation than the AAF, the Navy was ready in the summer of 1943 to project an offensive which the AAFAC had preached since its previous incarnation as the I Bomber Command. There doubtless still existed a difference of opinion relative to the priority to be attached to offensive operations. To the Navy, convoy escort probably still ranked above killer tactics.

Nevertheless, the Navy was prepared to throw everything possible into an effort to destroy the U-boats at sea as soon as the minimum requirements for defense had been met. And, thanks to the substantial defeat of the U-boats during May, June, and July, those requirements could be met at an earlier date than naval plans appear initially to have anticipated.

The question at issue therefore was not strategic or even tactical, but rather the larger one of jurisdiction over long-range, land-based air striking forces. With reference to this more comprehensive problem, control of the AAFAC constituted little more than a test case. But the importance of a test case is determined by the importance of the issue being tested, and the case of the AAFAC becomes consequently one of the most significant arising in the U.S. armed forces during the present war.

Chapter III

OPERATIONS

The Battle of the Atlantic

It was a large and already crowded stage onto which the AAF Antisubmarine Command stepped in October 1942. The Battle of the Atlantic had not yet reached its peak of intensity, nor had any decisive blows been struck, but several phases of the conflict had already come and gone and several agencies were engaged in an effort to defeat the Nazi raiders. At first, in 1939 and 1940, the U-boats had operated with immunity close to the British Isles and the coast of Europe. The British had made every effort to counter the submarine blockade and had, in fact, cleared the English Channel and North Sea waters with fair success. As yet, however, aircraft were used only to a limited extent, and long-range air patrols were unheard of. The summer of 1941 saw a marked increase in the use of air power, nearly one-third of the damaging attacks being credited to them. The result was that the U-boats moved farther afield, scattering their attacks as far west as 49°, and as far south as Africa. Effective air patrol remained relatively short-ranged, leaving the whole central ocean a free hunting ground for the enemy.

The next phase of the battle began upon the entry of the United States into the war. The resulting depredations off the U. S. Atlantic coastline General Marshall felt jeopardized the entire war effort.

THE CURVES FOR M/V'S SUNK, U/B's ATTACKED, AND U/B's SUNK SHOW 30-DAY CUMULATIONS PLOTTED AT END OF 30-DAY PERIOD

THE CURVE FOR U/B's AT SEA SHOWS A 30-DAY AVERAGE PLOTTED AT END OF 30-DAY PERIOD

By the middle of June 1942, he reported that 17 of the 74 ships allocated to the Army for July had already been sunk, 22 per cent of the bauxite fleet, and 20 per cent of the Puerto Rican fleet had been lost, and tanker sinkings had amounted to 3.5 per cent per month of the tonnage in use.[1]

By the fall of that year an entirely new act in the drama was begun. The enemy had gradually withdrawn from the Eastern and Gulf Sea Frontiers, partly because of the increased opposition he encountered in American waters and partly because the Allied invasion of North Africa made it essential for the U-boat fleet to turn from its aggressive campaign against shipping in general in order to concentrate defensively against the invasion convoys. The U-boat fleet continued, however, to operate actively and effectively in areas, such as the waters off Trinidad, where the traffic was relatively large and the antisubmarine measures relatively weak.

By the time the AAF Antisubmarine Command was activated, two things had become clear about the submarine war. One was that the Germans would, if at all possible, avoid areas provided with adequate antisubmarine forces. The other was that the most flexible and among the most powerful of those forces consisted of long-range bombardment aircraft, specially equipped and manned for the purpose of hunting and killing submarines. Though dictated primarily by the necessity of destroying as much Allied shipping as possible and preventing the Allies from implementing any logistical plan of major importance, German strategy in the Atlantic always remained sensitive to the state of Allied antisubmarine forces, especially air forces. Throughout the antisubmarine war, wherever adequate air cover was provided the submarines withdrew, if tactically possible. In the region of the British Isles, when the same submarine was sighted an average of six times a month it left the area, and when sighted an average of three times a month in American coastal waters it left them. As for the relative effectiveness of aircraft compared to surface vessels, Dr. Bowles, in March 1943, estimated aircraft to be about 10 times as effective in finding submarines as surface craft and at least as effective in killing them.[2]

The U-boat fleet, although strategically on the defensive, had still ample opportunity to operate effectively. The RAF Coastal Command and the Royal Navy had made the British waters unprofitable for it, and had seriously interfered with its free access to the submarine bases on the European coast. The AAF and U. S. Navy had cleared American waters as far south as the Caribbean. But the convoy routes, especially those in the North Atlantic, which bore the weight of Allied strategic supplies, remained relatively unprotected. For air cover, in the absence of adequate very-long-range equipment, could only protect an area a few hundred miles offshore. This left a large gap in mid-ocean without cover, and as yet the Allies did not have enough strength in carrier escort vessels to provide air cover for this area. Moreover, the Atlantic U-boat fleet was believed to be increasing rather than otherwise. Probably not more than 15 to

22 enemy submarines were operating in the Atlantic at the beginning of 1942. At the end of the year this force had risen to about 108, and the Germans were believed to be producing submarines at the rate of between 20 and 25 per month.[3]

After a highly successful month in November 1942, the Germans spent a relatively unprofitable winter. Their strategy was apparently to throw out mid-ocean screens in a primarily defensive plan to destroy Allied convoys. It may have been owing to this thinly deployed screen of submarines, extending from 56° north latitude to slightly south of the equator and through which convoys could frequently pass without detection, that few merchant vessels were lost that winter. It may also have been true that the Germans were conserving their forces for a total spring offensive. At any rate, toward the end of February and during the early days of March 1943, it became evident that they were adopting a new strategy involving a concentration of U-boats along the North Atlantic convoy routes. Concurrently with this shifting of forces, the enemy also planned to hold large forces of Allied antisubmarine aircraft and escort vessels in widely scattered control areas. This they could do without too much expenditure of submarines simply by sending small groups into the Eastern, Gulf, and Caribbean Sea Frontiers and the Brazilian, Freetown, and Mozambique areas.

The disposition of enemy forces in the North Atlantic followed a general pattern somewhat as follows. Two roughly parallel screens running in a northwesterly direction were thrown across the convoy routes in such a way as to make contact with both eastbound and westbound convoys. As soon as convoys were attacked, the two lines would break formation and gather around the convoy, resuming the parallel screen formation when all feasible measures had been taken to harass the Allied ships. This strategy worked well and accounted for most of the sinkings in the Atlantic, which rose once again to a dangerous total in March. In that month, too, the Allied nations immediately concerned in the Battle of the Atlantic took action to close the gap in their North Atlantic defenses. The Atlantic Convoy Conference met, and plans were laid to employ effective long-range air forces in Newfoundland, Greenland, and Iceland.

The battle of the North Atlantic reached its climax in early May with the attack on a convoy known as ONS-5. Frustrated by increasingly effective surface escort and air patrol, the Germans threw a large force of submarines into a running battle in a reckless attempt to retrieve some kind of victory from their dwindling spring offensive. So reckless was their attack that they lost heavily, and were forced to admit the failure of their attempt to close off the North Atlantic routes. In addition to an increasing number of air attacks of better quality than ever before, the Germans owed their defeat to the introduction by the Allies of aircraft carriers which were able to provide air coverage in any part of the ocean. Planned aerial escort of convoys by carrier-based aircraft had been inaugurated in March.

By early July the enemy had almost abandoned the North Atlantic and the vital war convoys could proceed unmolested. The estimated average daily density of U-boats in the area declined from 58 in May to 16 in June and only 5 in July. Ship losses decreased correspondingly from a peak of 88 in March to 14 in May and none in July, despite the fact that nearly 1,700 ship crossings were accomplished in June and July.[4]

Meanwhile, since October 1942, AAF bombers of the Eighth Air Force had joined RAF forces in bombing attacks on German submarine bases, construction yards, and parts plants. This action did little to reduce the number of U-boats at sea nor did it do as much as had been expected to retard the output of submarines, the estimated number of completions by early 1944 having been reduced by not more than 20.[5] Meanwhile, also, the RAF, with the brief help of two AAF Antisubmarine Command squadrons, was pressing an offensive campaign in the Bay of Biscay transit area. And both aircraft and surface forces engaged in the antisubmarine war were gradually increasing in effectiveness, as a result of improved weapons and devices, and the increasing experience of their crews.

It was clear, then, that the Allies, though hampered by lack of unified command, were successfully employing four main methods in their counterattack against the U-boats. First, they were maintaining defensive patrols in coastal areas to hamper and restrict enemy operations. Secondly, they were employing defensive convoy escort and offensive sweeps around convoys in order to prevent the submarine packs from closing in for the attack. Thirdly, offensive bombing missions were being pressed against U-boat bases and building yards. Finally, screens of surface craft and aircraft were being thrown in a continuous offensive action across areas in which U-boats were forced to concentrate.

A corollary to the increasingly effective antisubmarine campaign may be found in the increasing tendency of the U-boats to fight back. Prior to the spring of 1943, the standard practice on the part of U-boat commanders was to employ a passive defense against air attack and simply to dive on the approach of an enemy plane. If too many planes were encountered, however, a new problem arose. The submarine could not remain submerged indefinitely nor could it make the speed necessary for successful attacks while under water. The decision to employ an active defense came therefore as an admission of the effectiveness of air patrol. It also, of course, gave the attacking aircraft a substantial target for its depth bombs. During July of 1943 these defensive tactics, apparently adopted throughout the U-boat fleet, served to intensify the speed of the submarine war.

Especially vigorous was the action in the eastern Atlantic. It had been anticipated that the enemy, driven from the North Atlantic convoy routes, would move his forces south to the convoy routes between the United States and the Mediterranean. The latter lanes were not only carrying a substantial and steadily increasing amount of vital traffic in support of the North African and Sicilian campaigns, but, owing to lack of antisubmarine bases in the Azores, much of the route was out of range of land-based aircraft. This anticipation proved entirely correct, for the Germans formed heavy U-boat concentrations south and southwest of the Azores. These submarines enjoyed surprisingly little success. Several factors may have reduced the effectiveness of their groups. Convoys could be

Five charts: Merchant vessels sunk in the Atlantic, September 1941-August 1943. From charts published at intervals in AAFAC Monthly Intelligence Reports, 1943.

MARCH AUGUST 1912

SEPT. 1942 - FEB. 1943

MARCH-MAY 1943

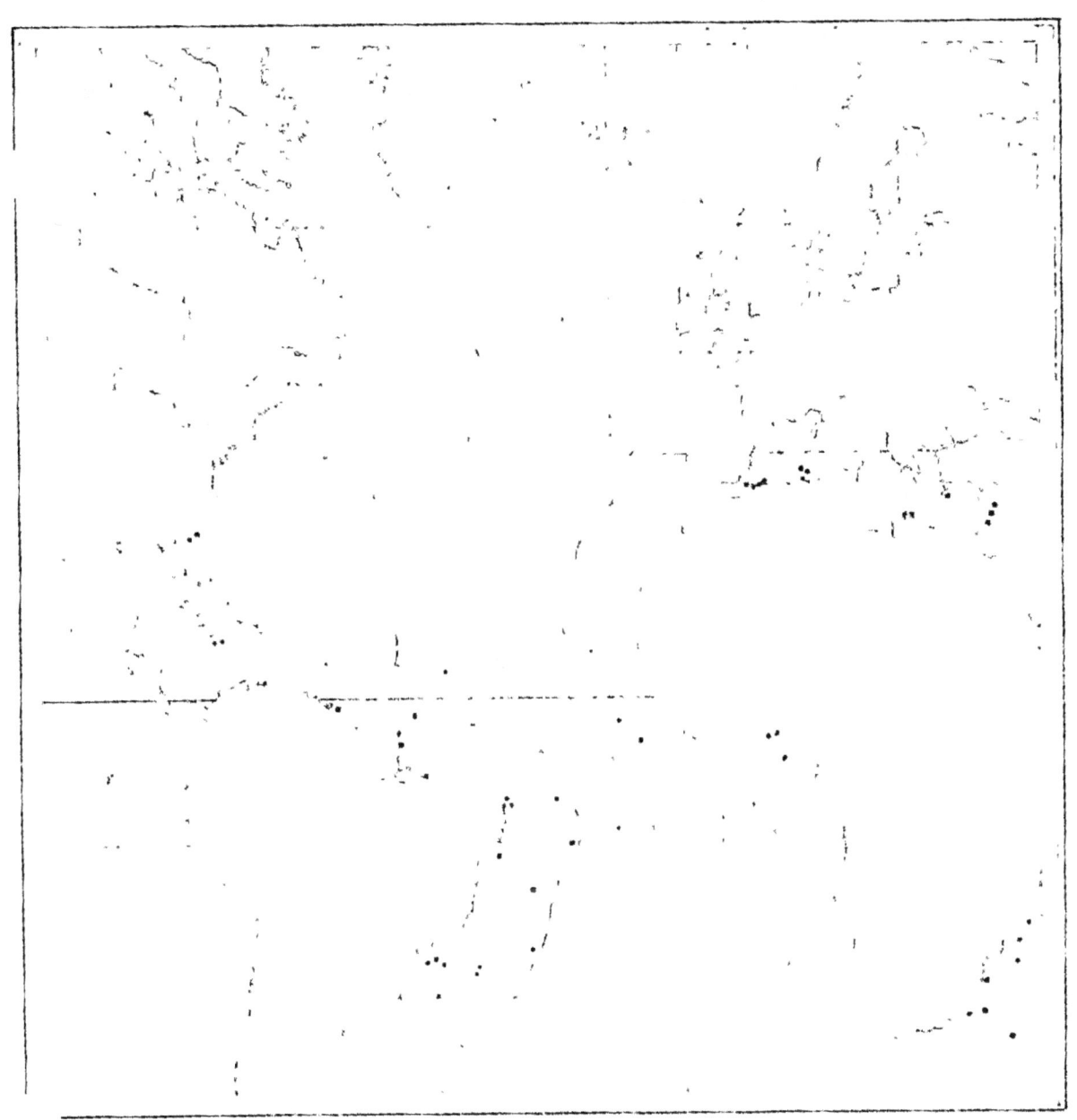

JUNE 1943 to AUG 1943

widely dispersed in the wide expanse of the mid-Atlantic; heavy escort was provided, especially for the high-speed troop convoys; and the small aircraft carriers operated effectively in this area.

Certainly another factor was the action of British and AAF Antisubmarine Command aircraft in the Bay of Biscay transit area and in the approaches to Gibraltar. AAF Antisubmarine Command squadrons were sent in July to reinforce the British offensive in the Bay of Biscay and long-range patrol of the approaches to Gibraltar had been increased in March by the transfer to Northwest Africa of two AAF Antisubmarine Command squadrons from the United Kingdom. In June and July these areas saw some of the sharpest action of the Atlantic war in operations which frustrated any further attempt on the part of the enemy to reorganize a concentrated offensive. During these operations, the Germans threw large forces of medium and heavy aircraft into defensive attacks on antisubmarine aircraft.

September saw a sadly reduced, if still potentially dangerous, submarine fleet being employed by the Germans in the Atlantic. The Germans had deployed an average force of about 103 U-boats in the Atlantic during the first five months of 1943. In contrast to these figures, probably not more than 50 were operating in the Atlantic by early September.[6] Moreover, the U-boats were now being manned by relatively inexperienced crews, since probably 7,000 trained crew members and officers had been lost in the submarines, estimated at upwards of 150, either sunk or probably sunk during the previous 8 months.[7] Most encouraging of all was the fact that from July to

September 1943 only one-half of 1 per cent of U. S. supplies shipped in the Atlantic were lost through submarine attack.[8]

In accomplishing this great change in U-boat warfare, which until the end of 1942 had run entirely in favor of the enemy, aircraft played a major role. By July 1943, aircraft were making 60 to 70 per cent of all attacks on U-boats and by the end of the year it was estimated that about 70 per cent of the submarines being sunk were lost to aircraft, either land-based or carrier-based. The answer to the U-boat menace had been found to an overwhelming degree in action at sea, and by air attack in particular.[9]

This, in rough outline, was the pattern of events in which the AAF Antisubmarine Command found a not inconspicuous place.

Operations in the Eastern Atlantic

The Bay of Biscay. The summer of 1942 had left the Eastern and Gulf Sea Frontiers almost free from the undersurface raiders. While the bulk of the Antisubmarine Command's operational squadrons were engaged in defensive convoy coverage or in the patrol of these un-infested waters, a few units were being allowed to test the command's doctrine of the strategic offensive, and to hunt the U-boats where they abounded, either in their home waters or where they were forced by strategic necessity to be. In November 1942, one squadron of B-24's, equipped with SCR-517C radar, was sent to England. In January another joined it. During the course of its career, the command sent, in all, six VLR squadrons to operate in the Eastern Atlantic. These units, ultimately organized into the 479th and 480th Antisubmarine Groups, contributed the most significant chapter in the AAFAC operational history.

Probably the most interesting aspect of these eastern Atlantic operations was the participation by the American squadrons in the Bay of Biscay offensive being conducted almost continuously by the British Coastal Command during the period covered by this study. Their participation was of brief duration, but the results were extremely instructive to students of antisubmarine warfare and destructive to the enemy.

The "Bay offensive" had, by 1943, become the pivotal point for the entire British antisubmarine effort. The strategic theory behind it was very logical. It was well known that most of the U-boats operating in the Atlantic, estimated at upwards of 100,[10] were based on ports on the western coast of France. In order to leave these ports for operations against Atlantic shipping and to return for necessary periodic repair and servicing, practically the entire German submarine fleet had to pass through the Bay of Biscay, thus producing a constantly high concentration in the Bay and its approaches.[11] Moreover, in crossing this transit area, the U-boats were obliged to spend an appreciable portion of their time on the surface in order to recharge their batteries. It soon occurred to the Coastal Command that the judicious use of a moderate air force in this area would be enough eventually to cripple the U-boat offensive.[12]

Throughout the first 6 months of 1942 the Coastal Command flew a small but steadily increasing number of hours in the Biscay transit area. During the next year, the flying effort in that area was maintained at a relatively high level, averaging between 3,000 and 4,000 hours per month.[13] The chief problems to be overcome were lack of very-long-range aircraft capable of covering the entire transit area from English bases, lack of a "balanced" antisubmarine force capable of attacking both by day and night, thus making it just as dangerous for U-boats to surface by night as by day, and lack of radar equipment of a kind the Germans could not detect. Early in 1943 a plan was being drawn up, based on comprehensive theoretical studies, calling for an increased and better-balanced flying effort in the Bay of Biscay. An area was determined in the approaches to the Bay, of such size that every U-boat in transit must surface at least once to recharge its batteries. The expected density of surfaced U-boats in the area was then calculated. It was estimated that a certain number of sorties by specially equipped planes would be required, by day and night, to insure that every submarine in transit would be subjected to attack. It was planned to make extensive use of Mark III radar, which the Germans were apparently unable to detect, in conjunction with the Leigh searchlight in order to make night operations effective. It was claimed that a force of 260 suitably equipped aircraft could account for about 25 U-boats killed and 34 damaged per month.[14] Even a force of about 40 long-range aircraft was considered enough to make the enemy abandon the Bay ports, because the U-boats in transit had no retreat from a well-equipped air force.

And to abandon the Bay ports would mean defeat in the Atlantic, for the Germans could not use Norwegian ports without risking a similarly concentrated offensive in a similar transit area off Scotland and Ireland.[15]

The question had arisen whether this air force would be used to better advantage in a defensive-offensive campaign in the area where the U-boats actually operated. But it was decided that, inasmuch as the Bay offensive, if pressed constantly, would lead to a breaking point, and therefore to total defeat of the U-boats in the Atlantic, it should have priority over the necessarily defensive campaign against the enemy in his operational area. In the open sea the U-boat could choose its time and place, surface or submerge, more nearly at will than was possible in the vital transit area. On the ground of morale alone it was believed the Bay offensive could do irreparable damage to the U-boat fleet.[16]

This was the strategic situation into which the 1st and 2d AAF Antisubmarine Squadrons were projected in February of 1943. They had been dispatched to the United Kingdom originally for the purpose of training in Coastal Command methods. When thoroughly indoctrinated, they were to proceed to North Africa for action with the Twelfth Air Force.[17] While in England, however, plans were altered somewhat. The British were at this point (early 1943) in serious need of long-range antisubmarine aircraft. Though their operations in the Bay had been successful, it was believed that the U-boats were able to remain submerged long enough, with possible brief night surfacing, to carry them beyond the outer limit of the British medium-range planes. It was therefore decided to use the two American squadrons of B-24's to supplement the few available long-range British aircraft in a thorough patrol of the outer area, far to the west. The medium-range equipment would then be concentrated in the inner area. These areas were called Outer and Inner Gondola, respectively.[18] In view of the then chronic shortage of aircraft, the sustained effort of this Gondola operation was planned to continue for only 9 days, and was dated to coincide with an estimated inrush of U-boats coming away from two convoy battles then in full conflict. The period was actually 6 to 15 February 1943. The results confirmed the wisdom of the plan. Fourteen sightings resulted in nine attacks in Outer Gondola. Only four sightings and one attack came from the inner area. Of the enemy contacts made in the outer area, 90 per cent were by the U. S. aircraft. Thus, Air Marshal Slessor, Air-Officer-Commanding-in-Chief, wrote, some months later, "The two U. S. squadrons . . . played the major part and incidentally 'blooded themselves in' most successfully in the Anti-U/Boat War on this side of the Atlantic."[19]

This is all somewhat ahead of the story. And the Gondola offensive is really only part of the story. It was no simple task to transplant two American squadrons and train them under foreign conditions to such a point that they could turn in a record such as that outlined above. Many U. S. bombardment squadrons had preceded them to England and as components of the Eighth Air Force had become successfully operational. But they had from the beginning formed part of a well-organized and sizeable American force, and had pioneered in an entirely different type of warfare from that to which the 1st and 2d Antisubmarine Squadrons were committed. The latter units, in fact, found the way but poorly prepared for them in the United Kingdom.[20]

To begin with, on its arrival at St. Eval on 7 November 1942, the advance units of the 1st Antisubmarine Squadron found that no one knew anything of the plans for it. The decision to send it and the 2d Antisubmarine Squadron had been made in haste and in great secrecy, and it took the commanding officer, Lt. Col. Jack Roberts, some time to find out where his unit should operate and under whose control. After a series of conversations with the Commanding General of the Eighth Air Force, it was finally settled that the squadron should be attached to the VIII Bomber Command for supply and administration, and that it should remain at St. Eval under the operational control of the RAF Coastal Command. When the 2d Antisubmarine Squadron arrived in January 1943, it was stationed at the same field and placed under the same administrative control.[21] On 15 January 1943 the two squadrons were combined in the 1st Antisubmarine Group (Prov.), under the command of Colonel Roberts, working as a detached unit of the 25th Antisubmarine Wing of the AAF Antisubmarine Command.[22]

It had been understood prior to departure from the United States that maintenance for aircraft would be provided immediately after arrival. Actually, there were no adequate facilities or personnel for this purpose. The VIII Bomber Command quickly detached 65 mechanics, ordnance men, armament specialists, and guards, but the men were not experienced in B-24 aircraft at that time, and they joined the group reluctantly since it meant leaving their own promotion lists. It proved to be a considerable problem to weld these men into an efficient maintenance team, but one that was fortunately soon solved.[23]

St. Eval was already overcrowded with squadrons of the Coastal Command. No hangar space was available for maintenance. The result was that all such work had to be done during the limited number of daylight hours in the open, the mechanics unprotected from the raw weather of a British winter. Nearly 50 per cent of the personnel immediately contracted heavy bronchial colds, a situation which presented a real problem to the flight surgeon who lacked even the simplest medicines. Furthermore, there were no quarters available for the officers and men at the station, so it was necessary to scatter them at considerable distances from the field. For quite a while, too, the American units had to eat British rations, since no separate mess facilities had been provided.[24]

St. Eval was far removed from any established Services of Supply or Air Service Command supply depots, finance offices, or Army post offices, nor had any adequate communications or supply channels been set up to reach it. As a result, the nearest depots were at first a difficult day's drive away. Later, a newly established depot was located that could be reached by a 5-hour drive.[25]

In addition to these initial difficulties, there were several serious administrative and operational problems which could scarcely have been solved until the units were in the theater. The squadrons had been sent to England with no idea of prolonged operations in that area. They, therefore, found themselves short of personnel, a situation which was not improved by generally prevalent illness. Officer personnel was especially overtaxed.[26] Moreover, since the group was at that time provisional, the commanding officer found himself without adequate authority in some respects. For example, he could neither promote deserving personnel nor demote a few recalcitrant individuals--in either case a condition detrimental to group morale.[27] The squadrons were immediately faced with innumerable problems in learning British control methods, navigational aids, communications, and other procedures. Even some British customs provided minor but troublesome problems. British military custom, for instance, draws a sharp line of demarcation among enlisted men between sergeants and those of lower rank, and provides each group with its own housing and recreational facilities. The American crews had to be similarly divided although such division was contrary to U. S. Army custom.[28]

Some difficulty arose over the nature of the "operational control" to be exercised by the Coastal Command. As in the case of the U. S. Navy's control, the term had not been clearly defined. Questions at once arose. Did operational control mean that missions could be ordered if weather conditions were, in the opinion of the group commander, too hazardous? Would he have a voice in determining assignments?[29] These and similar questions carried serious potentialities which could easily have wrecked current and future cooperation between Allied commands.[30] Officers of the group had, however, nothing but praise for the cooperation they received from the RAF Coastal Command. That organization gave freely of its long experience in antisubmarine warfare, a contribution which proved invaluable in guiding and training the novice squadrons. It left to the group commander final decision on all assignments as well as on all questions of recall or diversion of missions, whether owing to weather or enemy activity. The Army Air Forces Controller, who worked directly with the British Controller, had the full privilege of handling all control of American aircraft if in his judgment intervention was advisable. British radio communications proved to be excellent and the British control officers soon gained the complete confidence of all flying personnel. The British spared no effort in guiding aircraft to safe bases, regardless of risks involved, and fields were always fully lighted for landings despite the constant and often immediate threat of attack from enemy aircraft operating from bases only 100 miles distant.[31]

The 1st Antisubmarine Squadron flew its first mission in European waters on 16 November 1942, just 9 days after its arrival in the United Kingdom. Operations continued rather slowly for a while, since at first only three planes were available. Additional aircraft became operational during the following 90 days. Exactly 2 months later, on 16 January 1943, the 2d Antisubmarine Squadron flew its first mission. These small initial operations provided invaluable experience, for they demonstrated the operational problems that were to face all U. S. squadrons in European areas, and they served as laboratory tests that proved the amount and type of additional training needed for newly arrived units.[32]

The job of training to meet the conditions of operation in the eastern Atlantic, and under the control of the British, was a large one. Much instruction had to be given in the use of British depth bombs, in British methods of diverting aircraft to alternate fields when weather proved suddenly adverse, and in British control and radio procedures which differed substantially from American. Recognition of enemy and friendly aircraft had to be exact in an area covered by enemy as well as by friendly patrols. Enemy capabilities, tactics, and methods of combat had to be learned. Extra training in navigation was especially important since many of the navigational aids to which U. S. navigators were accustomed, such as radio beams, could not be used in the ETO; and even a small navigational error in returning from a 2,000-mile sea mission might put the aircraft over enemy territory.[33]

As for equipment, the new SCR-517C radar proved the principal problem. The aircraft of the squadrons had been equipped with this latest device immediately prior to leaving the United States. A supply of spare parts was lost en route, the equipment had not been "shaken down" before departure, the radar operators in the organization had not been trained in its use, and experienced mechanics could not be found in the United Kingdom. Once these initial difficulties had been surmounted, the radar sets proved their worth, accounting for many sightings that probably could not have been made with British equipment.[34] The B-24 aircraft themselves gave very little trouble. The only serious difficulty arose in adapting them to carry 10 to 12 of the British Torpex 250-pound depth bombs without shifting forward the center of gravity of the airplane.[35]

The chain of command in the Coastal Command was similar to that in the AAF Antisubmarine Command. The 1st Provisional Group operated under the Station Commander, St. Eval, who received his orders from Headquarters, 19 Group, RAF, which corresponded to the wing organization in the AAF Antisubmarine Command. The squadrons reported daily to the Station Controller the number of planes and crews available for missions the following day. The Controller then assigned take-off times. Crews reported for briefing 2 hours prior to scheduled take-off and received lunches, pyrotechnics, and all other equipment and information relative to the mission.[36] Operational missions generally were of 11 to 14 hours' duration in order to make full use of the long-range potentialities of the B-24. Such long missions, searching far out over the ocean, proved exceedingly fatiguing to the combat crews, especially when executed under adverse weather conditions. When it is considered that these squadrons arrived in the United Kingdom at the beginning of the worst months normally experienced in a country not noted for its fine winter climate, it can readily be seen that the long-distance patrols were only for tough and young men.[37] Missions at first were planned every third day, but it was found that, in the interests of the mental and physical health of the men, 3 days would have to elapse between missions.[38]

The following table indicates the extent of operations of the group from the United Kingdom:[39]

Month	Missions	Hrs. Flown	U-boat Sightings	U-boat Attacks
Nov. 1942	9	77	0	0
Dec. 1942	30	231	2	2
Jan. 1943	58	490	1	0
Feb. 1943	111	1,052	15	8
Mar. 1-5, 1943	10	116	2	1
	218	1,966	20	11

In view of the fact that few aircraft were available during November and December 1942, and that the 2d Antisubmarine Squadron did not fly its first operational mission until 16 January 1943, the record of nearly 2,000 hours of operational flying during the months of worst British weather is highly satisfactory. The record of sightings and attacks is also good. On the average, 1 sighting was made for every 98.3 hours of flying time, and 1 attack for each 177.8 hours of flight, a record far more satisfying than that being achieved during the same period on the U. S. Atlantic coast where the scarcity of U-boats necessitated many thousands of hours of flying for each sighting.[40] Most striking of all, however, are the figures for the Gondola campaign in early February. This action proved to be the climax of the operations of the 1st Provisional Group (later the 480th Group) during its stay in the United Kingdom.

On 20 occasions, aircraft of the group, while operating from the United Kingdom, sighted enemy U-boats. In 11 instances attacks followed. In the remaining 9, the U-boat had been submerged so long before the arrival of the attacking aircraft that no depth bombs were released, a procedure quite in accordance with instructions. In these early months of operation a great deal of difficulty was experienced in adjusting release mechanisms to function properly with the British type of depth bomb. In 3 out of 11 attacks made, the depth bombs "hung up" and so frustrated what might otherwise have been excellent attacks. Of the 8 attacks not thwarted by mechanical failure, the assessed results were:[41]

    1 probably sunk
    1 so severely damaged that it probably failed to reach port
    1 severely damaged
    3 insufficient evidence of damage
    2 no damage

The aircraft of the group did not conduct these early operations unopposed. For many months Allied aircraft had been free to fly over the Bay without opposition from enemy planes, but, as the Allied air patrols increased and crossing the Bay became correspondingly more difficult, the enemy began to put medium-range twin-engine fighters over the area in increasing numbers. This tendency was becoming apparent during the period when the 480th Group operated from the United Kingdom. Some months later, the 479th Group encountered much greater opposition from the JU-33's. During the winter months, aircraft of the 480th Group engaged enemy planes on four occasions. As a result, two JU-88's were at least damaged and quite possibly destroyed. They were last seen losing altitude rapidly and smoking heavily. On another occasion one of the group was known to have engaged in aerial combat but failed to return to its base or render any report by radio. Two other aircraft failed to return to their base, but no indication remains as to the cause of their loss.43

The successful operations of the 480th Antisubmarine Group from St. Eval were not accomplished without cost in lives and aircraft. In all, 65 officers and men lost their lives, and 7 B-24's were destroyed. Of the latter, 2 were lost in crossing the Atlantic to England, 2 failed to return from a mission, their fate unknown, 2 crashed, and the seventh was doubtless destroyed in aerial combat.43

In March 1943 the 480th Group was ordered to Port Lyautey, French Morocco, to engage in antisubmarine patrol of the vital approaches to the TORCH area. The final missions from the United Kingdom were flown on 5 March. In 6 weeks of full operations and during the preceding 2 months of limited operations, the 480th Group had made a very solid contribution to the antisubmarine effort in the eastern Atlantic. Of the 49 sightings and 26 attacks made during the critical month of February by all units operating on antisubmarine duty from the United Kingdom and Iceland, the 1st and 2d Antisubmarine Squadrons alone accounted for 15 sightings and 5 completed attacks. Even more important was the pioneering work done in foreign operations, a contribution which led to the solution of many troublesome administrative and technical problems. Their withdrawal was noted by the British Coastal Command "with keen regret."44

The campaign of early February in the Gondola area had demonstrated the feasibility of a sustained and concentrated air offensive in the Bay of Biscay. After the departure of the 480th Antisubmarine Group, the Coastal Command continued to hit the U-boats in transit as heavily as its resources would permit.[45] The British also agitated with increasing insistence for an Allied offensive, launched on an unprecedented scale, in the Bay area. In March it was proposed by the British that a combined British and American contribution of 180 additional VLR, ASV-equipped aircraft and crews be organized, to be added to the force of 100 aircraft then said to be devoted by the Coastal Command to the Bay patrol. This force would constitute the tactical elements of a specially staffed British and American organization to be assigned the specific mission of offensive air operations in the approaches to the Bay of Biscay during the period May to August, inclusive.[46] The plan, involving as it did the creation of a distinct task force, separate in organization, did not coincide with AAF plans which conceived the Bay project as but one aspect of a single air task of much broader scope, namely, the protection of the Atlantic lines of communication against submarine attack. Furthermore, it was pretty obvious that any implementing of the Bay of Biscay plan would have to be done by the AAF at the expense of ETO heavy-bombing operations, for the U. S. Navy was not planning to do more than add 45 planes to those already engaged in North Atlantic antisubmarine activity.[47] The AAF was both unwilling to compromise its current commitments of heavy bombers and crews to the Eighth Air Force and reluctant to incur further commitments with regard to the Atlantic antisubmarine campaign until it could be finally determined what organization would ultimately be responsible for U. S. air operations against submarines in the Atlantic.[48] The British authorities felt strongly that the Bay offensive would do more than any other single factor to end the "present unsatisfactory progress in the Battle of the Atlantic." And time, in this instance, was at a premium: 3 to 6 months later, the Germans might be shifting their efforts to Norway, thereby necessitating an entirely new project, and one less feasible than that proposed in the Bay of Biscay.[49]

Support for this view came from an unexpected source. The U. S. Navy, which had been hitherto officially against the use of antisubmarine forces in a purely offensive campaign, came, in June 1943, to favor the plan and urge its adoption. Admiral King, early in June, had suggested that two Army VLR squadrons be sent from Newfoundland to the United Kingdom to participate in the Bay of Biscay project. There were, he pointed out, more VLR aircraft in the Newfoundland area than were set up as a minimum requirement for that area by the Atlantic Convoy Conference (ACC 3).[50] Finally, in the latter part of June, the 4th and 19th Antisubmarine Squadrons were ordered from Newfoundland to duty in the United Kingdom. These units became the backbone of the 479th Antisubmarine Group, activated in England in July 1943.[51]

Meanwhile, the British had gone ahead with plans of their own for a concentrated offensive in the Bay and its approaches. The losses, which had been inflicted on the U-boats in May, forced the German command to withdraw their fleet from the North Atlantic convoy route and to operate against independent shipping in scattered areas. This shift in enemy strategy forced the British to redouble their efforts in the Bay transit area, for there alone could the enemy be found with any degree of certainty. Accordingly, it was decided in early June to concentrate in the Bay offensive all available aircraft not required for close escort of convoys, and to reinforce these by surface support groups withdrawn from the convoy routes. The resulting joint antisubmarine striking forces were deployed in two new antisubmarine areas in the Bay known as "Musketry" and "Seaslug."[52] Reinforcement of the patrol of these areas, especially in their southern reaches, came from the Allied forces in the Moroccan Sea Frontier and at Gibraltar. The newly intensified offensive met with early success. The enemy attempted to counter it by sending their submarines through the bay in close groups of two, three, sometimes even five. This practice, while it concentrated a formidable screen of antiaircraft fire against individual patrolling planes, presented a tempting target for a well-balanced antisubmarine force. On 30 July a whole group of three U-boats was sunk in a combined air and surface action.

The 479th Group began its work in the United Kingdom with a double advantage in its favor. Not only had the project been less hastily organized than that of the 480th, but it profited from the pioneering work done in the field by the older unit. Upon the arrival of its flight echelon at St. Eval (the first 13 airplanes landed there on 30 June, the remaining 11 on 7 July), the group was placed under the Eighth Air Force for administration and supply and under the 19 Group, RAF Coastal Command, for operational control. It was decided not to keep it at St. Eval but to turn over to its use a new field at Dunkeswell, Devonshire. At this field the men of the 479th enjoyed the advantage of a relatively separate establishment, under the control of Col. Howard Moore, commanding officer of the group, with Group Captain Kidd of the Coastal Command exercising only a general supervision.[53] The 87th Service Squadron, the 1813th Ordnance Service and Maintenance Company, the 1177th Military Police Company, and the 444th Quartermaster Platoon arrived in England with the group's ground echelon and were attached to it at Dunkeswell. It is not surprising, then, that the 479th escaped some of the more vexing administrative and logistical problems which faced the 480th on its arrival. The men of the 479th even received American rations at this new station.[54] The incomplete state of construction at Dunkeswell did, it is true, impose some discomfort on the new occupants. Nevertheless, the group at once settled down to training under the novel conditions of operations in the United Kingdom. The problems met in this regard were much the same as those encountered by the 480th.[55] On 13 July aircraft of the 479th Group flew their first operational missions.[56]

Not long afterward (29 July) Air Marshal Slessor spoke of the "most welcome reinforcement" provided by the two squadrons of the group "for the 'Musketry' area where hunting has been quite good this month."[57] The 479th had, indeed, taken an extremely active part in the Musketry campaign. During the 19 days, from 16 July to 2 August, aircraft of the 4th and 19th Squadrons sighted 12 submarines and attacked 7 of them. Of those attacked, 3 are known to have been sunk, 2 with the aid of RAF aircraft patrolling in the vicinity. Enemy tactics thereafter changed. The U-boats abandoned the policy of staying on the surface and fighting the attacking aircraft and henceforth made every effort to avoid surfacing during daylight hours. After a successful attack on 2 August, only 1 additional sighting occurred during the entire remaining period of operation, to 31 October; and even this sighting did not result in a successful attack.[58]

Most of the attacks (six out of eight) made by the 479th Group were made in the face of determined countermeasures on the part of U-boat crews. In a desperate attempt to nullify the air offensive that was bidding fair to strangle their submarine fleet, the enemy had resorted to the policy, ultimately disastrous to itself, of remaining surfaced during an attack and fighting back with antiaircraft fire. One B-24 was believed lost as a result of this action.[59]

Much more serious was the opposition encountered from enemy aircraft, though just as indicative of the enemy's desperate plight. German aircraft over the Bay in July and August accounted for 2 aircraft and 14 lives. JU-88's were encountered throughout the entire period of operations, often in very large groups. The average number was 6.6 enemy aircraft per encounter. It is therefore cause for surprise that so few planes of the 479th were lost. Even so, of course, the strain on the crews of the single B-24's in the face of such large groups was very great. Crews were instructed to avoid combat whenever possible, but in many instances the enemy pressed the attack vigorously. For a tabulation of the results of these encounters, in which the antagonists may be said to have fought to a draw, the reader should consult Appendix 3.[60]

It is not the province of this study to evaluate the entire Biscay offensive. It continued long after the AAF Antisubmarine Command had ceased to exist, and until the submarine menace itself had been substantially reduced. But some assessment must be attempted, at least for the period during which AAF Antisubmarine squadrons participated. It has been suggested that the campaign was a failure.[61] Certainly the tangible results obtained in August failed to measure up to those of July. In July, 26 per cent of all attacks made on U-boats were made in the Bay, and the B-24's of the Antisubmarine Command operating in that area had to fly an average of only 54 flying hours per sighting. The situation altered radically in August. Only seven damaging or destructive attacks were made in that month, as compared to 29 for July. Sightings fell off proportionately, and the 479th Antisubmarine Group certainly spent most of its time in August combatting enemy aircraft rather than in attacking U-boats. Yet throughout the month of August, plotting boards regularly carried from 10 to 20 U-boats in the area, which is approximately the same concentration as characterized the previous month. Nor can the decrease be charged to any relaxation of the offensive effort.

The failure to sight the enemy in August may be explained in part as the result of the installation of radar by the Germans in their submarines. Increasingly, the aircraft on antisubmarine patrol found that the "blips" disappeared from their radar screens at average distances of 8 or 9 miles, indicating that the enemy was detecting patrol aircraft at safe distances. The Germans also altered their tactics considerably in order to cut down the heavy losses sustained by them in July. They abandoned the practice of remaining surfaced and fighting back during air attacks, and resorted again to an over-all policy of evasion, hugging the Spanish coastline so as to confuse radar contact, and surfacing only at night in that farthest-south part of the Bay which lay at the extreme limit of the English Wellingtons equipped with Leigh-lights. Some credit must also be given to the persistent use of aircraft to counter the pressure of the Allied air offensive.[62]

Nevertheless, it must be remembered that the tactics to which the Germans resorted--fighting back in July, hugging the Spanish coast in August, and using extremely heavy air cover in both months--are themselves eloquent evidence of the effectiveness of the Bay offensive. And the effect of antisubmarine activity cannot be determined entirely by the amount of damage directly inflicted on the enemy. The constant patrolling of the Bay forced the submarines to proceed so slowly through the transit area that their efficiency in the open sea was greatly reduced and the morale of their crews seriously impaired.[63] Yet, even in terms of submarines sunk or damaged, the Bay campaign inflicted heavy loss on the enemy. During its most active 3 months (June to September) it accounted for the following score:[64]

	By aircraft	By surface craft or submarine
Sunk and probably sunk	19	4
Damaged	9	4

The Moroccan Sea Frontier. Closely related to the Bay of Biscay offensive was the action in the Moroccan Sea Frontier. In fact, the two at times overlapped, aircraft from the latter reinforcing the campaign in the transit area, at least in its more southerly reaches. In any event, the antisubmarine warfare in the approaches to the Straits of Gibraltar was always likely to be affected by strategy in the Bay, probably even more than other Atlantic areas, all of which were affected in one way or another. As the summer Bay offensive reached its climax in late June and early July, the U-boats tended more and more to skirt the Spanish coast to Cape Finisterre, and from there to deploy in a southwesterly direction toward the waters between the Azores and the coast of Portugal. The result was a concentration, during the first 2 weeks of July, of enemy submarines in that area, which thus became part of the narrow transit lane.

It is a matter of question what exactly were the strategic motives back of this movement. Undoubtedly it sprang in large part simply from a desire to evade patrolling forces in the Bay. But it also appears to be true that the U-boats were spending considerable time in that region on antishipping patrol. It may very well have been that they were ordered to spend several days in these waters on their way to and from their Biscay bases.[66] The object was apparently to create a screen off the coast of Portugal to intercept Allied convoys proceeding from the United Kingdom to supply the Allied campaign then being developed in the Mediterranean. It was a bold move, for it brought the U-boats within range of antisubmarine aircraft operating from Northwest Africa and Gibraltar, and it coincided with the brief and desperate attempt of the submarines in the Bay to counter the air offensive by antiaircraft fire. The enemy also relied on the relative ease with which air protection could be provided in the form of JU-88's and the longer range FW-200's. There is difference of opinion concerning the precise number of U-boats patrolling off the coast of Portugal in the first half of July, the estimate ranging from 8 to 25. But it is certain that a considerable concentration came within range of African-based Liberators.[67]

It is at this point that the B-24's of the 480th Group reenter the picture. They had been moved to Port Lyautey in March and had extended the patrolled area in the Moroccan Sea Frontier by several hundred miles. These squadrons were specially equipped to answer the challenge made by the U-boats as the latter swung across the convoy lane in early July. Their offensive really began with a sighting on 5 July in which the pilot made a perfectly executed run

116

on a submarine, but was foiled by mechanical failure of his bomb bay doors. On the 7th, two attacks were made, one of which resulted in the probable sinking of one U-boat. The other may also have been destroyed, although it was officially assessed as probably severely damaged. The following day a fifth attack occurred which resulted in another probable kill. On 9 July three attacks were delivered, one of which was assessed as severe damage, one as slight damage, and one as no damage at all. Next day another attack resulted in doubtful damage, and again on the 11th an attack of undetermined effect was executed. On the 12th, 13th, and 14th, an attack was made each day, resulting in one submarine definitely destroyed and two damaged. Thus, during this short period of 10 days, the 2 squadrons made 15 sightings and 13 attacks, which are believed to have resulted in 1 submarine known sunk, 3 probably sunk, 2 severely damaged, and 1 possibly damaged. Only 6 attacks were considered unsuccessful.[68]

After this decisive, if local, defeat, the enemy obviously decided to abandon his policy of active defense. The U-boats now dived, whenever possible, on sight of antisubmarine aircraft, and not a single submarine was sighted by AAF aircraft in the area thereafter. It was also immediately after this brief "blitz" that the Germans began to patrol the area with heavily armed JU-290's, and it is logical to presume that the action of the 480th Group had a good deal to do with that development.[69]

In order to put this July offensive in its proper perspective, it will be necessary to review the history of operations in the

Moroccan Sea Frontier from the time when Col. Jack Roberts and his 480th Antisubmarine Group reported at Port Lyautey in March 1943.[70]

The 480th Group encountered in Africa something more than the usual problems involved in transfer to a new theater. Most of the difficulties arose from the fact that the group was now placed under the operational control of the U. S. Navy. It was assigned to the Northwest African Coastal Air Force for administration, and attached temporarily to Fleet Air Wing 15 for operational control, pending decision as to the control and disposition of all Allied antisubmarine units in Northwest Africa and Gibraltar.[71] Colonel Roberts felt that this arrangement was most unsatisfactory for several reasons. The group had been the first of the AAF Antisubmarine Command units to operate free from U. S. naval control. It had been thoroughly indoctrinated in RAF Coastal Command procedures, which differed markedly from those of the U. S. Navy, and the officers of the group felt that, for the job at hand, they were much superior. Morale was adversely affected by poorer radio communications, less efficient briefing and operational control, poorer air-sea rescue facilities, and RDF than those to which the unit had become accustomed.[72] An example of the resulting friction was that, with five intelligence officers capable and experienced in briefing and interrogating crews, the group was not allowed to provide watch in the control room or to conduct briefing. Since the briefing provided by Fleet Air Wing 15 was not considered adequate by Colonel Roberts, crews had to be re-briefed by an officer of the group before going on a mission.[73] Worse than that, intelligence data necessary for successful missions frequently got to the group too late to be of any real value. And, with practically no operational authority, there was little that Colonel Roberts could do about it. Nor was much attention being paid to estimated U-boat positions in routing patrol aircraft, which resulted in poorly planned missions. In general, it was felt that the best use was not being made of a highly trained organization.[74]

Basically, the trouble lay in the difference of strategic thinking between Navy and AAF Antisubmarine Command:[75]

> The unsatisfactory nature of our present status and operations is due /Colonel Roberts wrote in May/ . . . to the difference in the fundamental conception of Moroccan Sea Frontier and this Hqtrs as to how best to defeat the submarines, whether offensively (on sweeps and covering threatened convoys) or defensively (covering all US convoys at all times to the exclusion of offensive sweeps and coverages).

As will appear in the following pages, the Navy had performed its initial function adequately by patrolling the approaches to Gibraltar to within 400 miles and had helped to force the Germans beyond that limit. But the long-range and very-long-range aircraft of the Antisubmarine Command had a new and different mission to perform, namely, that of reaching beyond the 400-mile line and striking the submarines prowling in the outer waters. The two missions thus required two different approaches, a fact which the Moroccan Sea Frontier failed to appreciate.

Since the problem of command in the Gibraltar-Northwest African area was currently under discussion in the spring of 1943,[76] Colonel

Roberts vigorously urged, as a solution, placing antisubmarine operations in the area under British control at Gibraltar. The RAF Coastal Command was operating antisubmarine squadrons from both Gibraltar and Agadir--to the north and south of Port Lyautey respectively. So he believed the best interests of all concerned would be served by coordinating operations from all three bases under Coastal Command control. "I am . . . convinced [he wrote in May], as are all of my subordinates, that our Wing can operate 'independently' under the central control of ACC Gibraltar with much greater efficiency and effectiveness than under present U. S. Navy control." This statement, he warned, was made without malice toward any individuals of the Navy "hereabouts," for they were "generally a fine bunch with whom our relations are on a most pleasant basis." He then added, significantly, "The majority of them privately concur with me in my expressed ideas on antisubmarine organization in Northwest Africa."[78]

In fact, by June, improvement was becoming evident in the general control exercised by Fleet Air Wing 15, and in the quality of services furnished at Port Lyautey, although no change in the official status of the group, or in the quantity of services, had taken place. Group intelligence officers were being given equal authority and responsibility with naval, and air-ground liaison was "reasonably satisfactory."[79] Army and Navy intelligence officers were rotating duty shifts in the Control Room. And the group was exercising increased authority, "actually if not officially," in the laying out of patrols, "the Navy exhibiting little interest in anything other than convoy coverage."[80]

The Navy did not, of course, furnish all the problems facing the 480th Group in Africa, though it provided the largest of them. In addition to the myriad of problems incident on stationing several hundred men in a strange territory and climate, Colonel Roberts had to build up his unit from a strength of not more than 16 or 17 VLR aircraft to one of 24 VLR (H).[81] This increase in aircraft, especially in the modified B-24D, involved considerable training of crews both old and new, and considerable adjustment of equipment.[82] As of 23 June 1943, the group reported 19 VLR (H) aircraft on hand, with 6 en route from the United States.[83]

The 480th Group arrived in Africa as a well-trained unit. Thanks to the experience gained under the tutelage of the Coastal Command, the group officers felt that their organization was better prepared for antisubmarine tasks than any other American unit.[84] And the quality of the new crews received from the OTU at Langley Field had steadily improved.[85] The chief training problem consequently arose in connection with the new equipment being received and the unfamiliar flying conditions prevailing in the Moroccan Sea Frontier, where scarcity of clouds made tactics learned under the heavier northern skies inapplicable.[86] The commanding officer was especially conscious of the value of continuous training, and, once such facilities as a triangulation bombing range and a blind-landing system had been set up, he maintained a steady training schedule.[87]

Morale constituted an ever-present, though happily not a serious, problem. At first the crews felt insecure under what they considered inferior radio control from the Navy, and in view of the fact that rescue facilities were lacking. Recreation facilities remained limited, relaxation consisting mainly of athletics and an earnest endeavor to consume enough liquor before 2000 to make a pass, normally expiring at that hour, worth the trouble of securing. Unfortunately, the 480th Group was the only "front line" unit in what was considered to be a rear echelon, or rest area, and the Provost Marshal persisted in subjecting it to the same type of restrictions ordinarily imposed on inactive units. Morale in general, however, remained high until, in August, rumors of the impending dissolution of the AAF Antisubmarine Command left all personnel in an uncertain and frustrated frame of mind.[88]

The 480th Antisubmarine Group found in the Moroccan Sea Frontier a field especially well suited to its talents. Since the invasion of Africa on 8 November 1942, a major objective of the German submarine fleet had been to harry Allied convoys heading for Northwest Africa and Gibraltar. At first they had met with some success. On 11 November 1942, four merchant vessels and one destroyer were sunk while riding at anchor off Fedala (20 miles from Casablanca) by what appears to have been a mass U-boat attack. Allied aircraft, however, soon made hunting in these shore-line waters too costly for the enemy to continue. This work had largely been done by the British who made 37 sightings between 7 and 30 November, resulting in 21 attacks. By the end of December the PBY's had made 6 attacks in the area.[89] The result was that the enemy retired to positions 400 miles or more from

Casablanca and Port Lyautey. Instead of having to guard only a 200-mile span, the U-boats then had to guard an arc several hundred miles long; and for some time they actually took up positions along the arc of an approximate circle centered at Gibraltar. After January, all sinkings occurred more than 600 miles from the nearest aircraft base. During all this time the U-boats showed little tendency to approach within range of land-based aircraft, for, although thousands of hours were flown, no sightings were made until the arrival of the Liberators in March. These long-range aircraft were able to reach both the U-boats on patrol beyond PBY range and also those traveling the great-circle submarine lanes to South America and South Africa. During the period March to June, a total of 12 sightings were made, mostly beyond the 400-mile limit. Meanwhile, aircraft operations from Casablanca had been discontinued and PBY's began patrols from Agadir in April.[90] By June, the location of American antisubmarine forces in the Moroccan Sea Frontier was approximately as follows:[91]

  Port Lyautey - Army 15 (480th Antisubmarine Group)
         Navy 12 (VP-92 and part of VP-73)
  Agadir - Navy 6 (remainder of VP-73)

Thus it became the peculiar task of the 480th Group to carry on long-distance patrols, beyond the extreme range of the PBY's, making the maximum use of the SCR-517 radar. Missions began promptly on 19 March in spite of temporary shortages of spare parts, maintenance personnel, and equipment.[92] Three planes a day ordinarily went out on operational missions, laid out by Fleet Air Wing 15, under the supervision of the Moroccan Sea Frontier at Casablanca. The area covered was at first from 31°00' N. to 35°00' N., extending west to the prudent limit of endurance (1,050 nautical miles).[93] Later missions were ordered almost as far north as Cape Finisterre.[94] Within 2 days of the beginning of operations, the group made the first sighting that had occurred in the area since December, and in the ensuing months of its stay at Port Lyautey it made roughly 10 times as many sightings per hour of flying time as the Navy PBY's operating from the same region at the same time. This result was owing in part to the extra range of the B-24, but also to the alert visual search of the B-24 crews and to the superior efficiency of their radar, which came nearer than the PBY equipment to making the theoretically expected number of sightings in the patrolled regions by a factor of 4.[95]

Of these sightings, all made in the period March to July 1943, inclusive, more than 90 per cent resulted in attacks on U-boats, and of these 20 attacks, 10 per cent were sure kills. In all, more than 25 per cent of the U-boats attacked probably failed to reach port.[96] Assessments run as follows:[97]

```
2 U-boats known sunk
3    "    probably  "
1    "    probably or severely damaged
5    "    possibly or slightly      "
9    "    no damage or insufficient evidence of damage
```

This fine record is largely owing to the high quality of flying technique and sound tactics employed by the pilots, to the well-

coordinated use of radar, and to the aggressiveness of the crews. Especially noteworthy is the use made of cloud cover. Clouds were available for use in 73 per cent of the sightings, and were actually used in nearly 60 per cent. In other words, of the 16 sightings in which cloud cover was available, it was used in 13 cases. Of the other 3, 2 involved flying below clouds on convoy coverage, and the other flying below clouds in darkness, both perfectly correct procedure.[98]

As a result of superior flying technique, 16 of the 20 attacks were made while the enemy craft was still visible, and in 13 instances the U-boat was still fully surfaced or with decks awash at the time of attack. Here the B-24's again surpassed the PBY's for, in all but 2 of the 13 sightings made by the latter from November to 15 July, the U-boats were able to submerge before the arrival of the aircraft. In one of these instances, the submarine deliberately chose to remain surfaced and fight back with AA fire.[99] This result arose in part from the slower speed of the Navy planes and from less effective radar.

At least 12 of the sightings made by the group were first picked up by the SCR-517 radar equipment at an average range of 18 miles. At least 5 of these sightings would certainly not have been made without radar, and in 6 others the contact would otherwise have been doubtful.[100]

The spirit of the crews played a very large part in securing the high record of attacks and kills. They showed general willingness to encounter enemy fire and an ability to carry out attacks in the face of strong opposition. In six instances the submarines fired on the attacking planes, yet with the exception of the first case in which resistance occurred, the aircraft pressed home their attacks. Several planes were damaged by this sort of encounter, and about 12 crew members injured.[101]

As in the Bay of Biscay, encounters with enemy aircraft in the Moroccan Sea Frontier proved more serious than resistance from the submarines themselves. As in the Bay, also, the early operations of the group were not seriously opposed by enemy aircraft, but opposition became more and more severe as the effectiveness of the antisubmarine patrols increased. In the Moroccan Sea Frontier it was not the relatively short-range JU-88 that opposed the aircraft of the 480th Group but the powerful long-range FW-200, which in many ways is comparable to the B-24 itself. The first combats of this nature occurred in the last half of July, when the antisubmarine "blitz" conducted by the 480th Group during the first 2 weeks had goaded the enemy into desperate action. By August the FW-200's began to appear, heavily armed with rapid-firing 20-millimeter cannon which gave them a marked fire superiority over the B-24. From that point on, the crews of the 480th found their mission to be very hazardous, and the casualties increased rapidly. The final record is, however, one of which the group may well be proud, for, during its entire African operations, through October 1943, it is estimated to have destroyed 5 FW-200's, 2 DO-24's, and 1 DO-26; probably destroyed 1 JU-88; and damaged 2 FW-200's and 2 JU-88's. In doing so the group lost 3 B-24's as a result of action by enemy aircraft.[102]

In all, the 480th Group put in a more than satisfactory amount of work in the Moroccan Sea Frontier prior to the dissolution of the Antisubmarine Command, even allowing for the excellent flying weather prevailing in the area. The following table demonstrates this fact:[103]

	Antisubmarine sweep	Convoy coverage	Total hours flown
March	400	–	400
April	1,122	397	1,519
May	674	733	1,407
June	1,119	541	1,660
July	1,544	624	2,168
August	883	795	1,678

This table also demonstrates the relatively high proportion of flying time devoted to escorting convoys, a type of operation unlikely to produce many sightings of enemy submarines. From November 1942 to the middle of July 1943, no unthreatened convoy (defined as one having no plotted U-boat positions within 100 miles, or within 100 miles of its course for the ensuing 24 hours) was attacked.[104] Conversely, of the 22 sightings made by aircraft in the area between 5 December and 15 July 1943 over 90 per cent occurred within 80 miles of a plotted U-boat position. The average error was only 41 miles.[105]

Facts of this sort confirmed the officers of the 480th Group in their belief that their aircraft would be much more profitably employed in hunting in areas of high probability (defined as regions enclosed by arcs of circles, 60 miles in radius, drawn about predicted U-boat positions) than in convoy coverage. They recognized, of course, that their very long range allowed them to pick up convoys much farther out to sea than was otherwise possible, a practice which the convoy commanders greatly favored. And it was also true that a minimum of actual danger from unplotted submarines made a certain minimum of air coverage advisable on all convoys.[106] Nevertheless, the results obtained in areas of high probability more than justified the diversion of as many planes as possible in those directions. Since such areas occurred mainly out of range of the naval planes (beyond the 500-mile limit) they fell principally to the Army B-24's.[107] As experience was gained, it became evident that by far the best ratio of hours per sighting could be obtained beyond 500 miles and on adroitly routed missions.[108] As the Army became more and more influential, officially or unofficially, in routing patrols, a gradual improvement in that respect took place.

The campaign of 5-15 July, narrated above, gave the group a splendid opportunity to prove not only its fighting ability but the validity of these tactical principles. Deployed on missions carefully routed toward those areas off the Portuguese coast where intelligence sources indicated the enemy had concentrated its forces, the aircraft of the group turned in what is probably a record for a unit of the sort.[109]

The effect of this campaign of July may be estimated to some extent by the fact that, after 14 July, the 480th Group made no further contacts with enemy submarines during their stay on the west coast of Africa. The Germans' attempt to defy heavy air coverage had proved disastrous to themselves and it was once again demonstrated that submarines either could not or would not operate in areas at all well covered by antisubmarine aircraft. In August patrols and convoy protective flights continued and were even extended. Employing tactics similar to those used by the RAF Coastal Command in July, a "shuttle run" was made in the early part of the month by the 2d Squadron between Port Lyautey and Dunkeswell. On the trip to Dunkeswell the squadron covered a convoy; and on the return flight it conducted an antisubmarine sweep, thus combining two principal functions in one operation. Two such runs were made in August, but no submarines were attacked.[110]

The antisubmarine warfare in the Moroccan Sea Frontier generally may be similarly evaluated. Between the British squadrons at Gibraltar and the Navy squadrons in the Moroccan Sea Frontier, the Allied antisubmarine forces had, prior to the arrival of the Army B-24's, forced the enemy to withdraw from the immediate approaches to the vital area.[111] The operations of the 480th Group forced them to withdraw to a point at which they could no longer seriously menace the convoys pouring through the Moroccan Sea Frontier, bound for the Mediterranean theater. And in July, when convoys were sailing down from the United Kingdom to supply the Sicilian campaign, they were able to pass through the greatest concentration of U-boats then at sea without loss from submarine activity, thanks to the effective air and surface escort provided.[112] This relative immunity granted finally to the Moroccan and Gibraltar area was a triumph for combined convoy escort and offensive antisubmarine sweeps, and it vindicated the principles underlying each form of antisubmarine activity within its own peculiar limits.

The operations in the Eastern Atlantic were experimental in a great many ways. For one thing, they gave the AAF Antisubmarine Command the opportunity to test its strategic doctrine. In the course of their rather brief duration, experiments were carried out in the difficult matter of administering the activities of units operating far from their parent organizations, and in the even more difficult problem of operational control. And, by no means least of all, invaluable experience was obtained in antisubmarine tactics in an area where operations had to be conducted on a more than theoretical scale.

As a result of these efforts, the AAF Antisubmarine Command was able to draw certain interesting, if tentative, conclusions. The offensive strategy had worked. If not the be-all and end-all of antisubmarine warfare, it had at least to be considered an essential element. In administration, the policy of sending units on detached service from the wing headquarters in the United States soon proved to be unsound and was replaced by one in which the overseas squadrons were given "separate, special" group organization. An effort had been made to extend that principle to the point of creating overseas wings, but AAF headquarters was opposed to expanding the AAF Antisubmarine Command organization on such a scale.[113] Operational control had been exercised over the AAF Antisubmarine Command units by both RAF Coastal Command and U. S. Navy. The comparison was striking, and not always to the advantage of the latter. The AAF Antisubmarine Command had always recognized its British counterpart as a pattern, and the experience of actual cooperation under the operational control of the older organization had only confirmed the younger in its preference. Yet even in Northwest Africa the problem of naval control was greatly mitigated, if not exactly solved, as a result of the tact and vigor of the commanders involved. Finally, the detached antisubmarine units learned more in a week of operations in the eastern Atlantic about such things as defense against aircraft attack, proper attack procedures, and the use of cloud cover and radar equipment than they could have done in weeks of operations elsewhere. It was with a sense of anticlimax and frustration[114] that they heard, in August 1943, that they were to be relieved of their mission just when they felt they were really achieving their objective and when they were, in fact, as efficient an antisubmarine team as could be found at that time.

Operations in the Western Atlantic

The Eastern and Gulf Sea Frontiers. In contrast to the intensive, if sporadic, activity of the overseas squadrons, the story of antisubmarine operations in the western Atlantic is one of endless patrols, few sightings, and still fewer attacks. While the units of the 479th and 480th Antisubmarine Groups were enjoying the best

of hunting in the Bay of Biscay and in the Moroccan Sea Frontier, flying at worst only a few hundred hours per contact, units in many parts of the U. S. strategic area were flying many thousands of hours per sighting in regions with an average U-boat density of 1 in a million square miles of ocean. In the Eastern and Gulf Sea Frontiers almost no enemy activity had been encountered since September 1942. To the south and north, in the Trinidad area, and in that part of the North Atlantic convoy route lying off the coast of Newfoundland, the Germans were still trying hard to stop the flow of vital materiel. Even in those areas, however, the hunting was often poor.

Yet the Navy felt obliged to patrol not only these threatened areas but the relatively quiet waters of the Eastern and Gulf Sea Frontiers with as many aircraft as might be spared from other more urgent projects. The enemy, it was argued, had withdrawn, but he might return. He was not too preoccupied with the invasion convoys to overlook a rich and unprotected merchant shipping lane. And, as Admiral King put it, the submarines could shift their area of operation more rapidly than the air defenses could be moved to meet them. Accordingly, an "irreducible minimum" of aircraft would have to be maintained on the coast of the United States, despite the meager returns in contacts with the enemy.[113]

The only question was, how small did that minimum have to be before it became truly irreducible? Was it necessary to provide such heavy coverage--at one time as many as 15 out of 25 squadrons?

Was it an economical way of using units specially trained in the work of destroying submarines to deploy them in areas where there were few if any submarines, when in other parts of the Atlantic the undersea raiders abounded? These were debatable questions, the debate resolving itself finally into a conflict between the AAF Antisubmarine Command ideal of a mobile offensive force and the Navy's doctrine of a relatively fixed defense. Since the operational control of antisubmarine activity lay in naval hands, the Navy won the debate. The result was that many of the fully trained and equipped antisubmarine crews could say of their operations as one squadron historian said, somewhat wistfully, of his entire squadron: "The tactical achievement of the squadron cannot be elaborated on by enumerating the number of submarines sunk. It has been our misfortune never to have had the opportunity of sighting a submarine." When he added sturdily that "this fact has never reduced the crews' efficiency and patrol missions have been conducted in an alert manner," he epitomized a large portion of this story.[116]

This work of patrol and convoy escort was shared by AAF Antisubmarine Command, air units of the U. S. Navy, and the Civilian Air Patrol. It must be remembered, however, that the CAP planes were light, single-engine civilian types, limited in their range to a narrow zone along the coast where the depth of the water normally restricted submarine activity, and that the planes used by the Navy in the Eastern Sea Frontier were mostly single-motor observation types, with a limited radius of action compared to the Navy PBY and the medium and heavy bombers used by the Antisubmarine Command.[117]

From October 1942 to February 1943, no damaging attacks were made in the Eastern and Gulf Sea Frontiers, and few positive sightings of enemy submarines. This startling lack of combat action was by no means the result of any reduction in antisubmarine patrol activity which remained heavy on the part of both Army and Navy squadrons. It was simply that there were few, if any, U-boats to see. From an estimated 10 enemy craft in August 1942, the average density in these areas had dropped in October to 3.4 and was further lowered in November to 1.7. In December, January, and February there was no positive evidence of any enemy activity at all, though some depth bombs were dropped on suspicious spots in the water. In all, these operations during the winter of 1942-43 probably did more damage to the aboriginal marine life in the patrolled areas than to the mechanized intruders. But there is no doubt that the negligible density of enemy submarines in its turn resulted partly from the continued heavy air coverage.[118]

The spring and summer months of 1943 brought some increase in enemy operation. In February, the average density rose to 1.8, a significant increase if still not a major threat in over a million square miles of ocean. For the rest of the time the AAF Antisubmarine Command patrolled these frontiers, the Germans kept from one to three U-boats busy--and not without effect. In addition to keeping a disproportionately large antisubmarine force patrolling these waters, they managed in May to destroy the first merchant vessel sunk in the Eastern Sea Frontier since July 1942.[119] Naval aircraft and a B-25 were in the vicinity of the attack on the tanker Pan Am (a straggler from convoy NK-533) but were unable to make contact with the submarine. A U-boat, possibly the one that sank the Pan Am, was detected several times and was attacked by a Navy plane with possible damage resulting to it. Later in the month, a B-24 from the 18th Antisubmarine Squadron based at Langley Field, Va., made a fairly promising attack in the same general area.[120] Again in June the tanker Gettysburg was sunk by a submarine (31°00' N. 79°00' W.). A Navy blimp had been escorting the tanker until separated from it by a thunderstorm. A plane of the 25th Antisubmarine Squadron later directed a passenger ship to the 18 survivors. In July the Bloody Marsh, a U. S. tanker, met a similar fate. In August a patrol vessel was sunk (37°22' N. 74°25' W.). On the 28th of August a B-25 of the 25th Antisubmarine Squadron attacked a U-boat (31°31' N. 78°45' W.). Unfortunately, the enemy managed to escape before any serious damage could be dealt it.

In spite of the poor hunting in the Eastern and Gulf Sea Frontiers, the range and efficiency of the AAF Antisubmarine Command Squadrons in the area were gradually being increased by the substitution of B-24's for the medium-range aircraft originally employed, and by constant processing of crews, old as well as new, in the Operational Training Unit at Langley Field.[121] By March 1943, the effect of increased long-range aircraft was becoming evident in an increase of over 3,000 flying hours in the month for Army planes.[122] On the 23d of that month, 23 B-24's were reported, distributed among the 4th, 6th, 9th, and 18th Squadrons. By August it was possible to report 75 B-24's among 9 of the squadrons based in the United States.[123]

If this were the whole story of operations in the Eastern and Gulf Sea Frontiers--and as far as actual contact with the enemy is concerned, it is the whole story--it would be a disproportionately small one in relation to the number of squadrons involved. And it might seem strange that so great an effort was being made to increase precious long-range equipment in what was essentially an inactive theater. Happily the story is much larger, for it includes also a prodigious program of technical development and crew training. When the Antisubmarine Command was activated, a beginning only had been made in the task of securing the proper weapons and auxiliary devices for antisubmarine warfare, and of training personnel in their use. Close liaison had to be maintained between the command and the various research organizations, and the new command had to put into effect a training program that was at once uniform and flexible enough to keep up with the constantly developing methods of antisubmarine warfare.

The responsibility in both materiel development and training rested not only on headquarters but also on the squadrons based in the continental United States, for it was with their help alone that the dual program could be implemented. It was originally contemplated that the Operational Training Unit at Langley Field would accomplish most of the training work for the entire command; but that objective was never completely achieved because the tremendous need for available aircraft made it necessary to carry on training to a considerable extent in conjunction with patrol operations. Even when the flow of personnel through the OTU had become fuller and steadier, stress was still placed on squadron training. The U. S. coastal area constituted a more or less inactive theater and it was felt that those squadrons tied down to patrol over those waters could profitably be used to supplement the training program. Training, therefore, became the principal contribution made by the home-based units. The story of this program will be told in a later chapter.

The Caribbean and South Atlantic Areas. As the Germans withdrew their submarines from the Eastern and Gulf Sea Frontiers, during the late summer of 1942, they concentrated for a time in the Caribbean area, specializing in the waters off Trinidad. The Caribbean had been a favorite hunting ground for the enemy since his entry in force into the U. S. strategic area. By September 1942, however, the convoy lanes off Trinidad offered one of the few profitable areas of operations in the western Atlantic. During the winter months, the Caribbean shared with the northern coastal waters a relative immunity from submarine attack. In December and January, a total of 10 merchant vessels were sunk, all outside the Caribbean, in the area east of Trinidad. In February, none were lost. In March, five sinkings occurred in the Caribbean, the first in the island ring since September. During the following months, from one to four enemy submarines were kept in the area, seldom, however, doing much damage.

The enemy withdrawal from the Caribbean, late in 1942, was part of the same strategic movement that took the submarines from the Eastern and Gulf Sea Frontiers. Unable to continue his original policy of destroying Allied shipping faster than it could be replaced, Admiral Doenitz had withdrawn the bulk of his submarine fleet in an attempt to cut off the "invasion" convoy. But it was apparently also a part of his strategic plan to leave a minimum force of U-boats in convoy and shipping areas of secondary importance. The nuisance value of these scattered raiders was enormous, for they kept a large force of surface craft and aircraft tied down to convoy coverage and routine patrol. In accomplishing this effect, only an occasional merchant vessel had to be sunk, and the operation could be carried on with the least possible risk to the submarine, since it could proceed in a leisurely fashion, evading searching patrols wherever possible.[124]

The problem, then, was to provide enough effective air coverage for the Caribbean to keep the U-boat threat to a minimum. For, no matter how greatly motives of high strategy had figured in the withdrawal of the enemy from the American areas, the fact still remained that the Germans normally stayed out of reach of effective air patrol, and deliberately sought out those areas in which it was lacking. So, from the beginning of its career, the AAF Antisubmarine Command was requested to plan for the deployment of an effective force in the Caribbean areas.

Operations in the Cuban area were undertaken in accordance with an agreement between the U. S. and Cuban governments drawn up 19 June 1942,[125] and were controlled directly from Headquarters, 26th Antisubmarine Wing, Miami, Fla.[126] These operations, undertaken successively by the 23d, the 8th, the 17th, and the 15th Antisubmarine Squadrons, supplemented those of the squadrons based in the Florida and Gulf areas.[127] The net result was similar to that obtained by the squadrons based in the United States. Yet, as in other coastal waters, the enemy continued to keep a few U-boats operating in the Cuban area and managed to sink a few ships. In July 1943 a probable strength of four U-boats accounted for two merchant vessels. It was felt, therefore, that an antisubmarine squadron of the AAF Antisubmarine Command should be kept in that region.[128]

A similar, though somewhat more exciting story, may be told of operations in the Trinidad area through which passed probably three-fourths of the Caribbean shipping. Pioneer work in this part of the world had been done for the AAF Antisubmarine Command squadrons by the 40th Bombardment Squadron, later designated the 4th Antisubmarine Squadron. From August to November 1942, that unit had threaded its way among the intricacies of command channels in the Caribbean Sea Frontier and had at least prepared succeeding squadrons for the sort of problem they were likely to face.[129]

And problems in plenty they faced, too. The weather itself proved a serious handicap to sustained operations, what with tropical hurricanes and torrential rainfalls; and night maintenance had to be entirely abandoned because of the prevalence of malaria-bearing mosquitoes.[130] If a pilot were unfortunate enough to be forced into a jungle landing, he might never get out alive. One pilot landed in the jungle at Zanderij Field, Dutch Guiana, only 15 minutes from his base. After 4 days of hard work a rescue party reached him.[131] On top of all this, the native population of Trinidad either disliked the Americans or British with an intensity that promised little in the way of hospitality, or else their unusually high venereal disease rate promised a little too much.[132]

The most serious problem came, however, not from the climate or the native population, but from the command situation into which the AAF Antisubmarine Command squadrons were plunged. Being on detached service from the 26th Wing, these squadrons had to be given a place in the administrative and operational structure already set up in the region; but, being temporary in status and late in arriving, they found no very satisfactory place in that system. As in the Eastern and Gulf Sea Frontiers, antisubmarine activity was under the operational control of the sea frontier commander. AAF Antisubmarine Command squadrons were placed under the administrative supervision of the area defense command. But in addition to the Caribbean Sea Frontier and the Caribbean Defense Command, many lesser headquarters existed between the highest echelon and the single AAF Antisubmarine Command squadron serving at Trinidad. Under the Caribbean Defense Command, air forces were normally administered by the Sixth Air Force, but, since the latter had delegated all its antisubmarine functions to the Antilles Air Task Force, all Army aircraft engaged in that work were under the jurisdiction of the Task Force. The 25th Bomb Group, with its headquarters at Trinidad, was attached to the Trinidad Detachment of the Antilles Air Task Force, and it was to this group that the AAF Antisubmarine Command squadrons were assigned. This, more or less, was the chain of command for administration. Air force supply and higher echelon maintenance came from the Trinidad Area Air Service Command under the Trinidad Sector Command.[123]

On the operational side, the jurisdiction of the Caribbean Sea Frontier, to which the Antilles Air Task Force had been assigned, was almost entirely decentralized among four subregions at Guantanamo, Puerto Rico, Trinidad, and Curacao. Between these subordinate commands, communications appear to have been somewhat cumbersome, and coordination frequently slow or entirely lacking. Such an operational structure would have been perfectly adequate as a system of static defence, but in antisubmarine operations, which demanded the highest possible mobility based on the most rapid and complete transmission of intelligence possible, it proved to be much less suitable, and no doubt led to a less economical use of the antisubmarine forces available than might otherwise have been the case. Even more annoying to the 26th Wing headquarters was its inability to order units into the Caribbean, or to exchange units, without securing specific authority from the Joint Command in Washington, and without having given advance notice of the movement to the Commander, Caribbean Sea Frontier and having secured concurrence from him or any other interested Caribbean headquarters.[134] With submarines likely to make their appearance suddenly and in force, this was an awkward arrangement since it bound the officer commanding AAF Antisubmarine Command units in the area to the point where he could not act quickly enough to counter such a move.

Operations from Edinburgh Field, Trinidad, were controlled more or less directly from Naval Operating Base, Trinidad, located at Port of Spain, the air officer of which had final decision concerning the time and nature of each mission. Control over operations was exercised from a joint control room, established on lines similar to those at Miami and New York City. Information was received by headquarters, 25th Bomb Group, at Edinburgh Field, and from a local control room relayed to the AAF Antisubmarine Command squadron stationed there.[135]

The first antisubmarine command squadron to go to Trinidad was the 9th. The air echelon, consisting of 42 officers and 72 enlisted men in 10 B-18K type planes, arrived at Edinburgh Field on 2 December 1942, Maj. Glendon P. Overing in command.[136] Living conditions at the field were generally considered good, possibly better than in Miami. In addition to the 9th Antisubmarine Squadron, the 10th Bombardment Squadron, a flight of the 417th Bombardment Squadron, and some Navy blimps operated from the field, all on primarily antisubmarine duty.[137] Patrol missions began once for the B-18's. To the chagrin of all present, the number of submarines active in the Trinidad area declined sharply after the arrival of the 9th Squadron. In January

1943 no vessels were sunk in the waters around Trinidad, as compared to 5 in December and 13 in November.[138] And it is very doubtful whether the increased air coverage provided by the 9th did more than confirm the Germans in a policy of strategic withdrawal already agreed upon, or possibly hasten the rate of that retreat. As the threat of a U-boat concentration decreased, sweeps gave way to convoy coverage, and some tactical time was given up to an accelerated training program.[139]

Equipped with aircraft of medium range only, and patrolling an area in which seldom more than one U-boat operated, the 9th Squadron could hardly be expected to turn in a long list of attacks. Prior to its return to the United States in the latter part of March 1943, it had, however, made seven sightings and two attacks, both probably embarrassing to the enemy. In fact, in March, though flying only one-tenth of the total hours flown in the Trinidad area, it was fortunate enough to record three of the four sightings made during the month in those waters.[140]

The 9th Squadron had been separated from its ground echelon for 3 months. During that time it had gained a great deal of experience in use of radar and in operational flying. It was decided that the squadron should be reunited and given transition training in long-range aircraft in order to make the best use of this experience.[141] The air echelon of the 7th Antisubmarine Squadron and part of the ground echelon were accordingly ordered to Trinidad to replace the 9th.[142]

With 10 radar-equipped B-18's, the 7th continued the work of patrolling the convoy lanes, both those from the west and those, especially of the bauxite ships, plying along the South American coast. Occasionally, convoys passed to the north and northeast of the island and, in order to provide more complete coverage, planes would be sent to St. Lucia and to Barbados for several days.[143] Although from 4 to 12 patrols were flown daily, weather permitting, and three-fourths of the time with radar equipment, the 7th Squadron had even less luck than the 9th in making contact with the enemy. From the end of March until the middle of July, when it was relieved by the 8th, the 7th Squadron obtained only one contact and made no attacks.[144] In fact, the only unusual incident resulted when the delicate political situation in Martinique required that the squadron patrol the island, two planes having been based at St. Lucia for that purpose.[145]

In July 1943 the enemy staged what amounted to a concerted offensive in the Trinidad area. The average density of U-boats increased to 4 daily, sinkings of merchant vessels increased to 4, and attacks on submarines reached 13. Of these attacks, the 8th Antisubmarine Squadron, having stationed flights of B-24's at Zanderij and Waller Fields to cope with the situation, accounted for 2. Of the rest, 4 were made by B-18's of the 35th Bombardment Squadron stationed at Zanderij, and 7 by Navy planes. It is interesting to note that this flurry of activity coincided with the desperate efforts of the Germans in the eastern Atlantic to proceed in spite of air coverage. In 10 of the July attacks the enemy elected to fight back.[146]

None of the three attacks delivered by the B-24D aircraft of the 8th Antisubmarine Squadron resulted in direct damage to the submarine, but twice they participated in effective killer-hunts.[147]

On 31 August, the 8th Squadron was replaced by the 23d, which undertook experimental operations in the area with 16 B-25G aircraft equipped with the debatable 75-millimeter cannon in the nose. The withdrawal of the AAF Antisubmarine Command from antisubmarine patrol, in August 1943, left these operations still inconclusive.[148]

The Caribbean and the South Atlantic areas both seemed to AAF Antisubmarine Command planners a fertile field for expansion. Early plans had included these areas.[149] An effort was also made in 1943 to establish a separate antisubmarine wing in the Caribbean in order to provide administrative machinery for a large-scale operation in that area and along the northeasterly coast of South America.[150] Most of these plans came to nothing, frustrated either by lack of equipment, lack of cooperation from the Navy, or lack of time--the command was dissolved before much could be done even on favorably considered plans. One project did, however, come close to realization. In the spring of 1943 it was proposed to survey the possibility of establishing antisubmarine coverage over the Atlantic Ocean in the general region of Belem, Natal, Sao Salvador, Ascension Island, Accra, and Dakar. This belt of ocean was little traversed by convoys, but frequently by independent vessels, and had been a fairly profitable resort for individual raiding U-boats. It was felt that this entire area could be covered if one or more antisubmarine squadrons, equipped with VLR (B)

B-24's, were based at Natal, Brazil, or some other base in that vicinity, using Ascension Island and points on the West Coast of Africa as advance or alternate bases.[151] AAF headquarters gave modified approval to the plan, suggesting in substance that it never does any harm to study possibilities of this sort provided definite commitments are not made.[152] In this connection it should be observed that the Navy hoped by the fall of 1943 to have enough B-24's to handle the job, and in June 1943, it was anybody's guess who would ultimately control the VLR aircraft engaged in antisubmarine warfare.[153]

A project was begun, somewhat tentatively, in May, when on the 10th of that month two B-24D aircraft from the 8th Squadron were dispatched to Natal under the leadership of the squadron commander, Lt. Col. E. S. Beake. This experimental detachment operated from Natal until the 27th, when it was moved, together with its ground echelon, to Ascension Island. During the following month, its strength increased to four B-24D's, one of which was normally based at Natal. Some confusion arose regarding its place in the command machinery of the South Atlantic, but finally it was placed under the Commander, South Atlantic Force, acting under the direction of the Commander in Chief, U. S. Atlantic Fleet. This arrangement was in accord with the procedure effective at the moment for control of all antisubmarine operations by the Joint Chiefs of Staff, with the Commander in Chief, U. S. Fleet acting as the executive agent for this unified command.[154] The detachment continued operations on this basis, with the official blessing of Vice Adm. Jonas H. Ingram, Commander, 4th Fleet, Recife, until its recall in August.[155] During the period of its special duty, it flew 98 missions. Although it made few contacts with the enemy, it gathered considerable valuable information regarding German use of radar and radar detectors.[156]

Nothing more came of the Antisubmarine Command's plans for the South Atlantic. Decisions concerning its fate, and that of antisubmarine activity generally, placed all such projects in abeyance.

The North Atlantic convoy route. In February and March of 1943, Admiral Doenitz made an all-out effort to render the North Atlantic convoy route unusable for Allied shipping. This attack was part of a general defensive strategy adopted to cut off or seriously harass the convoys bringing supplies to the invasion armies in Europe and Africa. And, as the North Atlantic convoys constituted the most important of these vital supply lines, the U-boat attack in the North Atlantic was the most concerted and desperate ever launched by the enemy. It therefore became essential to strengthen to the utmost the antisubmarine effort in that area; and to this end long-range air coverage was of paramount importance. So grave had the situation become by March, that President Roosevelt wrote on the 18th to the Chiefs of Staff, U. S. Army and U. S. Navy, asking how many B-24's could be operated at once from Newfoundland, Greenland, and Iceland, how many ACV's were on antisubmarine operations in the North Atlantic, and how soon the existing force of both could be brought to its maximum strength.[157] If sufficient long-range bombers and ACV's were not promptly engaged in this battle of supply, the President warned, both HUSKY and BOLERO, as well as the security of Great Britain, might be seriously threatened.

In answer to the President's urgent message, the Chiefs of Staff vouchsafed the following information.[158] Army, Navy, and Canadian air bases could support B-24's at the rate of 75 in Newfoundland, 40 in Iceland, and 6, for limited operations only, in Greenland. Plans to date did not, however, provide for numbers of this sort. For Newfoundland, the AAF had planned 12 B-24's by 1 May, and 18 by 1 June; and the U. S. Navy had 12 which it hoped would be ready by June. Six Army Liberators had been earmarked for Greenland by 1 June. Iceland was to be left entirely to the RAF, whose Coastal Command had 8 B-24's in operation, 12 promised by 1 May, and 12 more by 1 June. In addition to the B-24's, 12 AAF Antisubmarine Command B-17's were ready for immediate shipment to Newfoundland to help cope with the convoy problem, although they were not so well suited to the work as the B-24's, owing to their shorter range. The Navy had an ACV in the area and planned to deploy two more in April. The British planned to put two ACV's on the convoy route. In short, with the U-boat war nearing its peak of intensity, the Allies were only able to put a handful of the vitally necessary VLR aircraft immediately into the battle. Adequate forces were planned, and diversions from other projects were suggested,[159] but none could be made available before mid-summer.

This, then, was the desperate situation at the end of March. A few medium-range aircraft were being operated from Greenland and Iceland, and the 431st Bombardment Squadron (redesignated the 20th

Antisubmarine Squadron on 8 February) had for some time been operating a few B-17's from Newfoundland. But the pressing problem still remained to provide long-range air cover for that middle portion of the North Atlantic route which had hitherto been beyond the range of the land-based aircraft available.

The problem had been recognized from the first, and the increasing intensity of the U-boat war in the North Atlantic stimulated discussion of it at the highest level. But it took most of the winter and spring of 1942-43 actually to equip Newfoundland with three antisubmarine squadrons from the AAF Antisubmarine Command; and by that time the climax of the struggle had already arrived. All that the AAFAC squadrons could do was to hasten, as best they could, the impending defeat of the Nazi submarine fleet.

A leading part in the discussion had been taken by the Canadian government. In December, Canada had been asked by Prime Minister Churchill whether it could supply the necessary bases, crews, and aircraft to undertake the task of providing air protection for the gap of approximately 250 nautical miles west of mid-ocean which was not being given air protection. Canada was able to supply the bases and crews, but could not provide the aircraft. Neither, at the moment, could the British. The Canadian Joint Staff then asked the AAF for 15 LB-30 aircraft.[160] General Arnold disapproved the proposal on the ground that the AAF had no Liberators to spare.[161] In March, the Atlantic Convoy Conference proposed that the AAF Antisubmarine Command operate three squadrons of B-24's from Newfoundland.[162] By that time the situation in the North Atlantic had become so grave that every effort was made to equip and send these units as soon as possible.[163] It had been estimated that by 1 July 1943 the AAF would have the necessary VLR aircraft deployed as recommended by the Atlantic Convoy Conference, but General Arnold was concerned to implement the plan for Newfoundland immediately.[164]

Meanwhile, the four B-17's of the 421st Bombardment Squadron, which had been operating for months under the Newfoundland Base Command as a reserve striking force, had also been carrying on antisubmarine patrol as a secondary duty under the control of Navy Task Force 24. They had been providing convoy coverage in a small square off the southeast corner of the island, in addition to the various odd jobs assigned to the unit. In order to increase the antisubmarine forces in the area, this squadron had been redesignated the 20th Antisubmarine Squadron and assigned antisubmarine patrol as its principal duty, under the Navy Task Force.[165] In January, too, preliminary steps had been taken to extend long-range air coverage to Greenland. On the 25th the Director of Bombardment ordered the AAF Antisubmarine Command to conduct experimental operations from Greenland and to survey the facilities available there.[166] And approximately a month later a report on the subject was submitted.[167] Actual operations from Greenland had, however, to wait on the establishment of a regular B-24 patrol from Newfoundland, from which point all Greenland long-range operations were to be controlled.[168]

Finally, on 13 March 1943, a detachment of the 25th Antisubmarine Wing left New York, under Col. Howard Moore, to establish a headquarters at St. John's, Newfoundland. On 3 April, this detached headquarters began operations in the control room of the combined headquarters of the Royal Canadian Navy and Royal Canadian Air Force. The 19th Antisubmarine Squadron also arrived late in March, and the 6th Antisubmarine Squadron a few weeks later. These squadrons were stationed at Gander Lake with the 20th Antisubmarine Squadron which had been in operation there for some time. A control room was set up for their use. The recently arrived squadrons, the 6th and 19th, became operational on 5 April and 19 April, respectively. For the next three months the three squadrons conducted antisubmarine sweeps and convoy coverage from Gander under the supervision of the detachment headquarters.[169] In early June, the 4th Antisubmarine Squadron joined the units at Gander and the 20th Squadron returned to the United States. Late in June 1943, when their services were no longer required in Newfoundland, the detachment headquarters (which on 13 June had been transferred on paper from the 25th Wing to the AAF Antisubmarine Command itself) was ordered to England, together with the units operating under it, the 4th, 6th, and 19th Antisubmarine Squadrons. These squadrons became part of the 479th Group. The 4th and 19th arrived in the United Kingdom in mid-July. The 6th, which had been left behind for a few weeks, assumed responsibility for AAFAC operations in Newfoundland in the absence of the detachment command post.[170]

Operations originally were conducted under the immediate control of the detachment command post at St. John's and were subject, as usual, to coordination with the naval force in charge of that locality, in this case the FONF.[171] On 30 April 1943, operational control of ASWAC units based in Newfoundland passed to Canada, in accordance with recommendations of the Atlantic Convoy Conference (par. 6, App. A, ACC-1) for an appropriate division of area responsibility between the three countries most concerned with the North Atlantic antisubmarine war.[172] It was a natural division, for, as far as air forces were concerned, the RCAF operated a majority of the antisubmarine aircraft in that area.[173] The nature of this control remained general, however, and consisted of designating the missions to be performed, rather than prescribing how they were to be accomplished.[174]

By the time the detachment headquarters began operations, the tactical situation had been pretty thoroughly surveyed by the Canadian agencies concerned. The great proportion of Allied convoys sailing to the United Kingdom had, because of fuel limitations, to pass through a relatively narrow bottleneck as they rounded Newfoundland and proceeded northeast along either the great circle or the northern routes. The enemy, recognizing this fact, apparently deployed his attack forces in such a way as to take maximum advantage of it. By March it was estimated by FONF intelligence that the Germans were setting up a patrol line of approximately 20 "informer" submarines, spaced about 20 miles apart along a line which cut across the convoy lanes in the bottleneck within the general area bounded by 51° N. 49° W., 53° N. 47° W., 50° N.

40° W., and 49° N. 41° W.[175] This disposition of informer submarines afforded complete coverage of roughly 90 per cent of the North Atlantic trade convoys, and allowed the enemy to relay such information concerning these convoys as would be required for the main attacking forces, patrolling farther to northeast, to converge on each convoy with concentrated force and a significant economy of time, effort, and fuel.

According to this theory, then, the contact line became the most important target in the North Atlantic battle. To locate and attack its elements and so to put out the eyes of the U-boat fleet, became the primary objective of the antisubmarine forces operating from Newfoundland.[176] During April and May it appeared that the Germans were extending this contact line farther to the south by adding probably 10 more submarines to cover the approaches to the southern route. Probably not more than 15 U-boats were deployed as an attack group, but, with the advantage of accurate advance intelligence, they were able to make every craft count in their attack on the convoys. The U-boat offensive in the North Atlantic reached its climax in a running attack on ONS-5 (29 April to 5 May 1943), during which 12 merchant vessels were torpedoed--11 of them within less than 24 hours. The ONS-5 action, however, turned out also to be a turning point in the North Atlantic battle, for it was a costly victory, so costly that the enemy could ill afford many more such triumphs. Over 30 attacks were made on the U-boats by both surface craft and aircraft, resulting in 9 sunk or probably sunk and about 9 others damaged to some degree.[177]

It was in this sort of battle that the AAFAC squadrons found themselves during April and May. Convoy coverage and offensive sweeps in broad areas ahead of convoys were their normal missions. In general the latter were the most productive of tangible results. For a few weeks, sightings were relatively frequent. The 25th Squadron, with only a few of its 7 B-17's (equipped with Mark II radar) available for patrol, flew 370 hours during March and made 7 sightings which resulted in 2 attacks, neither apparently damaging to the enemy. April proved to be a fairly productive month for the 3 squadrons. After the attack on ONS-5 early in May, the Germans began to withdraw their U-boat fleet gradually. As the waters off Newfoundland became correspondingly quiet, operations of the AAFAC squadrons consisted largely of escort missions. The following figures illustrate the changes in the situation, as far as the AAFAC squadrons were concerned, during the 2-month period:[178]

Period	Escort Missions	Contacts	Sweeps	Contacts
2 April to 2 May	454 hrs. 7 min.	1	588 hrs. 30 min.	10
3 May to 31 May	1,161 hrs. 58 min.	0	234 hrs. 56 min.	1
	1,616 hrs. 5 min.	1	823 hrs. 26 min.	11

Few attacks resulted from the above listed contacts, and, of the 3 delivered, only 2 were assessed as damaging to the submarine. It must, of course, be remembered that the weather in the Newfoundland area permitted fewer efficient flying hours than in other areas of antisubmarine activity, with the exception of Greenland.

Part of the AAF Antisubmarine Command activity in the North Atlantic took place in Greenland. It had been announced by the high command on 16 March that a "Trans-Atlantic umbrella" consisting of Canadian, British, and American aircraft, was to be raised over the North Atlantic convoys in order to afford coverage for "every mile of the route from North America to Europe." Full responsibility for this broadening beneficence was to rest with the Canadian and British governments. Operations from Greenland and Iceland were necessary, in addition to those from Newfoundland, if this project were to be accomplished. The major part of the additional mid-ocean coverage had to come from Iceland, where the RAF and the U. S. Navy normally maintained patrols. But it was felt that even sporadic long-range operations from Greenland would be enough to discourage the enemy in the vital mid-ocean gap.[179] Accordingly, in spite of some of the most disheartening flying weather in the world (operations could be undertaken only 15 days in the month at the most suitable field in the country) it was decided to operate a small long-range force from Bluie West One. Surveys of the area had been undertaken in February, but nothing could be done to provide the necessary long-range equipment and control personnel until the Detachment Headquarters had begun to function in Newfoundland.[180]

Meanwhile, two AAF units, the 1st and 2d Provisional Bombardment Flights, were operating a few B-25D airplanes as an emergency striking force under the control of the Greenland Base Command. Although engaged in antisubmarine operations, the efforts of these flights were limited by the range of their aircraft and by lack of experience on the part of their crews. In addition to these small Army forces, the U. S. Navy had a few PBY-5A's and PV-1's at Bluie West One under its Greenland Patrol Force which also undertook antisubmarine patrol. Such coordination of antisubmarine effort as was available came from the commander

of this naval force.[181] It had not been contemplated to use Bluie
West One for more than an advance operating base for planes based in
Newfoundland. But it was not until close to the middle of May that
anything was done even to use the Greenland base in that limited
capacity or to open a control room there.[182] By that time the crisis
in the North Atlantic had already passed, and the enemy was withdrawing
from the northern waters.

By June 1943 convoys were passing safely through lanes where a
few weeks previously they had undergone the severest punishment.
Admiral Doenitz had, in the face of increased Allied counterattacks
and increased Allied activity in the Mediterranean, found it impossible
to maintain his Newfoundland line. For a few weeks he had given everything he had to an all-or-nothing showdown in the North Atlantic. After
the attack on ONS-5 he apparently decided to play for smaller and surer
stakes. In his defeat, the three AAFAC squadrons had labored hard and
not without effect, despite the few contacts obtained. There is no
question that the increased long-range patrol that they were able to
provide did much to reduce enemy mobility and to weaken enemy morale.

Antisubmarine Tactics and Attack Narratives

It was a strange type of warfare that the antisubmarine crews
undertook, unlike any other in which the AAF had engaged. Hours of
monotonous search were necessary. In areas of low U-boat density,
some crews never saw a submarine, yet they had to maintain constant

vigilance. Even in areas where the hunting was good, a crew might fly hundreds of hours without a sighting, then, in a matter of seconds, be required to go into action. For this kind of work crews had to be carefully trained to insure that no fumbling would mar an attack when the big moment finally came. Moreover, flying a thousand miles or more over open water requires expert navigation. Radio communication must be reliable and the crew must be able to identify surface craft and aircraft with the utmost accuracy.

It is the attack itself that distinguishes antisubmarine flying most sharply from all other types. To be effective the depth bombs had to be laid within 20 feet of the submarine's pressure hull, and the aircraft was forced to drop close to the water, often to a scant 50 feet above the waves, in order to place them accurately. Each battle became a duel between the U-boat and the attacking plane, for the antisubmarine aircraft normally traveled alone. It might only last a few minutes, and during that time the crew had to function as a well-coached team, with all mechanical equipment in perfect condition.

It was hazardous work, too. Many crews had to face antiaircraft fire at close range or attack by enemy aircraft, often in considerable numbers, sent in to cover U-boat concentrations. Should the plane crash at sea, the crew knew it had few chances of surviving. The greatest danger to the aircraft came about during low-level attacks which made safety precautions generally useless; and under the best of conditions the plane would sink in a matter of seconds. Even if the crew survived a landing at sea it faced a disheartening prospect, for it would usually be hundreds of miles from land, dependent mainly on luck and the sometimes doubtful aid of its emergency equipment.

Experience had evolved certain basic principles for the conduct of antisubmarine operations by long-range aircraft.[183] Patrol missions were planned in such a way that a given stretch of ocean would be covered in a more or less comprehensive pattern of flight, the crew depending when possible on its radar equipment to supplement the visual observation of its members. In this way a single plane could detect the presence of an enemy craft in a strip of water many miles wide. A radar-equipped plane might be expected to patrol effectively a 25-mile channel.[184] Sweeps of this sort were normally routed toward areas in which U-boat concentrations were suspected, or in which individual raiders had been reported.[185] Frequently the antisubmarine planes would be required to fly search sweeps in the neighborhood of convoys, the theory in this case being to prevent the enemy from closing in on its prey or even following it. Of course, if a submarine could be located and attacked, so much the better; but simply by forcing the enemy to dive and remain submerged for long periods, during which his speed would be greatly decreased, the patrolling aircraft could prevent a "wolf pack" from delivering a rapid and coordinated attack.[186]

The big trick in this business of submarine hunting was to catch the submarine on the surface, or at least partially visible, and to deliver the attack before it had time to crash-dive. Analysis of attacks on submarines demonstrated that in approximately 35 per cent the submarines were still partly visible at the instant when the depth

bombs were released, and that in about 30 per cent of cases the enemy had disappeared less than 15 seconds. Attacks made after 15 seconds had small hope of success. Analysis further indicated that, in about two out of three instances, the submarine sighted the aircraft first.

It thus became an essential point of tactics to surprise the U-boat crew. Every possible use had to be made of camouflage and natural cover. Clouds, when available, provided by far the best cover; and by flying in and out of their bases, even by flying above formations of less than 5/10, the pilot was able to enjoy considerable concealment without materially reducing his chances of sighting submarines. Attacks from down sun, up moon path, and up to a dawn or dusk horizon proved effective. Camouflage of the plane itself also helped. Some were painted either Mediterranean blue or gray or olive drab on their upper half and off-white on their lower, with good effect.[187]

Even with the best of cover and camouflage, the attack had to follow the sighting with the greatest possible speed. If the U-boat elected to dive, as it normally did, it could be out of sight in 30 seconds. If a maximum time of 45 seconds were allowed for the dive, and 15 more during which the submarine would be within range of depth bombs, the attack would have to be completed in 1 minute.[188]

It was not always possible, therefore, to approach the U-boat at the best possible angle. If practicable, the pilot would cross his target at a small angle (15 to 45 degrees was considered best).[189] In this way, without complicating his aim, he could considerably increase the probability that at least one depth bomb would do lethal damage. Normally a plane carrying only six depth bombs would drop them all on the first attack. If more were carried the second stick would be reserved for a subsequent attack. The bombs were spaced in such a way that at a normal height of 100 feet, the 325-pound charges would fall in a pattern of 60-foot intervals and those of 650 pounds at 70-foot intervals, thus making it possible for two of them to straddle the submarine and either tear its pressure hull seriously or even break it in two. Care had always to be exercised to attain the 100-foot level long enough before the attack to make the final approach in level flight. Nor was it wise to execute a run at too great speed, which simply increased the likelihood of error.

During the attack the aircraft gunners had to be prepared to bring machine-gun fire to bear on the U-boat, especially if the enemy crew showed signs of fighting back. Even under ordinary circumstances, it was considered advisable to fire along the hull of the submarine in the hope that penetration of its thin armor might do embarrassing damage to the fuel tanks or high-pressure air tanks.

If, as was usually the case, the aircraft crew could not be certain of the effect of their attack, or if they had not been able to make an attack at all, they were instructed to remain as long as possible in the area of the contact, or until relieved by other aircraft or by surface vessels summoned to the scene by radio. As long as a submarine is forced to remain submerged, the area to be searched is restricted to a minimum. In this way a concentration of forces in a cooperative killer hunt had a very good chance, if followed up persistently, of finally destroying the submarine. Sometimes, if the aircraft still had bombs, or had failed to release them at the initial contact, the pilot would drop a marker at the point where the submarine had disappeared, and resort to baiting tactics. After withdrawing some 30 miles, and staying away for 30 minutes to 1 hour, depending on his gas supply, he would return to the contact area on the chance that the enemy had surfaced again.

It was often difficult to determine the amount of damage inflicted, even by a well-executed attack, on an enemy submarine. Depth bombs themselves gave off a dirty oil residue which might easily be mistaken for the oily evidence of damage. Air bubbles appearing immediately after the depth bombs had detonated might only signify that the submarine was blowing or venting some tanks to adjust a temporary upset. Oil rising at this point might indicate damage to the external fuel tanks. If small air bubbles rose in a continuous stream, it was likely that the external connections to high-pressure air were damaged. This was annoying but not serious to the submarine. The U-boat might break surface momentarily after an attack and take up strange angles, stern or bow up. Yet even these signs might only mean a temporary loss of trim or control, rather than any serious damage. Large air bubbles that caused a disturbance on the surface and lasted for some time could be considered as evidence of trouble, and if accompanied by oil it meant that the enemy was in a desperate condition. In cases of this sort, if the submarine failed to reappear soon on the surface it would be considered sunk. Probably the only certain evidences of a "kill" were the appearance of survivors, or of bodies, or of a large amount of debris.

Most of the principles, outlined above, are exemplified, together with a number of unusual instances, in the following accounts of some of the more interesting attacks made by aircraft of the AAF Antisubmarine Command, which appeared in the monthly intelligence summary, published by that organization.

On 31 December 1942 the 1st Antisubmarine Squadron made its first important attack in the Bay of Biscay. It was a well-executed attack, making good use of the newly acquired radar equipment under adverse sea conditions. The attack was carried out at 1249 (GCT) by a B-24D, piloted by Capt. W. L. Thorne, while on patrol in 51°20' N., 20°58' W. An A.S.V. contact was first made while the airplane was 8 miles distant at an altitude of 1,000 feet. The pilot homed on the signal, on a course of 300°, gradually reducing altitude, and sighted the submarine about 4½ miles away traveling on the surface at a speed of approximately 8 knots, course 320° T. No wake was visible because of the heavy seas. The submarine began its crash dive as Pilot Thorne started his run. Attacking from 4 points abaft the starboard beam of the submarine, at a speed of 200 m. p. h. from 175-foot altitude, 9 Torpex Mk XI depth bombs were dropped with a fuse setting of 25 feet and at a spacing of 16 feet. The stick straddled the hull just behind the conning tower. Three depth bombs fell to starboard, two over the hull, and the remainder to the port side. Approximately eighty-five .50-caliber rounds were fired at the disappearing hull and conning tower by the port ventral and tail gunners. The three depth bombs that fell to the starboard should have moved in and exploded directly under the stern of the U-boat, and the plume of the depth bombs contained a black streak believed to have been oil. As the point of attack was circled, an oil patch estimated to be 500 feet in diameter was observed, in the center of which numerous small bubbles were noticeable. A flame float was dropped, and the plane left the area on baiting procedure, returning 50 minutes later without seeing any further evidence of damage.[190]

Tidewater Tillie was the B-24 in which 1st Lt. W. L. Sanford and his crew of the 2d Antisubmarine Squadron executed two attacks on enemy submarines which resulted in one probably sunk and one known sunk.

The first attack took place on 10 February about 800 miles west of St. Nazaire while the squadron was operating out of Great Britain. While patrolling at 800 feet at the base of a solid overcast, the left waist gunner sighted a U-boat on the surface 10 degrees off the port bow and about 4 miles away. A radar contact had been obtained in the same position a few seconds before, but owing to sea conditions, it had not been verified until the visual sighting was made.

When first observed, the conning tower was clearly seen, but, as the aircraft approached, it disappeared and about 40 feet of the stern was seen projecting out of the water at an angle of 20 degrees.

As the aircraft attacked, no churning was visible from the screws of the apparently motionless U-boat. Six Mk XI Torpex depth bombs, spaced for 19 feet, were released from 200 feet at 200 m. p. h. The entire stick overshot: the first depth bomb was observed to explode about 20 foot to starboard of the submarine as the tail gunner fired 75 rounds at the exposed part of the hull.

As the pilot circled to port the U-boat settled back on an even keel with the conning tower visible and both decks awash. A second attack on the still motionless submarine was made with three more depth bombs. The tail gunner fired another 75 rounds and saw the first depth bomb explode on the port side, while a second exploded to starboard. The U-boat appeared to lift slightly, lurching with the force of the explosion, and then remained motionless on the surface.

While Lieutenant Sanford circled to make a third run, the sea was seen to be churned just astern of the U-boat, and the conning tower settled beneath the surface, without way, 15 seconds before the last three depth bombs were released. The detonations occurred about 200 feet ahead of the patch of disturbed water, but no plume resulted. Instead, a dome-shaped bubble appeared, followed by a large circular slick of brown fluid which was described by the crew as definitely not depth-bomb residue. Nothing further was seen, and 30 minutes later the L-2 set course for base.

When first sighted, the U-boat apparently was attempting to dive at too steep an angle without sufficient way. This gave the pilot an opportunity to maneuver for two additional attacks which resulted, according to official assessment, in "probably sunk."

On 22 March, while operating out of a North African base, Lieutenant Sanford, again in Tidewater Tillie, made another attack in the vicinity of the Canary Islands which resulted in the complete destruction of the U-boat.

The B-24, camouflaged Mediterranean blue on its upper surfaces and cloud white underneath, was patrolling at 1,300 feet, in and out of the cloud cover, when the co-pilot sighted a broad wake about 5 miles on the starboard beam. The pilot continued on his course into the next cloud, then made a 90-degree turn, immediately losing altitude. As the plane emerged from the cloud, the wake, still about 5 miles distant, was observed to be caused by a U-boat proceeding fully surfaced on course 180°. Lieutenant Sanford decided to continue his run straight ahead and attack from the beam with the sun behind him rather than maneuver for a quartering or following attack. With the aircraft at 200 feet and making about 200 m. p. h., the bombardier released four Mk XXIX depth bombs spaced at 60 feet, allowing about 1,000-foot range on the water.

The explosions enveloped the after portion of the U-boat which continued on its course for 11 seconds, then began to settle by the stern. The entire bow section from the conning tower forward was projecting out of the water and in about 1 minute slipped beneath the surface. Several survivors were observed clinging to debris which was strewn about the area, and a large oil slick developed. Half an

LT W L SANFORD 2ND A/S SQ 10 FEB 1943
——— 1ST ATTACK ——— 2ND ATTACK ——— 3RD ATTACK

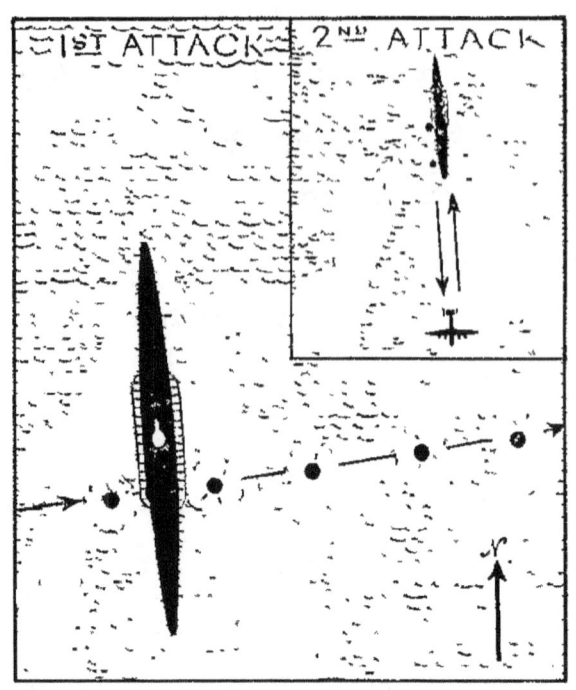

LT KUENNING 480TH GROUP 9 JULY 1943

LT DAMANN 2ND A/S SQ 9 JULY 1943

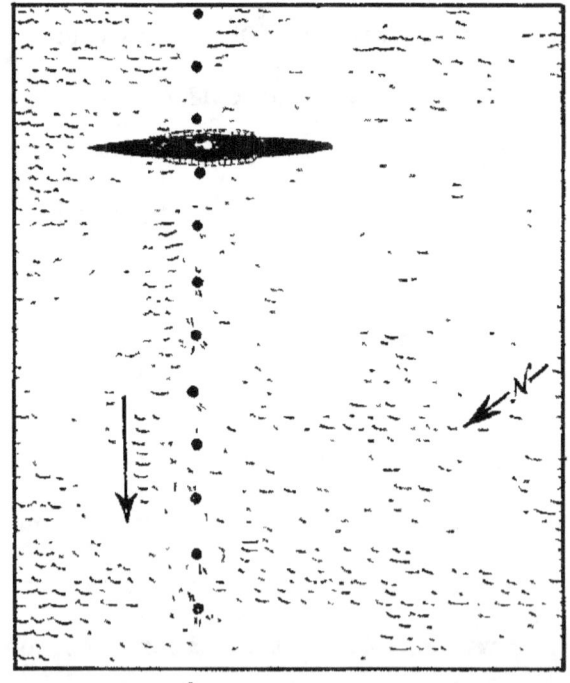

LT HAMILTON 4TH SQ 2 AUG. 1943

hour later, as the plane was about to depart, a mass of brown, paint-like substance came up in the middle of the slick. This may have been rusty bilge oil discharged when the U-boat began to break up on the bottom.

The submarine was described as painted white with no markings. It had a streamlined conning tower and a very sharp bow. Three men were observed in the conning tower as the plane passed over. One of them tried to man the antiaircraft gun.

The attack was evidently a complete surprise and was achieved by a combination of effective camouflage, clever use of cloud cover, attacking out of the sun, and accurate bombing.[191]

On 20 February 1943 a B-24 of the 1st Antisubmarine Squadron, piloted by Lt. W. S. Johnson, was on patrol over the Bay of Biscay in the area 49°30' N. 21° W., some 800 miles from base. It was flying at 1,600 feet through broken clouds that extended down to about 700 feet when the navigator in the nose sighted the broad wake of a fully surfaced U-boat about 3 miles away. The pilot immediately dived to attack, entering the clouds and emerging when about 1 mile distant from the U-boat.

Apparently the aircraft had not been spotted since the U-boat was still on the surface. The B-24 went in with its bow gun raking the conning tower. Six depth bombs spaced for 36 feet were dropped from 200 feet and were seen to straddle the hull just aft of the bow. The force of the explosions lifted the bow, and, as the plume fell away, another explosion was seen on the port side in the vicinity of the conning tower. This explosion caused no plume but a boiling hump appeared on the water. Fifteen seconds later the conning tower disappeared without any noticeable heading, and a bluish-grey oil slick about 400 feet long formed on the water. Some small bubbles were seen rising in the center of the slick, and the navigator reported seeing a greenish patch, possibly air, rising to the surface.

Baiting tactics were employed but nothing further was seen. Ninety minutes after the attack the aircraft left the area and returned to base. This attack probably resulted in severe damage.[192]

Early in March 1943 there took place in the Caribbean a good example of a killer hunt in a convoy area. Early on the evening of 3 March, while returning from a convoy escort mission in the Trinidad area, a B-18B of the 9th Antisubmarine Squadron picked up a good instrument contact at 17 miles. Haze and darkness restricted visibility to less than 1 mile, so the pilot had to home on the target, increasing speed and losing altitude at the same time. From three-quarters of a mile a wake was sighted and as the plane passed over at 400 feet it was identified as a fully surfaced submarine on course 330°, speed 12 knots. While the target remained on the radar screen the pilot immediately turned and lost more altitude. The attack was made 90° to the course of the submarine which was still visible when the bombs were released. Two Mark XXIX and two Mark XVII depth bombs were released from 100 feet and were seen to enter the water about 50 feet ahead of the swirl. Apparently the U-boat had just submerged as the bombs hit. All charges were observed to explode directly in the track of the submarine, but because of darkness no evidence of damage could be seen.

Edinburgh Field dispatched another B-18B as soon as the message from the attacking plane was received. About 2 hours later this plane obtained an initial radar indication about 8 miles distant at 45° to starboard in a position 12 miles northeast of the scene of the first attack. The pilot approached the target and, when 1 mile away, altitude 200 feet, he turned on his landing lights. The submarine immediately opened fire with two guns, one firing slightly higher than the other. Tracer bullets were plainly seen as the pilot banked steeply to the right, turned off the landing lights and drew out of range. The B-18B returned and positively identified it as an enemy submarine on course 300° making about 15 knots. The U-boat crash-dived immediately, making it impossible for the plane to make a second run.

A square search of the area was begun and 2 hours later a radar contact was made at 11 miles, bearing 60° to port. The plane homed on the target, dropping to 200 feet, and made three passes over the fully surfaced submarine in an attempt to line up on the target. On the fourth pass, the submarine was still proceeding on the surface at 15 knots, course 75°. Two Mark XXIX and two Mark XVII, spaced for 20 feet, were seen to enter the water, straddling the submarine between the conning tower and stern. At least three explosions were observed; the other bomb may have hit the U-boat, or hit so close to it that the explosion was not seen. Following the attack the area was searched for 30 minutes for evidence of damage but nothing could be seen due to darkness.

These two attacks, delivered under difficult circumstances, probably saved the convoy from an attack and caused possible damage to the enemy submarine. When the submarine was sighted again at 2110 by the B-18B which relieved the original plane, its course of 300° and speed 15 knots indicated that the submarine was persisting in its original intent. The fact that it opened fire on the plane and failed to submerge while the plane made four passes is not positive indication that the first attack resulted in damage sufficient to prohibit the prompt execution of a crash dive. However, it appears very probable that the net result of the two attacks was sufficient damage to hinder the enemy greatly in his efforts to evade the extensive search by airplane and surface craft which ensued.

Six days later a Navy PBY was hunting 500 miles east of these attacks for a possible crippled U-boat limping its way back home. From 4,500 feet, a fully surfaced submarine was sighted about 8 miles distant on a course of 83° and making 8 knots. Making good use of cloud cover, the aircraft maneuvered to attack out of the sun. Diving to 75 feet, four Mark XVII depth bombs were dropped in salvo, landing alongside the hull about 10 to 15 feet away. As the bombs exploded the submarine appeared to rise out of the water, then split in two at the center. Debris, smoke, and water were thrown 50 feet in the air. At least 11 survivors were seen in the water.[193]

Celebrating the arrival of the 6th Antisubmarine Squadron in Newfoundland, Lt. E. J. Dudeck in a B-24D made an excellent attack on 19 April 1943. The B-24D, camouflaged white, was flying on a course of 147° W. through weather conditions that were fair for submarine hunting, with the sun obscured by low stratus clouds at 1,000 feet and with visibility varying up to 8 miles. At 1448Z, while Lieutenant Iudeck was taking full advantage of cloud cover, a submarine was sighted at 355° about half a mile distant, proceeding on a course of 10° N., at about 8 knots.

At the moment of sighting the U-boat, the airplane crew was engaged in transferring fuel, and fast action was necessary since the enemy apparently had already spotted the plane and started to dive. The pilot immediately pushed the plane into a dive for the attack while the crew scrambled to their stations. The conning tower disappeared 10 seconds after the original sighting, but six Mark XVII depth bombs, spaced at 35 feet with 25-foot depth settings, were released 5 seconds later, while 10 to 15 feet of the diving U-boat's stern were still visible. The U-boat appeared to be a dirty grey color, about 200 feet long, with a 3-inch gun mounted forward of the conning tower.

The pilot led the visible stern of the U-boat by about 150 feet and while the first depth bomb was about 35 feet short and the fourth, fifth and sixth were over, the second and third appeared to straddle each side of the U-boat slightly ahead of the conning tower. A large yellowish green oil slick was observed immediately after the attack and air bubbles about 1 foot in diameter appeared 50 feet ahead of the last-observed position of the stern. The plane remained in the vicinity for 1 hour and 45 minutes and a B-17 later searched the area for 2 hours. No further evidence of damage appeared.

The attack, executed accurately in a minimum of time, appears to have been carried out in a superior manner. While evidence of a definite kill was lacking, the probabilities favored at least severe damage to the U-boat.[194]

On 2 May 1943, Capt. E. J. Larson and his crew in a B-17 of the 19th Antisubmarine Squadron had a field day off the coast of Newfoundland. They appear to have happened upon one of those U-boat packs by means of which the Germans were currently attempting to close the North Atlantic convoy route. A period of poor weather had restricted flying for several days previous, and even on this day haze, light rain, and fog prevented all the scheduled missions from taking off. Another result of the protracted low-pressure area which hung offshore was to draw in the U-boat pack which usually patroled from 500 to 600 miles off Newfoundland to within 300 miles. A convoy, ONS-5, was in the vicinity of Greenland at this time and proceeding on a southerly course for Halifax. Apparently the submarines were working into position to intercept it. Captain Larson was dispatched to sweep an area about 500 miles ahead of the convoy.

In the course of the afternoon three U-boats were sighted and attacked by this plane. The first contact was obtained at 1945Z when an enemy craft was seen 3 miles away proceeding with decks awash. The submarine appeared to be of the 740-ton type with deck guns fore and aft and a streamlined conning tower 12 to 15 feet long. It was painted solid black. The aircraft attacked on a course of approximately 45 degrees to the U-boat, dropping four Mark XVII depth bombs from 50 feet spaced at 30 feet. The top of the conning tower was still visible at the time of release. All the bombs were seen to detonate. With respect to the conning tower the first explosion was estimated about 40 feet short, the second 10 to 20 feet short, the third a direct hit, and the fourth about 10 feet over. As the bombs exploded, the conning tower appeared to lift about 3 feet and then settled under. Tracers from the nose and top turret were seen to hit in the conning tower area. After the attack, a heavy black oil slick 500 feet in diameter was seen.

Two hours later a conning tower was sighted 2 miles away, in a position about 50 miles from the first contact. This U-boat, which was also painted black, appeared to be of the 500-ton type with a small conning tower and a deck gun forward. The aircraft attacked on a course of 180 degrees to the U-boat with .50-caliber machine guns only, since all depth bombs had been expended in the first attack. As the B-17 circled, the U-boat was seen to submerge in a normal dive.

A half hour later another submarine was sighted in the same area. It was not moving and the deck was dry as if it had been surfaced for some time. A high, rust-colored conning tower and one deck gun forward was observed. As the aircraft went in to attack, six men were seen on deck; one, at the gun, may have fired upon the plane. At least two men were left in the conning tower when the U-boat crash-dived. One appeared to be hit by the fire from the ..50- and .30-caliber machine guns.

In all three attacks the aircraft was patrolling at about 300 feet. Visibility varied between 3 and 6 miles. All contacts were first picked up on special equipment which was used continuously, and without which the crew believed the sightings could not have been made. It is to be regretted that the limited bomb load of the B-17 prevented more serious damage to the enemy.[195]

On 19 June 1943 a B-24D of the 2d Antisubmarine Squadron, piloted by Capt. William Sanford, took off from Port Lyautey on convoy escort duty in the early morning hours. At 0633, with visibility 15 miles (still restricted by darkness), at an altitude of 1,200 feet, the radar operator reported two indications at 30 to 32 miles, in a position about 10 miles behind the convoy. Captain Sanford lost altitude as he neared the area and opened the bomb bay doors, but the contact was lost. Turning to starboard, he climbed again to 1,500 feet, and soon another indication was picked up 80° to starboard at 7 miles.

As the plane started its run, it let down to 400 feet, and from a distance of 1 mile sighted a 517-ton German U-boat with decks awash, making a speed of 12 to 15 knots on a course of 90°. The submarine immediately opened fire on the plane with cannon and machine guns, to which the plane's navigator replied with 25 rounds from the nose gun, scoring hits on the deck and conning tower. The U-boat's fire ceased when the B-24 came within 100 yards, but the navigator fired another burst for good measure.

The U-boat was still on the surface, making no attempt to crash-dive, when the bombardier released six Mark 47 350-pound depth bombs, with a 60-foot spacing and 25-foot setting. The plane, which was flying 200 m. p. h. at 100 feet, attacked from the starboard beam at an angle of 100° to the course of the submarine. The tail and left waist-gunners reported the explosions were seen 10 to 20 feet ahead of the U-boat's stern with numbers 3 and 4 straddling the hull. The force of the explosions lifted 5 feet of the submarine's stern out of the water at a 30° to 40° angle. As the plane passed over, the U-boat's guns fired again, but less heavily this time; and a few seconds later the submarine slid under the surface, bow first. The German gun crew was evidently left in the water, for they were still firing when the U-boat submerged. The screws were apparently damaged or destroyed in the attack, for there was no sign of churning when the stern sank. A large piece of debris was left on the surface.

Having dropped a flame float and circled to port, the plane made a second attack up the U-boat's track 40 seconds later. This time the remaining two depth bombs were released, guiding on the flame float, and the debris left from the first attack was scattered by the explosion. An oil slick 300 to 400 feet long and 20 feet wide was seen, but darkness obscured the scene, making observation of further results impossible. The B-24 reported to the convoy and after resurveying the area resumed its patrol.

This attack was assessed as resulting in "probably slight damage." It was one of the few successful night attacks made by the Antisubmarine Command.[196]

On 7 July a B-24D airplane of the 1st Antisubmarine Squadron, piloted by Lt. T. A. Isley, was out hunting about 250 miles southwest of Lisbon with ceiling and visibility unlimited and scattered clouds at 1,500 feet. The aircraft was flying at 170 m. p. h. in and out of the base of the clouds, when a radar contact was obtained at a distance of 15 miles. Lieutenant Isley immediately altered course and a fully surfaced U-boat was sighted at 8 miles distance, making 6 to 9 knots on a course of 20° true. As the aircraft let down still about 4 miles away, the U-boat was observed crash-diving. It was obvious that an attack could not be made while the U-boat was still on the surface, with the result that careful judgment was required if the attack was to be a success.

Lieutenant Isley estimated that fully 10 seconds had elapsed since the conning tower disappeared before six Mark 47 depth bombs were released by intervalometer. The bombs were spaced at 60 feet, fused at 25 feet, and released from 300 feet. The explosions straddled the advance track of the U-boat approximately 200 feet ahead of the swirl at a target angle of 360°. This angle of attack afforded a broad coverage of the submerged course of the U-boat, and soon indications of results appeared. About 45 seconds after the explosions, a large, black oil bubble rose to the surface, continued to erupt oil for 5 minutes, and spread over an extensive area 600 to 700 feet in diameter. Lieutenant Isley remained in the area for 40 minutes after the attack but observed no further evidence of damage. COMINCH considered this submarine to be severely damaged.[197]

On the same day and in the same general area, another aircraft of the 1st Antisubmarine Squadron, while patrolling at 3,000 feet, obtained a radar contact at 7 miles. Almost simultaneously, Lt. W. S.

McDonnell, the pilot, sighted a fully surfaced 517-ton U-boat proceeding northwesterly at about 8 knots. He immediately altered his course to starboard and let down to make the attack.

As he approached, the U-boat swung off to starboard and opened fire from the conning tower with its 20-millimeter gun. The pilot pressed the attack despite the AA fire, and as the aircraft passed over the U-boat from the port side at a target angle of approximately 270°, 7 Mark 47 depth bombs, spaced at 60 feet, were released by the bombardier. Both the navigator and the top turret gunner returned the fire of the U-boat, strafing the conning tower and the deck. The explosions of the bombs straddled the target, which was seen to break in two abaft the conning tower. Members of the air crew then observed the after section of the U-boat rise 10 or 12 feet into the air, roll to starboard, then settle and sink with no forward motion.

As the aircraft was attacking, a 20-millimeter shell from the U-boat struck the top center panel of the nose. Several members of the crew were seriously injured by the burst, including the navigator, bombardier, radio operator, and assistant radio operator. In addition, the aircraft itself suffered minor damage, as the shell knocked out the radio compass, the hydraulic system, and most of the engine instruments. With the plane damaged and most of the crew injured, Lieutenant McDonnell headed for home.

Although Lieutenant McDonnell was not able to remain in the area to observe further results, photographic evidence indicated a perfect straddle, and the testimony of the crew suggests that the U-boat was destroyed.[103]

The following day, 3 July, another attack was made by a plane of the 2d Antisubmarine Squadron, about 150 miles north of the previous day's action. The aircraft, piloted by Lt. J. E. Darden, was flying at 3,000 feet through a broken overcast when radar contact was made on a U-boat off to starboard and 18 miles distant. Approaching through the base of the clouds, Lieutenant Darden, planned the attack so that he would come down out of the sun in a steep dive. The maneuver worked out according to plan. Upon sighting the U-boat ahead 8 miles distant, proceeding at 12 knots in a southeasterly direction, the plane dove steeply, leveled off, and passed over the submarine at an altitude of 50 feet. The target angle was 270° and four Mark 37 650-pound depth bombs were observed to straddle the U-boat between the bow and the conning tower. The tail gunner observed the surfaced U-boat running directly into the center of the explosion.

This attack had not been delivered without opposition; once again, the U-boat commander elected to remain on the surface and defend himself with AA fire. From 800 yards on in, the B-24D was under fire, suggesting that the use of the sun almost achieved a complete surprise attack. As the aircraft passed over, however, one burst struck the starboard side of the nose, but caused only minor damage. Fire was returned during the attack by the top turret, nose, and tail guns. Lieutenant Darden made a sharp climbing turn to port after delivering the first attack, and prepared for another run. The enemy craft was now circling, out of control, in a series of tight turns, gradually losing speed and trailing a long stream of brown oil. A large cloud of dark smoke poured from a point directly abaft the conning tower, and, in addition, the stern was submerged completely with the bow rising higher out of the water.

The aircraft returned for a second attack at a 50-foot altitude and a target angle of 80°. On this occasion the U-boat's AA fire was more effective, scoring numerous hits on the wing, fuselage, and bomb bay, cutting the hydraulic and fuel lines and damaging the radio equipment and the command radio transmitter. Unfortunately, the damage to the bomb bay doors now made it impossible to release the additional two depth bombs as the aircraft passed over on this run. Machine-gun fire from the plane, however, continued to rake the U-boat, which now had slowed to two or three knots, continuing tight turns and gradually losing all forward motion. Finally it disappeared, stern first, settling slowly with no churning or other surface indications. There were still two depth bombs aboard, however, and the crew prepared for a third attack.

The bombardier, Lt. C. J. Proccaro, succeeded in opening the doors of the bomb bay despite the damage, and two more Mark 37's were dropped upon the settling U-boat, which was silhouetted beneath the surface. The explosions of these bombs straddled the conning tower and were accompanied by a third blast of greater intensity. This third plume appeared to be higher than normal, thick and dark in color.

This series of attacks had consumed approximately 20 minutes. It was skillfully executed, beginning with the use of the sun and cloud cover, and ending with a successful release of the remaining two depth bombs. Heavy and accurate enemy AA fire did not deter the pilot from completing very accurate runs over the target, and the bombardier released the bombs in both instances with superior skill. The results of the attack were visible on the surface, for heavy oil spread over the entire area. Owing to the damage sustained, and to minor injuries suffered by one crew member, the pilot was unable to remain in the vicinity to observe further indications of success.[199]

On the 9th of July a B-24 of the 2d Squadron attacked and probably destroyed a submarine. The plane was flying at 3,200 feet, taking advantage of 3/10 cloud cover when Lieutenant Gerhart, the bombardier, sighted a U-boat apparently just surfacing about 4 miles dead ahead. It was the 517-ton type, camouflaged slate gray.

Lt. T. E. Kuenning, the pilot, immediately put the aircraft into a dive, leveling off at 50 feet. Six Mark XI 250-pound Torpex-filled depth bombs were released, straddling the bow with one short and five over. The explosions occurred just aft of the conning tower. No enemy fire was encountered. No one was seen on deck, confirming the supposition that the submarine may have been surprised just as it surfaced.

The pilot circled immediately and, as the spray subsided, came in again for a second attack on the still surfaced U-boat. This attack was almost head-on, and two more Mark XI were released, exploding aft of the conning tower on the port side as the enemy craft appeared to be attempting a crash dive. As the plane climbed away to port, six crew members saw the bow rise 15 feet out of the water at an angle of 45°; then the hull slid backwards, sinking stern first. The entire action was over in 2 minutes.[200]

A very unusual attack in which radar played a very important role occurred on the 12th of July about 200 miles northwest of Lisbon. Lt. E. Salm, the pilot, was flying at 5,600 feet over a solid overcast, using radar continuously, when a contact was obtained about 13 miles dead astern. The pilot turned and descended through the overcast on instruments at 240 m. p. h., constantly receiving headings from the radar operator.

The B-24D finally broke through at 200 feet, and a surfaced U-boat was sighted on the starboard bow 1 mile away. Immediately the navigator and top turret gunner opened fire and tracers were seen to rake the entire conning tower area. No enemy personnel was seen, but lookouts must have been present. Seven Mark XI 250-pound Torpex-filled depth bombs were released while the aircraft was still in a slight dive. Because of the angle at the time of release, the spacing of the bombs was somewhat shortened, but in this case the shorter spacing probably resulted in maximum effectiveness, owing to the accuracy with which the bombs were released.

The crew saw the explosions straddle the submarine, and, as the pilot made a vertical turn at 100 feet, the U-boat broke in two and sank. The entire area was covered with oil, and large bubbles appeared for several minutes. While Lieutenant Salm continued to circle, low and very tightly because of the limited ceiling and restricted visibility, 15 survivors were counted in the water. The air crew dropped a dinghy and smoke flares. As the plane departed seven survivors were still seen in the water.[201]

This remarkable attack demonstrated what skillful use of radar equipment, coupled with the alertness and audacity of the pilot and crew, could do, even in the face of adverse weather conditions.

On 28 July an excellent example of a cooperative attack took place. On that date, Lt. A. J. Hammer of the 4th Squadron had set a course to return to base from the vicinity north of Cape Finisterre. Flying at 4,000 feet and in light clouds on a course of $30°$, the B-24D was approximately 150 miles north of the Cape when a fully surfaced U-boat was sighted 5 miles off to starboard. The U-boat, which appeared to be of the 740-ton type and well camouflaged, was proceeding at 10 knots on a course of $250°$.

Lieutenant Hammer immediately altered his course to prepare to attack out of the sun which was now down in the west. The U-boat had altered its course $90°$ to starboard shortly after it was sighted, and now was on a northwesterly course, continually zigzagging. As the aircraft closed in to attack, the U-boat opened fire at a range of $2\frac{1}{2}$ miles with two guns abaft the conning tower, but, despite the intense flak, no hits were scored upon the Liberator on this run. At 1,000 yards, the two top turret guns and nose gun opened accurate fire on the U-boat, registering hits all along the deck, knocking two men overboard, and temporarily silencing all AA fire.

From an altitude of 100 feet the bombardier released 8 Mark XI Torpex depth bombs, spaced at 60 feet, of which 5 fell short and 3 just beyond the conning tower, thus securing an accurate straddle at a target angle of approximately $270°$. The pilot circled to port to prepare for a second attack, and this time the bombardier released 4 Mark XI bombs spaced at 100 feet from an altitude of 50 feet and at a target angle of $90°$. The U-boat was still on the surface and all 4 of the depth bombs fell short, the last one falling only 5 feet from the hull. Unfortunately, during this second run, the turret guns jammed and the nose gun had exhausted its ammunition, which left no defense against the renewed AA fire of the U-boat. The No. 1 engine of the Liberator was completely knocked out, and additional damage was suffered in the tail assembly as a result of the intense AA fire.

At this point a second Liberator appeared on the scene, attracted by the depth-bomb plumes of the original attack, and before the U-boat could submerge, the new arrival, a Coastal Command B-24, commanded by Flight Officer Sweeney, was able to deliver a third attack. Seven more Torpex depth bombs straddled the U-boat, with the third one falling alongside the conning tower. Before the plumes had entirely subsided, the enemy craft had disappeared, but immediately surfaced on an even keel, then submerged once more with bow projecting high out of the water. Once again an attack was delivered by the second aircraft, and the U-boat disappeared. Two extensive oil patches spread over the sea, large air bubbles rose to the surface, and 10 men in life jackets were observed swimming amid the debris and oil. During the run in, the second Liberator had been hit in the No. 4 engine which was set afire, but fortunately both aircraft reached their bases safely. Despite damage to Lieutenant Hammer's aircraft, his crew suffered no injuries. This attack was assessed as a definite kill.[202]

A B-24D of the 4th Antisubmarine Squadron attacked and sank an enemy submarine on 2 August 1943. The aircraft was patrolling at 2,500 feet on top of scattered clouds about 400 miles west of St. Nazaire when a radar contact was obtained indicating a target 20 miles distant and $50°$ to starboard. Lt. J. L. Hamilton, the pilot, changed course and 5 minutes later the co-pilot, Lt. R. C. Schmidt, sighted a large wake about $30°$ to starboard and approximately 10 miles away. As the aircraft let down from out of the sun, a surfaced U-boat was sighted, apparently homebound on a course of $30°$.

When the B-24D was 1 mile away the submarine opened fire with light flak, scoring one hit on the left wheel, but most of the firing was very inaccurate. The aircraft's top turret opened fire at 1,500 yards distance, the front guns began at 600 yards, and both registered hits all along the U-boat decks. Antiaircraft shelling subsided as the plane made its final run at a target angle of $90°$.

From an altitude of 50 feet the bombardier intended to drop 8 depth bombs, but actually a train of 12 Torpex Mark XI depth bombs were released. The tail gunner observed the charges straddling the U-boat. The American A-1 bombsight was used but the plane's intervalometer, previously known to be unreliable, was not used on order of the squadron commander. The 12 depth charges were released by toggle and the crew estimated their spacing at 50 feet. As the plumes subsided, the tail gunner observed the entire U-boat lifted out of the water. It quickly settled by the stern as the bow raised to an angle of $30°$. The submarine continued to sink stern first and disappeared 10 seconds after the depth bombs were dropped.

After the aircraft had circled to port, at least 15 men were seen in the water. White and yellow pieces of wood and a large amount of oil were floating on the surface. The B-24D dropped two marine markers, and 5 minutes later tossed out a rubber dinghy to the survivors. Five men were seen to climb aboard the raft.[203]

This attack is an excellent example of radar and visual search, followed by a clever approach out of the sun. This tactic probably contributed to the aircraft's relative safety in the face of antiaircraft fire.

It has been pointed out in other parts of this study that the AAF Antisubmarine Command units operating in the Eastern Atlantic frequently had to give as much attention to enemy aircraft as they did to enemy submarines. No account of their activities would be complete without at least an example of the frequently violent action involved in these engagements. Most of the aircraft encountered were medium JU-88's, which were being employed for the primary purpose of intercepting antisubmarine planes. Later in the summer of 1943, the Germans also sent their heavy, four-engine FW-200's into the fight. The primary mission of these bombers was antishipping strikes for which their long range (they often operated as far as 700 miles from their bases) made them ideally suited. But their long range also allowed them to intercept the B-24's when the latter had flown far beyond the range (seldom over 300 miles) of the JU-88.[204] These heavy bombers gave the AAFAC crews virtually their only action in August when the submarines themselves had acknowledged their defeat and were staying carefully out of range of the B-24's.

It was with the FW-200's that probably the most dramatic of the many air engagements took place. On the 17th of August a B-24D of the 1st Antisubmarine Squadron was on convoy coverage 300 miles west of Lisbon, when two Focke-Wulf 200's were sighted. The B-24D was flying at 1,500 feet below an overcast when it received a radar contact, indicating a target at 12 to 15 miles, 30° left. After turning towards the target, a second blip was obtained at 8 miles, 5° left. The aircraft climbed to 2,300 feet and homed on the target. At 4 miles, it descended through the overcast to 1,000 feet. Finally, at a distance of 1 mile, two FW-200's were sighted, just beginning a parallel bombing run on the convoy.

The nearest FW fired a sighting burst at the approaching B-24 and banked to the left. Captain Maxwell, the pilot, followed on its tail and slightly above. The other FW closed in from astern. The three planes were in line at this point and all opened fire. The fire from the enemy aircraft appeared to be from 20-millimeter cannon. The first German aircraft dived to 50 feet, with the B-24 and second FW following. After 1 minute of combat, Nos. 3 and 4 engines of the B-24 were out. Large holes were seen in the wing and fuselage and the right wing was ablaze. Nevertheless, the B-24 continued to gain on the first FW, scoring many hits on the inner wing, fuselage, and port engines of the leading FW. As the B-24 passed over this aircraft, it was seen to break into flames and crash into the sea.

Meantime, the tail gunner and right waist gunner had been returning the fire of the trailing Nazi aircraft, and now the top turret gunner turned around to join in that engagement. The B-24, however, was almost out of control and the crew took up ditching stations immediately. There was no time for ditching orders. Owing to cut hydraulic lines, the bombardier was unable to release the depth bombs, but the navigator used the emergency release and jettisoned the bombs a minute before ditching.

The right wing of the B-24D hit the water first. The plane skidded sideways with little shock, making about a $180°$ turn. On the second impact, the aircraft broke in three pieces at the trailing edges of the wings and at the waist windows. The nose section floated for $1\frac{1}{2}$ minutes, but the other two sections sank almost immediately. The pilot and co-pilot escaped through the broken windshield, the navigator and radio operator through the escape hatch. Two others of the crew escaped through a break in the top of the fuselage near the waist windows, while the tail gunner went through the top of the tail turret which had partially broken off.

Two life rafts were then released and seven survivors, all of whom were slightly wounded with shrapnel, climbed aboard. Three men were lost including the radar operator, who, it is believed, was pinned to his seat by the radar set.

Meanwhile, the second FW could still be seen by the crew mushing along at 50 feet with No. 3 engine out and tail heavy. In 15 minutes, the crew members were picked up by one of the escort vessels from the convoy. Survivors from the first Focke-Wulf were also rescued a short time later. Seamen from two of the naval vessels said that they saw the second German bomber crash. At the same time, a radar indication on the screen of the escort leader disappeared at about 8 miles, tending to confirm the destruction of the second German plane.

It is to be noted that inthis and other encounters with FW-200's, 20-millimeter fire was experienced from both the front and rear of the "bathtub." The B-24D, however, appeared to be approximately 20 miles per hour faster, even with a full bomb load, and more maneuverable than its adversary.[205]

Throughout the sharpest of the fighting, whether with enemy aircraft or in attacks on submarines, the B-24 proved to be by far the best land-based aircraft for the job, especially in its modified form (B-24D). Indeed, the modified Liberator had no rival anywhere in the antisubmarine forces, except in the carrier-based planes developed by the U. S. Navy and employed effectively during and after the summer of 1943.

It is a pity that the AAF Antisubmarine Command was unable to profit more fully from the technical research undertaken in the field of antisubmarine warfare. No agency appreciated more keenly the potential value of improved devices and weapons; and it did all in its power to stimulate development along lines suggested by experience in that highly specialized kind of combat. The story of its efforts in this direction will be told in Chapter IV. At this point it will be enough simply to state certain general facts. First, it must be remembered that the Command did profit to some extent from the research done prior to its activation and during the course of its career. Most useful of all antisubmarine aids was radar, which, in the form of the SCR-517 type, did yeoman service during 1943 and accounted for many contacts that might not otherwise have been made.[206] Improved, though by no means ideal, low-level bomb sights were in irregular use by the summer of 1943. And by that time also the modified B-24D, with its greatly increased forward firing power, was ready for use. Early in 1943, more dependable bombing was made possible by the adoption of the flat-nosed depth bomb. The absolute altimeter was completed in time for it to be used effectively by this command, with the result that safer and more accurate bombing runs could be made at low altitudes. Most of the other projects, and their number was legion, were not completed in time to be of any use to the AAF Antisubmarine Command.

Great things were expected of the new detection devices, especially the magnetic airborne detector and the radio sonic buoy. And in the field of lethal weapons, rocket projectiles and retrobombing devices promised greatly increased precision in antisubmarine attacks. But as far as the command was concerned, their value remained largely potential. Indeed, the greatest tactical progress made by the command appears to have come about as a result simply of increased experience in the operation of those devices and techniques already in use when the command took over, or developed shortly thereafter.

Summary and Results of AAF Antisubmarine Command Operations

It is hard to find an adequate criterion for measuring the results of the Army Air Forces antisubmarine operations. In addition to locating and destroying hostile submarines, the mission of the AAF Antisubmarine Command included "assisting the Navy in the protection of friendly shipping."[207] In the 8-month period from January to August 1943, purely defensive escort missions totaled 43,264 hours.[208] Even these figures do not fully reflect the extent of the effort in protecting friendly shipping, for most of the flying in the western Atlantic was of a purely defensive nature. Of the total operational hours flown by the command, 86 per cent were accounted for by squadrons based on the western side of the ocean, yet this primarily defensive flying yielded only 29 per cent of the attacks.[209] Although it is obviously impossible to estimate the number of ships that may have been saved by this great defensive effort, the presumption is that it was large.

The following table will give some idea not only of the total activity of the AAF Antisubmarine Command, but that of the I Bomber Command as well:[210]

Attacks on Submarines

	Operational Combat Hours	Total Attacks	A	B	C	D	E	F	G	H	I	J	Not Assessed
I Bomber Command	59,248	81	1			6	7	12	25	9	1	9	11
Antisubmarine Command													
Eastern Atlantic	12,215*	37	5**	4	1	3	5	8	9	0	0	0	2
Western Atlantic	75,879*	15				2	3	1	2	1	0	1	5
Totals	147,342	133	6	4	1	11	15	21	36	10	1	10	18

* Through September 1943.
** Two of these kills were made with the help of RAF aircraft.

```
            A--Sunk . . . . . . . . . . . . . .  6
            B--Probably sunk . . . . . . . . . .  4
            C--Probably severely damaged to
               the extent that sub failed to
               reach port . . . . . . . . . . . . .1
            D--Probably severely damaged . . . 11
            E--Probably slightly damaged . . . 15
                             Totals           37
```

Key to other assessments: F--insufficient evidence of damage; G--no damage; H--insufficient evidence of presence of submarine; I--non-submarine; J--insufficient data for analysis or inconclusive.

Thus a total of at least 37 enemy submarines suffered from attacks by aircraft of the command and its predecessor. Of these, probably 11 failed to reach port at a cost to the enemy of some $55,000,000 to

$75,000,000 and the lives of more than 500 men.[211] Eleven others were severely damaged and 15 slightly damaged. The British had a rule of thumb that about 30 per cent of the "severely damaged" and 5 per cent of the "slightly damaged" usually fail to reach port. If such a measure were applied to the above figures, it would indicate that a total of 15 U-boats were destroyed. There is no way of telling how much inconvenience was caused by the attacks of lower assessment, but it would be reasonable to suppose that they failed in most instances to simplify the task of the U-boat commander.

In this connection the probable effect of aircraft attacks on the U-boat crews must be recognized. No submarine crew likes to make emergency crash dives since there is always the chance that some mistake will be made, some valve left open. Furthermore, the crews know that crash dives use up valuable electricity and if repeated too often will leave the craft in a vulnerable position. Frequent air patrols, insofar as they make frequent crash dives necessary, had a gradually corrosive effect on crew morale. There is little doubt, too, that depth-bomb attacks, even though non-damaging to the U-boat, are likely to damage the morale of the crew. And even slight damage is enough to spoil a long ocean trip in a craft as peculiar in its habits as the submarine. It may be leaking, it may be unable to withstand the pressure of a deep dive, its steering apparatus may be damaged. In any case, it is not safe.

The table presented above also reflects the great improvement in accuracy of aircraft attacks as the Army Air Forces gained experience in this field that was foreign to its training and traditions. Prisoner of war statements indicate that U-boat crews had little fear of attacks by aircraft at the beginning of the U. S. participation in the war, and the statistics seem to verify this evidence. Out of 51 attacks made by the I Bomber Command prior to 15 October 1942 (eliminating all attacks in which there was doubt as to the presence of a U-boat, three which were inconclusive, or which were not assessed) only 1, or less than 2 per cent, resulted in the known or probable destruction of a submarine, and 13, or over 25 per cent, in damage. In the 10 months following the formation of the AAF Antisubmarine Command, 43 attacks, computed on the same basis, resulted in the destruction, known or probable, of 10 U-boats, or over 23 per cent of those thus evaluated. Fourteen others, or almost 33 per cent, suffered damage to some degree. Thus close to 56 per cent of the validated attacks in this period were either lethal or damaging, as compared to 27 per cent during the period of the I Bomber Command operations.

The mission assigned to the AAF Antisubmarine Command did not mention combat with enemy aircraft, but there is truth in the cynical remark of a young pilot of the 480th Group at Port Lyautey in September 1943. "We are," he said, "not hunting U-boats any more. We are hunting Focke-Wulf 200's."[212] The crews were instructed to remember their mission and avoid combat with enemy aircraft whenever possible. But frequently such engagements were forced on the American flyers. The consolidated figures for these unsought operations, which follow, include encounters during the entire period, prior to 1 November 1943, during which these units were operational:[213]

	479th A/S Group	480th A/S Group	Total
Number of e/a encountered	165	55	220
Results to e/a			
Destroyed	3	8	11
Probably destroyed	1	1	2
Damaged	4	6	10
Probably damaged	8	0	8
Total destroyed or damaged	16 (a)	15 (b)	31
Results to our a/c			
Destroyed	3	4	7
Damaged	7	6	13
Total destroyed or damaged	10	10	20

(a) All JU-88's.
(b) 5 FW-200's, 2 DO-24's, 1 DO-26 destroyed, 1 JU-88 probably destroyed, 2 FW-200's damaged, 4 JU-88's damaged.

The AAF Antisubmarine Command made a distinct contribution to the antisubmarine effort. It was a contribution that increased in scope as time went on. And it is perfectly obvious that this contribution cannot be measured by the number of submarines sunk or damaged. It is, however, well to observe that it was only a small part of the total contribution by all agencies involved in the antisubmarine war. It must, for example, be placed in relation to the total of 136 submarines known sunk by all agencies during the 8 months from January to August 1943.[214] It must also be remembered that many more submarines would probably have been sunk or damaged by AAF Antisubmarine Command aircraft had the command been allowed to deploy its forces in accordance with its own aggressive policy. Whether such an offensive could have been mounted without correspondingly weakening the defensive patrols in the western Atlantic remains an open question. And it is true that only late in its career did the command receive enough VLR aircraft to make possible any extensive deployment overseas in that vital category. It is probable, however, that throughout its existence, more units were retained in domestic areas than the U-boat situation warranted.

Undoubtedly, at the time of its dissolution, the AAF Antisubmarine Command was rapidly reaching the point where its VLR forces could profitably have been dispatched in large numbers wherever the enemy might make his appearance. Its own plans tended stubbornly in that direction. Almost on the eve of its removal from antisubmarine duty, the command had submitted plans for an extended deployment in Australian, Indian, Mediterranean, and Chinese areas.[215] The following figures illustrate the rapid growth of the power at the command's disposal, expressed in terms of VLR aircraft. Shortly after its activation, the Antisubmarine Command reported 209 operational planes at its disposal. Only 20 of these were B-24's, assigned to the 2 squadrons in England. Of the remainder, 12 were B-17E's, and 125 were medium bombers, B-18's, B-25's, A-29's, and B-34's. The rest were observation planes, O-47's and O-52's.[216] By 27 August 1943 the number of B-24's had risen to 187, the remainder of the 286 operational planes consisting of 12 B-17's, 7 B-34's, and 80 B-25's. It was planned eventually to equip all squadrons with B-24's.[217] It is further worth noting that, of the 286 planes reported in August, 148 were equipped with radar.[218] Thus, although the AAF Antisubmarine Command was responsible for only about 8 per cent of the total aircraft engaged in antisubmarine warfare in the Atlantic by August 1943, the strategical importance of the command's aircraft was relatively much greater than that percentage would indicate. For of the VLR aircraft then in use, approximately 56 per cent were operated by the Army Air Forces, 31 per cent by the RAF, and only 13 per cent by the U. S. Navy, although the latter was rapidly acquiring a large force of B-24's.[219]

In a sense the real strength of the command, as it stood in August 1943, lay in its men and their experience. A significant proportion of its personnel had 18 months of actual experience in hunting submarines. The combat crews had mastered the complexities of long overwater navigation, of enemy ship identification, of radar operation, of air-sea rescue methods, and, most important of all, the technique of spotting and instantly attacking an inconspicuous, moving, and rapidly disappearing target. They had become expert in a form of bombing vastly different from any other form of air attack.

The conclusion, then, is inescapable that, however its operational history may compare with other agencies, the AAF Antisubmarine Command was, at the time of its dissolution, potentially the most powerful force of very-long-range antisubmarine aviation in existence. To many observers it seemed a pity that its great promise could not have been fulfilled.

Chapter IV

PROBLEMS OF LOGISTICS, RESEARCH COORDINATION, AND TRAINING

During the course of its operational history, the Antisubmarine Command faced certain problems of organization, training, and materiel development which were unique, at least insofar as AAF experience was concerned. The command had been invested with a responsibility of a hybrid character, in relation to current military concepts. The resulting problems had to be solved without reference to any body of experience except, perhaps, that then being established by the British. A great part of the energy and initiative of the command personnel had therefore to be expended on the solution of these problems. To complicate matters still more, the solutions usually depended on action by higher echelons since they involved the relation of the command to other agencies; in which case the command itself could only point out to higher authority the urgency of the matter, and recommend appropriate action.

The whole problem of logistics, for example, was one which involved liaison with various other organizations and, owing to the peculiar nature of the Antisubmarine Command's mission, the establishment of certain new procedures. Originally all, and to the end of its career most, of the AAFAC units were stationed in the continental United States, yet they were operating directly against the enemy. Unlike most other domestic units, they therefore required full equipment immediately. This meant securing a priority rating for supplies.

It was not until 13 January 1943 that a priority rating of A-2a was secured for all squadrons, thus placing them on the same level as a unit under warning orders for overseas duty. In April 1943, it was raised to A-1b, which gave antisubmarine squadrons the same status regarding supply as that of an overseas unit.[1] Beginning in May of the same year, squadrons were being put under warning orders for supplies in accordance with a definite schedule worked out between the Antisubmarine Command and the Assistant Chief of Air Staff, Operations, Commitments, and Requirements. Supplies were processed by the use of shortage lists just as if the units were going overseas. This method proved reasonably successful, and by August 1943 the domestic squadrons were about 85 per cent equipped.[2]

The procurement and distribution of ammunition presented certain difficulties. Since the Antisubmarine Command had neither bases nor base troops assigned to it, but operated from bases under the jurisdiction of other air forces and commands, it originally became entangled in a complicated system of supply involving coordination and liaison with First Air Force, Third Air Force, Air Service Command and Air Transport Command. Under this system AAFAC ammunition requirements had to be submitted to these four separate agencies who would incorporate them with their own requirements, and eventually issue supplies to the AAFAC units.[3] Some relief was gained by having requirements submitted directly to the Commanding General, AAF, who in turn issued Ammunition Supply Authorities (AMSA's) to the organizations having jurisdiction over the bases at which the AAFAC units were stationed.

AAF Regulations still authorized only personnel with base jurisdiction to control training ammunition. In February, this regulation was changed, and the command was allowed to issue AMSA's and distribute them to its units as required. Supply of combat ammunition was still not the responsibility of the AAFAC, but remained with the defense command, air force, or air command which had jurisdiction over the base. In March authority was granted by the Army Air Forces to maintain certain stock levels of combat ammunition on each base, to be made immediately available to units of the command whenever needed.[4] Overseas units were supplied by the theater commander except for training ammunition, requirements for which were submitted to the Antisubmarine Command which, in turn, would send the ammunition to the Eastern Defense Command port of embarkation for disposition.[5]

The Antisubmarine Command had, then, to fit itself gradually into a supply plan not originally designed to meet its needs.[6] It involved a constant need for liaison between the AAFAC A-4 section and the service agencies, especially Air Service Command and Air Transport Command. This was especially true before the assignment of a high priority to AAFAC projects, but it continued to be necessary throughout the history of the organization. To facilitate liaison, the Air Service Command released one of its officers to AAFAC headquarters, and the Supply and Logistics subsection, A-4, AAFAC maintained constant contact with the Air Transport Command. The value of those liaison channels appeared especially in connection with the movement of units overseas. As soon as a squadron received orders for foreign duty the

Overseas Section, Supply Division, Headquarters, ASC was immediately notified, and special project supplies were usually at the point of destination as soon as the squadron itself. The Air Transport Command set up priorities for shipment of AAFAC personnel and materiel upon coordination with that command.[7]

Expansion of I Bomber Command and AAFAC activities necessitated extending the system of communications beyond that used in the days when the Bomber Command was asked to begin antisubmarine operations. The usual peace-time communications facilities--teletype and telephone mainly--proved totally inadequate for routing information and instructions to a widely scattered patrol force. Joint action between Army planes and naval units failed frequently as a result of inadequate communication.[8]

By October 1942 the Bomber Command communications network extended from Canada to Mexico along the coastline, between stations from which Army and CAP planes operated. AGL stations had replaced the Navy service, and radar planes were beginning to be used in some numbers. When the Antisubmarine Command was formed, little change was made in this system. The 25th Wing took over the Joint Control Room in New York City. A new switchboard was installed with lines to those serving the 25th Wing, the 26th Wing, and First Air Force headquarters. With the addition of more signal personnel, the command took on more projects. When it went out of business it had worked out an effecient and rapid means of communication between command headquarters and control rooms, and between control rooms and the aircraft in flight.[9]

Radar equipment presented many problems. Not only was there constantly changing equipment to contend with, but, in a widely extended network, serious problems of congestion arose. When the 25th and 26th Wings were formed in the early days of the command, separate AGL frequencies were assigned to each, which did much to relieve the situation. In order to allow AAFAC planes to move to any part of the world on short notice, they had to be equipped with additional transmitters which covered a wide band of frequencies and allowed the aircraft to establish communications in any area.

Originally air-ground communication had been conducted by the I Bomber Command from a single mobile station on Governors Island. Arrangements subsequently made with the Navy to supplement this system with numerous shore stations proved unsatisfactory. The naval radio stations handled their own traffic first, so that messages from planes were often delayed as much as an hour in reaching the Army controller. A project was begun to install a series of permanent AGL stations to cover the extended areas of Bomber Command operations, and by the time the Antisubmarine Command was created, the Navy was relieved of the task of guarding the AGL frequencies.[10] These stations, operated by the 30th Antisubmarine Communications Squadron, were so located that the direct teletype facilities of the command were available to them, thus providing facilities for the immediate relaying of information between aircraft and controller. As the scope of operations, increased, additional installations were made. At the time of the dissolution of the command, a station was under construction at Port Lyautey, North Africa.

Wire remained the major means of point-to-point communication used by the Antisubmarine Command, although a point-to-point radio net was set up in connection with the permanent AGL stations. A network of teletype and telephone lines covered the eastern seaboard from Cuba to Newfoundland and as far west as Texas. This wire network served the tactical needs of the command excellently, at least as they existed in the western Atlantic.

A project for installing an AAFAC direction-finding network, based on general dissatisfaction with existing systems along the Atlantic seaboard, was under consideration when the command was dissolved.[11]

Special cryptographic equipment and systems had to be worked out to insure the speedy transmission of a large volume of highly secret information concerning merchant vessels, friendly submarines, convoys, and naval vessels operating in the American waters. Here again Headquarters, AAF discovered that the mission of the command was unlike that of any other units operating within the continental limits.

It was found, in the fall of 1942, that the existing method of manning the command AGL facilities, by placing men on detached service in various antisubmarine squadrons, was unfair to the highly trained personnel involved. On 15 February 1943 the 30th Antisubmarine

Communications Squadron was activated under a new T/O (1-1017), its personnel comprising all those then operating command AGL stations.[12]

The greatest logistical problem with which the command had to contend was that of securing the mobility necessary for effective antisubmarine operations. The entire concept of the organization had been based on the assumption that it should be able to move rapidly and at a moment's notice in order to counter the centrally controlled and rapidly shifting U-boat concentrations. Time and again it had been demonstrated that the submarine situation could change overnight, yet just as frequently the antisubmarine forces proved too cumbersome to react with the required celerity. When the submarine menace shifted from the U. S. Atlantic seaboard, a proportionate number of antisubmarine squadrons was not moved with it. Those units subsequently sent to the Caribbean area, to which the U-boats had withdrawn, found that the situation had already altered by the time they became operational. Likewise, in the North Atlantic, it took most of the early months of 1943 to get plans approved for deploying an adequate force in Newfoundland and the units themselves delivered, by which time the crisis had already arrived and was soon over. Only in the eastern Atlantic, in waters the U-boats had to traverse whether they liked it or not, did the AAFAC squadrons find the kind of hunting they wished.

Undoubtedly this slowness in delivering an effective counterattack retarded the antisubmarine campaign. It also threatened the morale of the AAFAC squadrons whose spirit was normally high. Such units as those sent to Newfoundland were well equipped and trained and possessed of a profound confidence in the importance of their mission. But they found themselves for the most part sharing in the patrol of ocean stretches virtually without enemy, a task which they felt could easily have been done by less highly specialized units. In short, they were not getting submarines. For a few weeks, the 6th and 19th Antisubmarine Squadrons had taken part in a campaign which promised much, and gave considerable, in the way of combat activity. The 4th had been moved to Newfoundland too late even to catch sight of a U-boat.[13] The experience of the 4th Squadron was, in fact, particularly frustrating. An old squadron in the game, it had been organized as an antisubmarine unit early in the war. In the late summer of 1942, it had been ordered to the Caribbean for a short period of operations in areas where the Germans were especially active. Its stay was too brief and its orders too confused to allow it much chance at the enemy. After its abortive Caribbean experience, the squadron flew patrol for a while from Westover Field without much action for its pains.[14] After undergoing B-24 transition, it contributed certain units to an emergency project in the Bermuda area where, according to the A-3 of headquarters, 25th Antisubmarine Wing, the entire project was about 3 days late, with the result that no contacts or sightings were made.[15] In June the squadron was sent to Newfoundland, but there again the shooting was over before it arrived. Finally, of course, this unit saw action in the Bay of Biscay in late July. Prior to that time, however, its pilots had built up an average of 1,000 hours each, with only three contacts among them all to show for their effort. To be sure, they were performing useful preventive patrols during those long hours, but the lack of tangible results could not help but dampen their enthusiasm.[16]

The reasons for this lack of mobility were many, and involve the entire antisubmarine organizational structure. Some resulted from flaws in the organization of lower echelons. During most of their career, the AAF heavy antisubmarine squadrons operated under the old heavy bombardment T/O and T/BA. Each squadron had assigned to it some 50 pieces of transportation, including trailers. They carried with the, wherever they went, field-lighting equipment, decontaminating units, and other implements that ran into tons of cases requiring careful crating and slow hauls by surface vessels up and down the coast. Air transport for those elements of the squadron that could be airborne was usually done by Air Transport Command planes. The Antisubmarine Command had never enough transport aircraft to provide its own transportation; and without that ability it was dependent on coordination with external agencies.[17]

What compromised mobility most fundamentally was the difficulty of operating through devious command channels and by means of liaison between various agencies concerned in the antisubmarine war. To begin with, the command was forced to operate through War Department channels and Navy liaison in such a way that much valuable time was always lost before a movement order could be approved and action undertaken. This was true of the Newfoundland situation, and particularly so of the summer project in the Bay of Biscay. Navy operational control tended also to slow up mobility because it was not originally founded on premises of mobility. Hence the freezing of many squadrons where they could not make the best use of their equipment. This point must not, however, be overstated. Admiral King was as eager as anyone to see that units were moved as rapidly as possible to Newfoundland and to the Biscay area during the later phases of that campaign.[18] The fault lay only partly in a desire to maintain a static defense. It lay also in the inability of all concerned to clear command and liaison channels rapidly enough to permit sudden shifting of the antisubmarine forces. The Germans, under unified command, could move their U-boat fleet with a minimum of delay. The Allies could only follow slowly, impeded by divided control both internationally and, in the case of the United States, within the national military organization.

The officers of the Antisubmarine Command itself saw the problems clearly enough. In the fall of 1942 they had submitted a plan calculated to streamline the Allied antisubmarine organization from the top on down to the individual elements.[19] And, in April of 1943, they drew up a plan to increase the mobility of their own organization. Specifically they proposed that the Commanding General, AAFAC be authorized to issue the necessary orders dispatching air echelons to any base within or without the continental limits of the United States from which hostile submarines might be subject to attack. In order to facilitate the physical transfer of units, they further proposed that bases be surveyed in all likely theaters for possible emergency use;

that the command be equipped with its T/BA allotment of transport aircraft to be used for rapid movement of personnel and equipment to operating bases; and that direct communications be authorized between the Commanding General of the AAFAC and other agencies involved in the transfer of antisubmarine units--Army Service Forces, Air Transport Command, The Adjutant General's Department, and the theater commands.[20]

Some steps were taken to remedy the situation. A new T/O was shaped for heavy antisubmarine squadrons,[21] though too late to be of much help to the command. The AAFAC headquarters maintained constant liaison with ATC and ASC. No increase in transport planes allotted to the command was approved, however, since to do so would mean diverting aircraft from the ATC on whose shoulders rested the primary responsibility for rapid transport.[22] On the international level, the Atlantic Convoy Conference defined areas of responsibility for each of the interested countries. And, finally, in assuming control of all U. S. antisubmarine activity the U. S. Navy took a long step toward the necessary unity of command, a step which, of course, eliminated the Antisubmarine Command entirely. The AAFAC went out of business, however, with the problem of mobility still largely unsolved.

Next to hunting submarines, the most important elements of the AAFAC mission were to promote the development of special antisubmarine equipment and tactics and to train personnel in their use. Research in antisubmarine devices and techniques had been made the special responsibility of the Sea-Search Attack Development Unit (SADU), operating at Langley Field under the Commanding General, AAF, through the Director of Technical Services.[23] Several agencies outside the AAF were engaged in the general problems of research in antisubmarine warfare, notably, the Antisubmarine Warfare Operations Research Group (ASWORG), a subcommittee of the National Defense Research Council, and the naval antisubmarine research unit known as the Air Antisubmarine Development Detachment, Atlantic Fleet (AirASDevLant). But the Antisubmarine Command found it necessary to insure, through its Research Coordinator, that the progress of technical development was in accord with the requirements and experience of its own operating units.

Prior to the activation of the Antisubmarine Command, the I Bomber Command had taken little part in promoting technical development. It was a small organization and found its hands full with its operational duties. Furthermore it was still officially a bomber command, and in considering modification of any equipment it had always to remember that tomorrow it might be back on bombardment duty. Some independent action had been taken by SADU and ASWORG, but liaison between them and the I Bomber Command was poor. As a result, a considerable amount of the work of these agencies failed to profit by the experience rapidly being amassed by the I Bomber Command.

When the AAFAC was activated an office was set up in the new organization for the purpose of insuring that research followed lines indicated by experience to be most profitable, and that the needs of the command were translated into technical projects. The A-3 officer, designated as the Research Coordinator, was charged specifically with assembling data on all new developments of any type which, in his opinion, might prove of value. This data he then presented to all command sections concerned, for criticism and suggestion. If the development appeared to have merit, the Research Coordinator requested either the Director of Technical Services, Headquarters, AAF, or the Materiel Command, AAF, to take such action as might be indicated. In most instances, this action consisted of installing certain types of airborne equipment in B-24's, the standard antisubmarine long-range plane, and of specifying desired tests. Occasionally, however, it meant that problems were presented which required the development of brand new devices.

The section eventually consisted of the Coordinator, his assistant, and two civilian scientists, the latter attached from the ASWORG of the National Defense Research Council.[24]

The Research Coordinator attempted to present to higher headquarters the technical problems confronting the command in the order of their importance, which meant that development requests were not confined to devices for the airplane. Action was instituted to demonstrate the need for installing the latest type of radio direction-finding equipment at all AAFAC stations, for installing radar beacons at stations where navigational aids were scarce and for installing Loran equipment at certain specified bases. Emergency rescue kits were also designed by this section and standardized for all antisubmarine aircraft.[25]

Probably the most important function of the Research Coordinator was to keep the attention of higher headquarters fixed on the more important problems. It was not as easy a task as one might at first think, for emphasis was often placed on projects which on the surface appeared plausible, but which in experience had been discarded as impractical. For example, many persons believed that antisubmarine airplanes should carry one or two heavy demolition bombs rather than four to six 325-pound depth charges. After studying this idea, the command discarded it because the bombs did not possess as great a lethal range, a conclusion reached independently by the U. S. Navy and the RAF Coastal Command.[26]

The Research Coordinator had no dearth of problems with which to grapple. There were those constant navigational difficulties which were not peculiar to antisubmarine work but which nevertheless were essential to its success. As long as it was possible for an airplane to get off its course, during a long-range operation, especially at night or in bad weather, constant attention had to be given to improving and extending the scope of such navigational aids as the radar beacon and Loran direction-finding equipment. The Research Coordinator advocated installation of adequate radio direction-finding equipment in all operating areas. The command experienced difficulty in obtaining desired results from the system in operation along the Atlantic coast. So it was decided to install an AAFAC direction-finding network reaching from Greenland to the Caribbean. Fifty units of receiving equipment were allocated for use in this special network and surveys began in

April 1943.[27] Final installation of the extended system was not made before the termination of the command. Radar beacons were, however, installed where needed in foreign bases.[28]

Radar, in general, was, of course, a major and constant preoccupation of all agencies engaged in the antisubmarine campaign. Throughout the experience of the Antisubmarine Command, effort was made to improve airborne radar equipment and to extend its use. There was no doubt that radar constituted a vital element in the successful pursuit of the command's mission. By February 1943, radar efficiency had so increased that it was possible for a skilled operator to identify landmarks at 100 miles, buoys at 35 to 40 miles, convoys, small ships, and submarines at even greater distances. Even the conning tower of a submarine could be detected at from 15 to 30 miles. But it was equally clear that radar had its limitations. It was not perfectly reliable and was difficult to maintain. It required the interest and cooperation of all concerned, from the command headquarters down to the individual crew member. Consequently, the training problem was a sizable one, especially as the command extended its activity overseas. It was difficult also to keep a steady flow of supplies available to radar-equipped units, a problem complicated still further by the constant changes being made in the standard devices. Despite these obstacles, it was planned to expand the use of radar as quickly as possible. Although the SCR-717 A equipment, considered superior, had never been field-tested it was decided to install it in all future VLR planes. It proved to be definitely superior in operation and maintenance to all previous models.[29]

The radio or absolute altimeter, a modification of the radar principle, answered a pressing tactical as well as a navigational need. In areas of abnormal barometric pressure, the ordinary sensitive altimeter, reacting to barometric changes, would give erroneous readings which could be disastrous in blind landing and might easily frustrate an otherwise well-executed, low-level bombing attack. For it is obvious that, whereas an error of 50 feet at high altitude would make little difference in the accuracy of the bombing, at 100 feet it would probably cause the bombardier to miss his target. In a few instances the errors balanced out, but the odds were great. The AYD altimeter, accurate to within 10 feet at altitudes of less than 400 feet, removed much of this uncertainty, and by May 1943 was approved as standard equipment on all AAFAC planes.[30]

Radar did not wholly solve the problem of submarine detection. A U-boat sighted by radar at a distance of 25 miles might, especially in the absence of cloud cover for the attacking plane, be completely submerged and beyond further possibility of detection by the time the plane reached the spot. And, by remaining submerged, the submarine was always well insulated from the air. The magnetic airborne detector (MAD) and the radio sonic buoy were developed in an attempt to meet this problem of underwater detection. A plane having sighted a submarine by means of radar might thus conduct an intensive search by using these new devices. Though potentially valuable devices the MAD and the sonic buoy (or sonobuoy) had limited success during the lifetime of the Antisubmarine Command.[31]

Night operations proved to be almost valueless on account of the variety of unidentifiable small craft likely to be met in the course of a patrol flight. Upon locating a surface craft, the pilot had first to fly over it, attempt to identify it, then circle and bomb it if he believed it to be an enemy craft. By the time he had completed these maneuvers, a submarine would have submerged and bombing would have been useless. In an effort to improve night operations, searchlights and rocket flares were developed. These valuable devices were, however, successfully tested just prior to the termination of the AAFAC.[32]

Having located the enemy, the antisubmarine crew faced problems of attack. When the I Bomber Command originally studied the problem of submarine bombing, it was felt that no bombsight was necessary for operations from altitudes of 50 to 100 feet. But tests proved that the average range of error in this sort of dead-reckoning attack amounted to about 175 feet. Furthermore, the standard round-nosed MK-XVII depth bomb was found to be erratic in its underwater travel, and ordnance data, initially received, provided no answer to the problem. Navy and Army ordnance authorities had to be pressed for exact data on depth charges, and every effort was made to develop an adequate low-level bombsight for the peculiar purposes of antisubmarine warfare.[33] Considerable progress was made along these lines. The flat-nosed depth bomb proved much less erratic than the round-nosed type, and several fairly efficient bombsights were in use by the summer of 1943. The latter, though effective, were still in the experimental stage at the termination of the command.[34]

Considerable work was done to develop superior lethal weapons. Among the most promising of these developments was retrobombing. MAD indications reach their height when the plane is directly over the contact. It was, therefore, essential to develop a method of releasing projectiles at this point with a nearly vertical trajectory. It was found that, by means of rockets, bombs could be projected to the rear with a speed approximately equal to the forward speed of the plane, so that the bomb trajectory would be vertical rather than parabolic. This method not only made possible "direct-over" bombing, but eliminated ricochet and erratic underwater travel. The Research Coordinator gave the device a high priority and predicted that it would prove to be "the number one Antisubmarine weapon."[35] Much thought was also expended on the development of forward-firing rocket projectiles. Though apparently effective, retrobombing and forward-firing rocket projectiles had not progressed beyond the experimental stage before the dissolution of the Antisubmarine Command.[36]

Other projects urged by the command included additional emergency equipment, suitable water markers, long-burning flares, droppable automatic radio homing beacons, and improved airplane camouflage, most of which were completed prior to the demise of the command.[37]

A sudden change in submarine tactics in the late spring of 1943 created a problem the solution to which involved the remodeling of the B-24 antisubmarine airplane. In an effort to escape from the embarrassment of continuous air coverage, the U-boats began to stay on the surface and fight it out with the attacking aircraft. In the face of this situation the standard B-24 showed certain weaknesses, chief being its inability to bring adequate forward fire power to bear on the enemy craft. As a countermeasure, the AAFAC had power-driven turrets installed in the nose. The nose was so designed that during an attack the bombardier and gunner could work simultaneously, the latter equipped with two .50-caliber machine guns. The project was begun in May 1943. By the end of August, 30 modifications had been received.[38] Although in use only a short time before the termination of the command, it was apparent that the front turret had tremendous value and could play an important part in the final defeat of the U-boat.[39]

The projects mentioned in the preceding pages represent only the more important ones in which the Antisubmarine Command was interested. Many others, some promising, some fanciful, came before the Research Coordinator. Of those mentioned, many were developed from specifications established by other organizations, but the AAFAC research section kept constant pressure on the agencies engaged in the work. Actual service testing was usually performed by SADU. Since this group was not under the AAFAC, but under the Director of

Technical Services, AAF, all requests for testing had to go through AAF Headquarters.[40]

The research section attempted also to see that the training of operating and maintenance personnel, and the provision of necessary supply channels paralleled procurement orders. This proved to be a major problem and efforts toward its solution met with little success. The difficulty lay in the organizational structure of AAF Headquarters, where experimental procurement, training, and supply were each the responsibility of a separate directorate. As a result, in the case of two of the most important projects, radar and MAD, the equipment was installed in the aircraft months before trained operating and maintenance personnel or normal supply channels became available.[41]

The *Antisubmarine Monthly Intelligence Report* declared in its final issue that "perhaps the most lasting contributions of the Antisubmarine Command in the battle against the U-boat are the various tactical and technical improvements, either developed by this organization or stimulated by it and completed by special research agencies."[42]

Be that as it may, the fact remains that most of the special projects undertaken had not been completed, or were not operational, when the AAFAC went out of the picture. It was the opinion of the Research Coordinator himself that the submarines were defeated primarily because they were smothered by quantities of air and surface craft and not because they were hunted out and destroyed with special devices which might have done the job more speedily.[43]

All important AAFAC projects were turned over to the Navy upon termination of the command.[44]

The Antisubmarine Command faced a training problem unparalleled in the history of the Army Air Forces.[45] As in the case of technical development, the I Bomber Command had no preparation for its hastily assumed antisubmarine duty. It had been training for its normal mission of bombardment, and, except for a limited amount of overwater reconnaissance, its units were entirely unacquainted with the tactics and techniques of antisubmarine aviation. Each unit commander had consequently to devise his own methods and give his own men whatever makeshift training he could manage in the operation of inadequate equipment. Only the simplest type of control could be exercised by command headquarters, which was at all times understaffed for the proper execution of its enlarged mission. For this reason, it was several months before proper control could be extended over subordinate units, and still longer before directives formulating uniform tactics and techniques could be published.

It was a chaotic situation that the AAFAC faced after its activation. The first thing to do was to extend control over subordinate units in such a way as to standardize training throughout the command. That would have been a task difficult enough to accomplish if it had not been further complicated by several additional problems. Since the antisubmarine mission was a specialized one, and unique in AAF experience, no provision had been made to provide replacement crews for the command. Training had therefore to be undertaken mainly within the command itself and on its own time, while its units were engaged in operational work. This practice had many bad features, inasmuch as training had often to be interrupted in accordance with operational requirements and as the crews, many of which had already learned improper techniques in actual combat, had to be taught proper methods. In addition, there was a shortage of AAF personnel qualified to give training in antisubmarine warfare. Especially serious was the need for qualified navigators, for that work required a knowledge of navigation unequaled in any other branch of the AAF.

Moreover, the methods and equipment of the Antisubmarine Command were constantly changing. Seven of the squadrons originally assigned to the command [46] were observation units, quite inexperienced in bombardment aviation. All squadrons had sooner or later to be converted from single- or twin-engine aircraft to heavy long-range bombers, and their personnel given adequate transitional training. As the work of research progressed and the experience of the command increased, new equipment and new tactics were constantly being introduced, bringing with them new training problems.

Supply agencies were not organized to give automatic consideration to the requirements of the command for training equipment and materiel, as they were accustomed to do in the case of the other types of tactical aviation. All AAF agencies gave these requirements consideration when specifically requested, but many of them were not constructed to cope with problems peculiar to antisubmarine operations. Especially serious was the lack of synthetic training devices. As a result of the Atlantic Convoy Conference, the Assistant Chief of Air Staff, Training directed that efforts be made at once to assist the command in procurement of this equipment. Prior to that time none had been received, and it was found that the command was low on the priority list for distribution of training devices. Although action was immediately taken to remedy the situation, by the end of its career only 10 per cent, approximately, of the equipment requested had arrived.

Fortunately, the domestic squadrons were not engaged in operations in close or frequent contact with the enemy. By the time the Antisubmarine Command was activated, the U-boats had practically abandoned the U. S. coastal waters. This was the only bright side of the picture as far as training was concerned, for it gave the command a good opportunity to train the majority of its units while they were engaged only in routine patrol operations, and squadrons could easily be rotated in the Operational Training Unit. In fact, the work of training became the principal mission for the domestic elements of the command. Of the 116,723 hours flown by the command between 1 January and 1 September 1943, 55,324, over 50 per cent, consisted of training operations.[47]

It was with these considerations in mind that the command set about building an integrated training program. Some changes in staff organization had to be made in order to place training in its proper relationship to the other staff offices. The traditional grouping of Plans and Training in one subsection of A-3 proved inadequate. Plans were closely allied with the activities of the Operations Section; and

Training, in addition to being dependent upon operational planning, was a full-sized job in itself. Accordingly, Plans and Training were divorced, Plans being transferred to the Operations Section as a separate subsection under the designation of Operational Planning.

Originally it was contemplated to establish a combination operational training unit and replacement training unit which would furnish completely trained combat crews and individual replacements for assignment to units of the command. In this way the command wings would be charged only with that training necessary for the maintenance of proficiency. In this way the units actively engaged in operations would be relieved of all but routine training activities. It was a sensible objective, but one never realized. Initial qualification of individuals continued to be carried on in the wings and squadrons. Such progress as was made toward the attainment of the objective was made after the first 6 months when the Operational Training Unit began to function with rapidly increasing efficiency.

The Operational Training Unit was the pivotal point for the entire training program, despite the many factors which always made a large degree of decentralization necessary. The 18th Antisubmarine Squadron, stationed at Langley Field, was relieved of its operational mission and given the responsibility for all operational training in the command. This was to be a temporary expedient which would be discontinued as soon as AAF Headquarters should authorize a separate training unit. The expedient remained in effect, however, until the command itself was inactivated. The new unit suffered from an inadequate table of organization, still that of a heavy-bombardment squadron. A new one came into being a few days before the inactivation of the command. It also suffered from lack of instructors, especially in navigation, and from a general lack of equipment and facilities.

Originally the OTU course was 4 weeks in length and covered B-24 transition, bombing and gunnery, navigation, and practice patrol. One hundred and two combat crews, each consisting of 10 men, received this course. Later, when increased delivery of B-24 aircraft made an increased number of trained crews necessary, the course was reduced to 3 weeks. One hundred and four crews received the shorter course. It was planned to give each squadron a thorough refresher course, as soon as delivery of B-24's had been completed, in order to compensate for the necessarily inadequate training packed into the few weeks of the original OTU course, and to keep crews abreast of new tactical and technical developments. This plan was never realized, however. Close liaison was, of course, maintained between the OTU and the Research Section. At the completion of the Antisubmarine Command's operations, 20 of the 25 squadrons assigned to it had completed their initial course at the OTU.

Bombing and gunnery training was the largest single problem. When the Antisubmarine Command was activated very little was known, based on practical tests, regarding the technique of antisubmarine bombing. The only available data was that obtained from the British

Coastal Command. Subsequently the U. S. Navy developed valuable studies on the underwater characteristics of depth bombs, and, when camera installations for photographing low altitude antisubmarine attacks became available, the command conducted tests of its own. But, even with increasingly useful data, training was still handicapped by lack of antisubmarine bombing ranges. The same was true of gunnery facilities. Requests for these facilities were approved by higher headquarters and construction begun on the various projects, but few of them were completed in time to be of any use to the command. The result was that training in bombing, technique of attack, and gunnery did not reach the level considered desirable. Nevertheless, by use of improvised facilities, considerable training was possible, especially in connection with the OTU at Langley Field, aerial gunnery remaining the weakest element.

The Antisubmarine Command began its operations in the fall of 1942 with a critical shortage of trained navigators. Its patrols made long flights necessary and pilots, co-pilots, and bombardiers alternated in performing the navigational duties, using elementary dead-reckoning and radio bearings. Because of this shortage, the policy was to assign one graduate navigator to each squadron to act as a local supervisor and instructor. Throughout the early months of the command's activity, the navigation training program was devoted to training of bombardiers and other combat crew members in dead-reckoning navigation. It was these men, developed in considerable numbers, who performed most of the navigation on patrols during the autumn and winter of 1942. In January 1943, graduates of AAF navigation schools began to be assigned in larger numbers, which greatly relieved the pressure on the generally inadequately trained personnel who had been doing emergency duty. The trained navigators, however, tended to be concentrated in the squadrons destined for overseas service, the result being that a celestial and dead-reckoning navigation school was set up under the 26th Wing at Miami which trained 60 officers prior to its dissolution in July 1943.

Training in the operation and maintenance of antisubmarine aircraft presented many difficulties over and above those involved in transition to the B-24. Even though it was known from the beginning that the B-24 was ultimately to be used throughout the command, the fact that their arrival in quantity would be delayed made it necessary to attain proficiency in operating and maintaining the various multi-engine types then in use. In an effort to raise the level of training, three methods were adopted. Some trained maintenance men were secured from the Technical Training Command. Some were sent from the AAFAC squadrons to the Technical Training Command schools and factory schools for specialized training. And many were simply given on-the-job training. Since training had to be undertaken in such a way that operations would not suffer, it was not possible to send more than a few men to schools for technical training.

By December 1942, it appeared that, for an indefinite period, about half of the strength of the command would consist of B-34's.

Accordingly, several officers and men were sent to Lockheed Aircraft Corporation factory, and two B-34 Mobile Training Units were obtained from the Technical Training Command. But most of the B-34's were withdrawn from the command just about the time this training program had been completed, and the maintenance personnel had to begin training all over again in B-25's.[48]

Training in the use of radar[49] naturally proved to be a major problem. Highly developed in any type of operation, radar became particularly specialized in antisubmarine warfare. Considerable attention was therefore given to proper radar training at the OTU. A member of the National Defense Research Council was assigned to that unit in June 1943 in order to assist in the development of teaching techniques. The big difficulty, of course, was in securing personnel with the right kind of basic training in this line of work. The officers, in general, had received good theoretical background in radar, but were unacquainted with the practical application of radar principles in antisubmarine activity. Operators and mechanics lacked both practical education, and, of course, experience. In addition to these personnel deficiencies, new equipment and techniques continually complicated the problem.

To offset these difficulties, a program was set up in June 1943, with the following objectives. All radar personnel would be procured well in advance of needs and assigned to a specific squadron. Until such time as their own squadrons should be equipped with radar, specialists would be assigned to fully equipped units for training and experience. All radar personnel would accompany their squadron on its periodic visit to the OTU. Mechanics would be split into small groups, each specializing in one particular new development which their organization had not received, and might not receive for some time, yet which they would normally expect to operate. In order to facilitate the assimilation of new equipment, factory-trained Western Electric technicians were obtained to act as consulting engineers, both in training and repair. To the same end, a "permanent" cadre was developed, (May 1943) usually consisting of one supervising officer, two experienced operators, and two experienced mechanics, who were to assist in training of new organizations.

By August 1943, this part of the training program was, like the rest of it, in a fair way to achieving for the first time the results desired.

From the training point of view, the dissolution of the Antisubmarine Command was premature. During the last months of its existence all training directives were completed, synthetic training equipment, ordered shortly after the command's activation, was being delivered, standardized procedures for the first time were being accepted willingly by the combat units, satisfactory aircraft and operational equipment were being received in sufficient quantity to ensure progress, and a suitable operational training organization, based on recently approved tables of organization, was about to be inaugurated. As the officer in charge of training not infelicitously put it, the situation of the command at the end of its existence was comparable to that of a man who, having worked industriously to put his automobile in running order, is then asked to step aside and let a stranger drive off with it.

Chapter V
CONCLUSION

The story told in this study resembles nothing else in the history of the Army Air Forces. The Antisubmarine Command grew out of a combination of necessity and confused jurisdiction. It came into being essentially because no adequate preparation had been made to meet the submarine emergency. Its forerunner, the I Bomber Command, had been asked suddenly to assume responsibility for a kind of patrol activity hitherto jealously guarded by the Navy as one of its own peculiar functions, and one for which the air unit had no special training. It possessed an air striking force and that was immediately thrown into the gap made by the U-boats in the scheme of Western Hemisphere defense. It was to give this extraordinary mission something like precise organization, and in a sense to legalize it as a function of the Army Air Forces, that the command was created. In an effort to fulfill its mission, the Army Air Forces, through its Antisubmarine Command, planned to carry the fight as soon as practicable to the enemy. On both the legal and the strategical ground this command became the center of a controversy which overshadowed in importance its actual operations.

Those operations, nevertheless, contributed significantly to the defeat of the U-boat in the Atlantic. It is more than possible that they might have contributed considerably more had they been controlled by AAF agencies. As it was, much of the strength of the command remained tied to areas of defensive patrols, lacking the kind of hunting for which the squadrons were being trained and equipped. Most significant is the fact that at the time of its dissolution the Antisubmarine Command was for the first time nearing a level of experience, equipment, and general efficiency toward which its personnel had been working since the days of the I Bomber Command. Many antisubmarine authorities therefore viewed with regret its withdrawal from the Battle of the Atlantic, especially at a time when the enemy appeared to be on the verge of defeat. It was felt that, regardless of the quality of Navy pilots or the nature of naval strategic doctrine, months would pass before the Navy could hope to build up a force of long-range antisubmarine aircraft as powerful and as experienced as that of the AAF Antisubmarine Command. And the ugly fact persisted that the enemy, though beaten, still possessed large numbers of U-boats in the fall of 1943, and his capabilities for inflicting damage on Allied shipping remained substantial.

Yet it would be romantic to suggest that the decision to eliminate the Antisubmarine Command was an operational decision, or even one arising from the basic controversy concerning the strategic value of antisubmarine air forces. The final deliberations turned not on the record of this command or its potentialities nor on the doctrine of the strategic offensive, toward which the Navy was itself gradually tending, but on the question of jurisdiction over long-range, land-based air striking forces engaged in overwater operations. On this level the controversy came close to testing the raison d'etre of the Army Air Forces itself.

On this level of policy, the antisubmarine controversy points to certain lessons of long-term importance. It emphasies, of course, the need for closely integrated and clearly defined command in joint operations. It also illustrates the essential unity of air power. The chief characteristics of air power are its adaptability and its fluidity. Plans laid on the basis of rigid distinctions of area and function are likely to end in confusion and frustration, a fact proved by the experience of the I Bomber Command during the early months of the war when it found itself handicapped by training which had been carefully restricted to overland operations and inshore patrol. And air power must be employed according to strategic and tactical doctrines shaped to suit its peculiar character rather than borrowed from older military theory.. In the light of these conclusions the settlement embodied in the Arnold-McNarney-McCain agreement appears to be a compromise, logically unsound, in which the division of air power into naval and Army branches was artifically perpetuated. Yet it was the only way around a problem which at the moment could not be eliminated, and it contained an element of reason in that it reinvested the Navy with a responsibility, originally and normally naval, namely, the protection of shipping. Yet it undoubtedly left the question of the ultimate control of strategic air power unanswered.

On the level of actual operations, the story of the Antisubmarine Command is less rewarding. Except for the activity of the 479th and 480th Groups in the eastern Atlantic, it is a story of hard work and frustration, in which is told how a great deal of effort and material was expended in an effort to build up a powerful fighting machine which was never allowed to function as its creators meant it to, and which was disassembled just when it was about to become for the first time fully operational. It is a story of much promise and relatively little fulfillment of great but largely unrealized potentialities. In August 1943, AAFAC equipment was nearing completion, the research program was about to provide the command with special weapons and devices which would greatly have enhanced its effectiveness, the training program was on the point of realizing the high plans laid down for it,. and the entire organization was on the verge of becoming the mobile, air striking force which General Marshall had hoped to see deployed on a broad, aggressive strategic plan. In this sense the story is a brilliant prelude to anticlimax.

GLOSSARY

AAFAC	Army Air Forces Antisubmarine Command
ACC	Atlantic Convoy Conference
ACV	Auxiliary carrier
AFABI	AC/AS, Intelligence
AFAEP	AC/AS, Plans
AFDTS	Director of Technical Service
AFRDB	Director of Bombardment
AFREQ	Requirements Division, AC/AS, Operations, Committments and Requirements
AMSA	Ammunition Supply Authorities
AOC	Air officer commanding
ASC	Air Service Command
ASF	Air Service Forces
ASWORG	Antisubmarine Warfare Operations Research Group
AWIG	Antisubmarine ing
CAP	Civil Air Patrol
CPS	Combined Staff Planners
DC/S	Deputy Chief of Staff
DF	Direction finder
EDC	Eastern Defense Command
ESF	Eastern Sea Frontier
ETO	European Theater of Operations
GSF	Gulf Sea Frontier
JCNW	Joint Committee on New Weapons and Equipment
JCS	Joint Chiefs of Staff
LR	Long range
MAD	Magnetic airborne detector
MIR	Monthly Intelligence Report
OPD	Operations Division, War Department General Staff
OTU	Operational Training Unit
RCAF	Royal Canadian Air Force
RCN	Royal Canadian Navy
RDF	Radio direction finder
SCR	Signal corps radio equipment
SDC	Southern Defense Command
VLR	Very long range
VP	Navy patrol (squadron)
WDGS	War Department General Staff

FOOTNOTES

Chapter I

1. Excerpts from Eastern Sea Frontier War Diary, Dec. 1941, in *Three Historical Essays Relating to Army Antisubmarine Activities* /Three Essays/, 26 April 1944, Tab I H, in AAFAC files; Report by Maj. A. Standish to Secretary of War for Air /Standish Report/, 1 Dec. 1943, 3, in AAFAC file 100.01.

2. Standish Report, 5. The following table of shipping losses is taken from memo to CG AAFAC from Maj. W. Jackson, Assistant A-2, AAFAC, 7 March 1943, in Three Essays, Tab I I.

	ESF SHIPS	ESF TONNAGE	GSF SHIPS	GSF TONNAGE	TOTAL SHIPS	TOTAL TONNAGE
Jan.	13	92,995	---	---	13	92,995
Feb.	14	94,054	5	34,531	19	128,585
March	27	167,257	3	26,221	30	193,478
April	24	133,265	2	5,256	26	138,521
May	5	23,336	42	226,415	47	249,741
June	13	73,585	20	88,705	33	162,290
July	3	17,563	15	56,137	18	73,700
Aug.	---	---	3	9,489	3	9,489
Sep.	---	---	1	6,511	1	6,511
Oct.	---	---	---	---	---	---
Nov.	---	---	---	---	---	---
Dec.	---	---	---	---	---	---

3. Standish Report, 2.

4. Later designated Eastern Sea Frontier.

5. Ltr., Commander, North Atlantic Naval Coastal Frontier to Chief of Naval Operations, 22 Dec. 1941, in Three Essays, Tab I A. Cf. Standish Report, 3.

6. The convoy system was inaugurated formally 15 May 1942. Ltr., Commander, Eastern Sea Frontier to Commander in Chief, U. S. Fleet, 14 May 1942, in Three Essays, Tab I M.

7. Standish Report, 6.

8. War Diary, Dec. 1941, quoted in Three Essays, Tab I B.

9. *Ibid.*, Jan. 1942, in Three Essays, Tab I E.

10. Ltr., Commander, North Atlantic Naval Coastal Frontier to COMINCH, 14 Jan. 1942, in Three Essays, Tab I C.

11. Extract from ESF War Diary, Jan. 1942, in Three Essays Tab I D.

12. Col. D. R. Lyon "History & Organization of the Army Air Forces Anti-Submarine Command" /Lyon History/, n.d., in AAFAC files 100.031, Monthly Antisubmarine Summary, Jan. 1943, 32. According to this account, the squadrons principally involved were the 20th, 43d, and 96th Bombardment Squadrons.

13. When activated, on 5 September 1941, the I Bomber Command consisted of a headquarters squadron, three heavy and one medium bombardment groups, a similar number of reconnaissance squadrons, and a single pursuit group.

14. Lyon History.

15. Ltr., Commander, North Atlantic Naval Coastal Frontier to COMINCH, 14 Jan. 1942, in Three Essays, Tab I C.

16. ESF War Diary, in Three Essays, Tabs I F and I G.

17. Lyon History.

18. Ltr., Hq. I Bomber Command to CG 1st AF, 14 Jan. 1942, in AAFAC file 112.

19. See below, 13-14.

20. Col. C. A. McHenry, "The Antisubmarine Command of the Army Air Forces" /McHenry History/, 13 Oct. 1943, prepared for release in the Army and Navy Journal. In AAFAC file 100.031.

21. Report from W/C P. F. Canning, RAF, to Capt. J. T. G. Stapler, USN, Col. H. D. Smith, 1st AF, and Lt. Col. R. B. Williamson, I Bomber Comd, 17 Feb. 1942 in AAFAC file 001. See also file 115.51.

22. The following table is from Standish Report:

I BOMBER COMMAND AND ENEMY ACTIVITY
EASTERN AND GULF SEA FRONTIERS

	I BOMCOM		Ships Sunk		
	HOURS FLOWN	U-BOATS ATTACKED	NO.	TONNAGE	EST. AVERAGE DAILY U/B DENSITY
Jan. 42	3,134	1	13	92,955	3.4
Feb.	4,766	3	19	128,585	5.9
March	7,247	4	30	193,478	5.7

	I BOMCOM		Ships Sunk		
	HOURS FLOWN	U-BOATS ATTACKED	NO.	TONNAGE	EST. AVERAGE DAILY U/B DENSITY
April	6,328	11	26	138,521	8.1
May	6,618	20	47	249,741	11.1
June	5,439	21	33	162,290	9.0
July	6,799	11	18	73,700	14.9
Aug.	5,685	6	3	9,489	8.5
Sep.	6,822	3	1	6,511	4.7
Oct.	6,410	1	0	0	2.2
	59,248	81	190	1,055,270	

23. Ibid..10.

24. Established shortly before Pearl Harbor, the CAP felt that it could be of service in the work of coastal patrol, and in February had submitted a plan for the employment of its forces. Memo, Maj. Gen. M. F. Harmon, C/AS, to Lt. Gen. L. F. McNair, C/S, GHQ, U. S. Army, 11 Feb. 1942 in AAFAC file 280. Originally under the operational control of the I Air Support Command, the CAP was placed under that of the I Bomber Command 19 August 1942. See AAFAC file 280.012.

25. See below, Chap. IV.

26. See below, n. 52.

27. Reference data attached to memo, Arnold to Marshall, 21 Feb. 1942 in Plans III-R-Bk. 1. Reference is made here to Act of 5 June 1920 (41 Stat. 954) as amended by Sec. 1, Act of 2 July 1923 (44 Stat. 780). Congress was declared competent to limit the jurisdiction of the armed forces in memo from Secretary of War, 28 August 1929.

28. Copy in Office of AC/AS Plans.

29. Ibid., par. 19 e, f, g.

30. Ibid., par. 20 c.

31. Ibid., par. 32 f.

32. Ibid., par. 20 and 23.

33. See correspondence in Plans III-R Book 1, under November and December 1941, for discussion concerning proposed revision of Joint Army and Navy Basic War Plan, Rainbow #5, and of Joint Action.

34. Ltr., Hq. 1st AF to CG I Bomber Comd., 5 Nov. 1941, in AAFAC files.

35. <u>Joint Action</u>, Chap. V, Sec. III, par. f. The last really effective opportunity for joint exercises was in connection with "Minor Joint Air Exercise No. 1," 17-22 April 1939. Prior to that maneuver, the 100-mile limit had been relaxed, but not in time for any practice to be undertaken; and subsequent practice flights of that sort were rendered impracticable by a regulation stating that permission for each must be received from the Navy 15 days ahead of time. Joint exercises in 1940-41 involved very small participation on the part of the First Air Force, owing to the general Air Corps policy of concentrating for the time being primarily on expansion. This entire subject is developed in Chapter IV, History of the I Bomber Command, Part One, page 256, received, in draft, from the unit historian /Draft History/, in AAFAC file 001.2.

36. Ltr., Hq. I Bomber Comd. to CG 1st AF, 8 Nov. 1941, in AAFAC file 001. See also other correspondence in folder, "Joint Army Navy Plans before Pearl Harbor."

37. <u>Joint Action</u>, Chap. III, par. 8 (1) (d) and Chap. V, Sec. II., par. j (2).

38. Report of Minor Joint Exercise No. 1, New England and New York Sectors, 17-21 April 1939, analyzed in Draft History.

39. Memo, Adm. E. J. King to Gen. Arnold, 20 Feb. 1942, in Plans III-R, Bk. 1; ltr., King to Arnold, 5 March 1942 in Plans III-R, Bk. 2.

40. Memo, King to Arnold, 20 Feb. 1942, and memo for Arnold, 15 Jan. 1942, in Plans III-R Bk.1. By 1 July 1944, 200 additional B-24's and 500 B-25's were to be made available to the Navy.

41. Review of correspondence, ltr., C/S, to COMINCH, 17 July 1942 and attached memo for record, in Plans III-R Bk. 1. In 1942, the Navy received 51. By August 1943, the AAFAC planned to have a force of 240 heavy bombers, including the two squadrons partially equipped with B-17's. Memorandum Report to the Secretary of War "The Acute Problem of Ocean-borne Transport and Supply" /Bowles Report/, by Dr. E. L. Bowles, 3 March 1943, 5, copy at present in AAFAC files. A report from the Chief, Statistical Control, Air Staff, Management Control, 19 March 1943, attached to memo from the President to Chief of Staff, U. S. Army and COMINCH, 18 March 1943, in AAFAC file 575.6, puts at 52 the number of B-24's delivered to the Navy.

42. Ltr., Arnold to King, 25 Feb. 1942, Plans III-R-2 Bk. 1.

43. Memo for Mr. R. A. Lovett, entitled "Unity of Command vested in the Army for Coastal Frontiers," n.d., in Plans III-R-2 Bk. 1.

44. Ltr., Arnold to King, 9 May 1942, in Plans III-R-2 Bk. 2.

45. Ltr., Maj. Gen. Follett Bradley, CG 1st AF, to Brig. Gen. W. T. Larson, CG, I Bomber Comd, 26 May 1942.

46. See below, n. 52.

47. Ltr., Arnold to Maj. Gen. W. H. Frank, CG, 2d AF, 29 May 1942, in AAF 384.7-A.

48. Ltr., Col. F. L. Anderson, Acting Dir., AFRDB to Bradley, 1 July 1942, in AAG 384.7-A.

49. Draft in AAFAC files, entitled "I Bomber Command." Cf. Standish Report, 2.

50. Ibid., Conclusion, 13. See Monthly Intelligence Report, AAFAC, July 1943, 14, for charts illustrating expansion and relocation.

51. Joint Action, Chap. II, Par 8 (a) and (b). Cf. Draft History.

52. Rad. from C/S, 25 March 1942, in AAFAC file 001.

53. Lt. Gen. Joseph T. McNarney's notes on trip to 1st AF and I Bomber Comd., 23 April 1942, in Plans III-R-2 Bk. 1.

54. Memo for Arnold, 20 May 1942 from AFRDB; memo for TAG from OPD, 27 May 1942; ltr., Hq. 2d AF to CG AAF, 15 June 1942; all in Plans III-R-2 Bk. 1.

55. Memo for Col. Glantzberry from Col. F. R. Pitts, 20 Aug. 1942; McNarney's notes, cited above, n. 53; both in Plans III-R-2 Bk. 1.

56. The I Bomber Command still, theoretically, had the job of general coastal defense in addition to its antisubmarine duties. See below, Chap. IV.

57. Memo AC/S, OPD to CG EDC, 20 May 1942; memo AC/S, OPD to CG AAF, 20 May 1942; both in AAFAC file 113.3. The latter is roughly the same as the former, except that it alone contains the directive requesting a reorganized bomber command.

58. Memo AC/S to CG AAF, 20 May 1942, and attached memo for CG AAF from Acting AC/S, 22 May 1942, in AAFAC file 113.3.

59. See AAFAC files 115.51 and 115.52.

60. Report, "The Coastal Command System of Operational Control," 17 Feb. 1942, in AAFAC 115.51. See conference with Comdr. R. B. Martinean, RAF Coastal Command, 17 July 1942, in AAFAC

file 115.52 for additional information on the English system.

61. Report by W/C S. R. Gibbs, RAF "on visits to units of the First Air Force," in AAFAC file 115.51.

62. Draft plans, n.d., unsigned, in AAFAC files 113.3 and 001.

63. Notes for conference on improvement in antisubmarine operations, 1 June 1942, in AAFAC file 113.3 and 001. Cf. memo for AC/S, OPD from AC/AS Plans, 4 June 1942, in Plans III-B-2 Bk. 1, which is virtually the same plan.

64. See draft plans.

65. Ibid. In the patrolled area an airplane density of 1: 15,000 square miles should be maintained.

66. Ibid.

67. Document, unsigned, 19 Dec. 1942, "The Strategic Control of our Antisubmarine Campaign," in AAFAC file 575.201.

68. Ltr., Air Marshall P. B. Joubert, RAF, to Lord Halifax, 16 Aug. 1942, in Three Essays, Tab II B. This letter was sent in answer to Lord Halifax's request for information concerning British experience which might be of help to the United States in its antisubmarine problem.

69. Memo for King from McNarney, 26 May 1942, in AAFAC 001.

70. Ltr., King to Marshall, 10 June 1942; ltr., King to Comdrs. ESF and GSF, 10 June 1942; both in AAFAC files 113.3 and 001.

71. Memo, Marshall to King, 19 June 1942, in AAFAC file 001.

72. Memo, King to Marshall, 21 June 1942 in Bowles Report (see above, n. 41), Tab XII B. This reference to an increase in allocation of Army planes was a repetition of an earlier suggestion. Ltr., King to Marshall, 10 June 1942, in AAFAC files 113.3 and 001.

73. See above, n. 22; Standish Report, 9-10.

74. Ibid., 10-11. Figures taken from COMINCH assessments.

75. Ibid.

76. See above, n. 2.

77. See Charts in Monthly Intelligence Summary, AAFAC, Nov. 1942, 8-9.

78. Analysis of U. S. Aircraft Attacks on U/Boats, Memo 20, prefaced by Antisubmarine Warfare Operations Research Gp., 7 Dec. 1942, p. 4. In this connection it should be noted that half, or a significantly larger proportion, of the radar contacts were made by Army planes.

79. History, 1st Search Attack Gp., Langley Field, Va., Chap. II, 21 and App. 19 B.

80. At least one German U-boat commander agreed with this interpretation. Early in June 1942, when the force of the U. S. antisubmarine measures was just beginning to be felt, the rescued captain of a U-boat sunk by a I Bomber Command plane off Cape Hatteras stated that he did not believe German submarine successes in American waters could be maintained, owing to the frequency of depth-bomb attacks. McHenry History.

81. Estimated at 859,000 tons for November, as compared to 575,886 for October. *Monthly Intelligence Summary*, AAFAC, Nov. and Dec. 1942.

82. See review of SADU activities in memo for CG AAF from Brig. Gen. T. T. Handy, AC/S, 27 June 1943; memo for S/W from Dr. Bowles, 7 Aug. 1942; both in AAFAC files 113.3 and 001.

83. *Ibid*. See also another plan submitted 22 August 1942 and constructed on roughly similar lines. Attached to ltr., Lt. Col. P. C. Ashworth to Col. R. L. Harper, 22 Aug. 1942, in AAFAC files 113.4 and 001.

84. Ltr., Marshall to King, 14 Sep. 1942, in Bowles Report, Tab XIV A.

85. Ltr., King to Marshall, 17 Sep. 1942, in Bowles Report, Tab XIV B.

86. Memo for CG AAF from McNarney, 22 Sep. 1942 in Bowles Report, Tab XIV C.

87. GO No. 84, 1st AF, 15 Oct. 1942, in AAFAC file 210. The original title, "Army Air Forces Anti-Submarine Command," was changed to Army Air Forces Antisubmarine Command on 20 Nov. 1942. Memo from Maj. F. E. Bauer, 20 Nov. 1942 AAFAC file 212. Although given prior approval by Navy authorities, the command was welcomed by Admiral King with marked lack of enthusiasm. In the 38th meeting of the Joint Chiefs of Staff, 20 Oct. 1942, he asked whether the announcement by the War Department of the constitution of the AAFAC, "now a *fait accompli*," was meant to convey the approval of the Joint Chiefs of Staff. Notes on JCS, 38th meeting, attached to JCS 93/1, in J/CCS Div., AFAEP.

88. Ltr., Col. F. C. Milner, CG, AAFAC, 28 Dec. 1942; memo from Milner, 28 Dec. 1942; ltr., Maj. Gen. G. E. Stratemeyer to Air Marshal L. S. Breadner, Ottawa, Canada, 9 June 1943; all in AAFAC files 211, 211.1, 212.

Chapter II

1. *Monthly Intelligence Summary*, AAFAC, Nov. 1942; Standish Report, 18. In October 1942, I Bomber Command reported 22 DB-7 B's and A-20's, 19 A-29's, 12 B-17's, 14 B-18's, 3 B-24's, 35 B-25's, 43 B-34's. Of these aircraft, only 27 were listed as radar equipped. *Ibid.*, 8. See App. 5 for station lists.

2. See n. 84 Chap. I.

3. See n. 83 Chap. I.

4. Bowles Report, Tab XIII.

5. Ltr., AAG to Larson, 28 Dec. 1942, quoted in Standish Report, 17.

6. In JCS 93, considered in 31st meeting of JCS, 1 September 1942, information was requested on 500 additional aircraft which the Navy wished provided for antisubmarine patrol. In JCS 93/1, (19 October 1942) General Arnold outlined a plan for the ultimate deployment of 416 Army planes. This plan was approved in the 38th Meeting of JCS.

6a. Ltr., TAG, to CG AAF, 17 Nov. 1942 in AG 320.5 (11-15-42); ltr., Maj. Bower to CG AAF, 6 Jan. 1943, copies in AAFAC files 212 and 215. The figure 19 is taken from JCS 93/1.

7. Ltr., CG AAFAC to CG AAF, 6 Jan. 1943, copies in AAFAC files 215 and 001.1.

7a. *Ibid.*

8. *Ibid.*, 1st ind., n.d.

9. R&R, Dir. of Technical Services /AFDTS/ to AC/AS, A-3, 6 Jan. 1943, in AAFAC file 001.1.

10. Memo, Dr. P. M. Morse, ASWORG, to AFDTS, 20 Jan. 1943, in Plans III-B-2 Bk. 1.

11. After a detailed analysis, he set 6,000 as an upper and 800 as a lower limit, leaving 1,000 to 2,000 as a compromise, provided they could be moved easily from base to base to follow U-boat concentrations. *Ibid.*

12. Memo ("unofficial") Dr. Morse to Larson, 5 Jan. 1943, in AAFAC files 001.1 and 591.

13. Memo for JCS from Joint U. S. Committee on New Weapons and Equipment, (JCNW), 4 Jan. 1943, memo from JCNW to Deputy C/S, 6 Jan. 1943,

both in Plans III-R-2 Bk. 1. The latter document closely resembles Dr. Morse's report in the number of aircraft considered necessary in the North Atlantic. A similar opinion was experienced by Brig. Gen. H. H. McClelland, AFDTS, in memo for McNarney, 23 Jan. 1943, in AAG, Bulk file, Antisubmarine Command correspondence prior to 1 April 1943.

14. Memo for CG AAF, from Brig. Gen. C. W. Russell, 3 Nov. 1942, in Three Essays, Tab II C.

15. He estimated that 105 enemy submarines were operating in the Atlantic and that Germany was building between 20 to 25 a month.

16. Memo for CG AAF, n.d. (probably January 1943), in AAFAC file 001.1.

17. 1st ind., Hq. AAF to Russell, 6 Feb. 1943 to brief of memo for CG AAF from Russell, n.d., in AAG 384, 7-A. See also ltr., C/S to COMINCH, 17 July 1942, in Plans III-R-2 Bk. 1, in which a similar viewpoint is foreshadowed. In a memo for the Chief of Staff, 5 October 1942, in Plans III-R-2 Book 1, Lt. Gen. B. H. Somervell, Commanding General, ASF, had urged the bombing of submarine bases and yards as the principal target for the Eighth Air Force, and a necessary prerequisite to successful logistical operations in the European theater. Arnold, summing up a discussion of the problem during the course of which he and Air Vice Marshal Slessor, RAF, had experienced divergent views, wrote in December what may be considered the official AAF position at the time:

> The submarine right now is a terrible menace and it must be a target for our bombers. Their destruction is one of our primary problems. I am convinced therefore that we must hit them first where their component parts are made; second, where they are assembled; third, at their operating bases; and fourth, in the open sea.

Ltr., Arnold to Slessor, 4 Dec. 1942, in SAS 370.31 (Office of the Air Secretary.)

18. R&R, AFAEP to AFABI, 28 Dec. 1942, in Plans III-R-2 Bk. 1.

19. An Evaluation of the Air Effort against Submarines, to 1 Jan. 1943, compiled by Intelligence Service, AAF, 8 Mar. 1943, in A-2 Library, US 9950 Shipping, K-17802.

20. Ibid. Cf. memo for CG AAF from Col. D. R. Lyon and Col. Adrian Williamson, 27 Feb. 1943, in AAFAC file 001.1.

21. Minority report submitted by Col. Williamson, one of two AAFAC members of Special Committee on Measures for Combatting the Submarine Menace. CPS 56/3, 1 March 1943, Annex B to App. C.

22. Memo for CG AAF from AFAEP, 21 Dec. 1942, in Plans III-R-2 Bk. 1; ltr, Hq. AAFAC to CO 25th Antisubmarine Wing, 3 Feb. 1943, in AAFAC file 001.1.

23. Memo for Brig. Gen. Upston, unsigned, n.d., (probably early in Feb. 1943, because in answer to a letter of 8 Feb. 1943), in AAFAC file 001.1. British ASV-2 equipment had been seriously compromised by the German detecting devices.

24. See below.

25. Memo, for Marshall from King, 8 Feb. 1943, in Three Essays, Tab II F.

26. Memo for Upston. (See note 23 above.)

27. Supplementary Report on the Air Effort against Submarines, prepared by A-5, 8th AF, 28 Feb. 1943.

28. See Monthly Intelligence Report, AAFAC, April 1943, 13. Memo for CG AAFAC from Maj. W. Jackson, n.d., AAFAC file 001.1.

29. Minutes of the Atlantic Convoy Conference, 4, in AAFAC file 575.5. On this score, the conference made some important recommendations which resulted in materially strengthening the convoy routes both in number of VLR aircraft and in the international organization. See ACC 3 and 3/1; Three Essays, II, 37-40.

30. Minutes of ACC, 2-3.

31. Memo for CG AAF from Cols. Lyon and Williamson, 27 Feb. 1943, in AAFAC file 001.1. In the course of the discussions of the subcommittee of the CPS on the submarine menace, it came out that the total strength in VLR aircraft planned by Britain, Canada, and the United States exceeded the number considered necessary by 208 (260 were required, 468 planned by all agencies). Ibid.

32. Memo for CG AAF from Russell, n.d., in AAFAC file 001.1.

33. Memo for DC/S from JCMW, n.d., in Plans III-R-2 Bk. 1, under 6 Jan. 1943.

34. Ibid. See also ltr., CG AAFAC to CG AAF, 22 June 1943, in AAFAC file 001.1; Memo, Dr. Bowles to Marshall, 3 March 1943, prefaced to Bowles Report.

35. Ltr., Lt. Col. Jack Roberts to Air Vice Marshal Lloyd, AOC, NW African Coastal AF, 6 April 1943, in Letters of Col. Roberts, AAFAC files. Other references to this problem may be found throughout Col. Robert's letters. See also ltr., CG AAFAC, to CG AAF, 6 Jan. 1943, in AAFAC file 001.1.

36. "Proposed Reorganization of ASW Forces," AAFAC Liaison Office, 21 Jan. 1943, in AAFAC file 001.1.

37. Memo, King to Marshall, 8 Feb. 1943, in Three Essays, Tab II F.

38. Notes on 54th Meeting, CCS, 31 Dec. 1942, attached to CPS 56/D.

39. Subcommittee created 5 Jan. 1943 as a result of CPS 56/D, dated 2 Jan. 1943. Memo for CG AAFAC from Cols. Lyon and Williamson, 27 Feb. 1943, in AAFAC file 001.1. Representatives were present from the following agencies: RAF, AAF, RN, USN, RCAF, and RCN.

40. Ibid.

41. CPS 56/3, Annex B to App. C.

42. Plan attached to memo, Cols. Lyon and Williamson to CG, AAF, 27 Feb. 1943, in AAFAC file 001.1.

43. "Proposed Reorganization of ASW Forces," issued by AAFAC Liaison Office, 21 Jan. 1943, in AAFAC file 001.1.

44. Memo for DC/S from JCNW, in Plans III-R-2, Bk. 1, under 6 Jan. 1943.

45. Notes on 76th Meeting, JCS, 27 April 1943 and on 82d Meeting, CCS, 30 April 1943, attached to CCS 203.

46. Minutes of ACC, 3.

47. Ibid., 11.

48. Ltr., the President to C/S, and COMINCH, 18 March 1943, copies in AAFAC file 575, 6 and 001.1. Specifically, the President asked for a statement as to the number of B-24's the two services could operate at once from Newfoundland, Greenland, and Iceland, how soon the maximum number would be operating from each of these bases, how many ACV's were in use, and at what rate they might be increased. See below, n. 70.

49. For status of foreign squadrons, as of 1 April 1943, see App. 7, this study. Memo for Arnold from Giles, 2 April 1943, in AAFAC file 001.1.

50. Ltr., Chief of Bomb. Br., AFREQ to CG AAFAC, 2 April 1943, in AAFAC file 001.1.

51. Memo, Arnold to Stratemeyer, 29 March 1943, in AAFAC file 001.1. This subject had received much attention in CCS and CPS deliberations. In CCS 189, 16 March 1943, a recommendation had been made to CCS from JCS to the effect that the urgent need for an immediate increase

in VLR aircraft in the antisubmarine campaign should be met by diverting 128 heavy bombers from the bombing of Germany. On 25 March 1943, Air Commander Strafford pointed out that only 8 VLR aircraft were available in the North Atlantic where heavy losses in shipping had occurred in the previous 2 weeks. Notes on CPS 49th Meeting, attached to CPS 49/D, 20 March 1943. In CCS 189/2, it was recommended that during April and May 1943, first priority in equipment and labor at all ASV modification centers be given to B-24's for antisubmarine service, and that the entire VLR, ASV-equipped B-24 output from modification centers during those months be similarly allocated, even at the expense of other theaters. These recommendations were accepted, substantially, in CCS 189/3.

52. Ibid.

53. R&R, comment 2, AFOCR to AFAEP, 29 April 1943, in AAFAC file 001.1. Planned allocations of VLR B-24 aircraft to the AAFAC were listed as follows:

Month	Number	Month	Number
April	40	September	67
May	26	October	52
June	21	November	54
July	31	December	36
August	56		

54. Memo for King from Marshall, 16 April 1943, in Plans III-R-2 Bk. 1.

55. JCS 268, 19 April 1943, memo by C/S.

56. Bowles Report, 20-21. The over-all average of attacks against submarines indicated that one sighting in 40 was fatal to the enemy. In England, the average had been considerably better than this; in America, considerably less. Ibid., 28. Dr. Bowles proposed using the British Coastal Command system of operational control, in which submarine positions and predictions would be given to the AAFAC each day, whereupon the command itself would then lay out its plans for the next day's operations. He deprecated the restrictions imposed on antisubmarine activity by the Navy's insistence on adhering to arbitrary sea frontier boundaries, both at home and abroad. Ibid., 20 and 21.

57. Memo for Marshall and McNarney, 3 March 1943, attached to Bowles Report. For 1943, production schedules called for 6,400 B-24's in all. In 1942 the Navy had received 51 B-24's, and 343 were scheduled to go to the Navy in 1943. By August 1943 the AAFAC could only count on 175 additional long-range planes for its operational force. Ibid., 5. Cf. n. 55, above.

58. Memo for Marshall from S/W Stimson, 14 March 1943. Copies in AAG 384.7 and AAFAC 1001.1.

59. Ltr., Hq. AAFAC to CG AAF, 11 April 1943, in AAFAC file 001.1.

60. Memo for JCS from AC/S, (JCS 268).

61. Memo for King from Marshall, 11 May 1943, in Plans III-R-2 Bk. 1.

62. Notes on 75th Meeting, JCS, 20 April 1943.

63. JCS 268/1, 3 May 1943.

64. Notes on 77th Meeting, JCS, 4 May 1943.

65. Memo for Marshall from King, 30 April 1943, in Plans III-R-2 Bk. 1. He suggested that, since the convoy systems in the South Pacific and the Southwest Pacific should be the same as that in the Atlantic, the Commander, Tenth Fleet should control it.

66. Notes on 77th Meeting, JCS.

67. *Ibid.*

68. Memo for King from Marshall, 11 May 1943 in Plans III-R-2 Bk. 1. It appears, however, that, pending a decision on the Tenth Fleet proposal, antisubmarine forces were, in fact, administered by the JCS with COMINCH as their executive, a procedure which, in the above memo, General Marshall had admitted would cause complications. See Joint Directive from JCS to Comdr., S. Atlantic Force, and CG, S. Atlantic, 4 June 1943, in AAFAC file, Operations, Ascension Island.

69. Memo for C/S from OPD, 8 May 1943, in AAFAC file 001.1.

70. Memo for King from Marshall, 11 May 1943, in Plans III-R-2 Bk. 1. General Marshall also nominated the man for the job, Maj. Gen. Willis H. Hale, then air chief in Hawaii.

71. Rad. issued by King, 19 May 1943, in AAFAC file 218.1. The organization became effective 20 May 1943.

72. See Chap. III, n. 219 for figures on Navy allocations.

73. Memo for CG AAF from Brig. Gen. B. W. Chidlaw, 13 June 1943, in Plans III-R-2 Bk. 4.

74. Memo for King from Marshall, 28 June 1943, in AAFAC file 001.1.

75. See above, n. 30.

76. Memo, Stimson to Marshall, 14 March 1943, in AAFAC 001.1.

77. Ltr., Allied Antisubmarine Survey Board to COMINCH, 29 April 1943, in AAFAC 001.1.

78. Notes on 79th Meeting, JCS, 10 May 1943.

79. CCS 241, 21 May 1943.

80. Minutes, 93d Meeting, CCS, 22 May 1943, ref. CCS 241/1.

81. Minutes, 88th Meeting, JCS, 22 May 1943, ref. CCS 241.

82. Notes on 98th Meeting CCS, 14 June 1943, ref. CCS 241/5.

83. Memo for Col. W. C. Sweeney, OPD from Larson, 10 June 1943, in AAFAC file 001.1.

84. Memo for DC/S from Acting AC/S, OPD, 7 June 1943. Cf. attached draft of memo for King from DC/S; both in AAFAC file 001.1.

85. It was officially concurred in by General Marshall, 14 June 1943, on the basis of the informal concurrence of General Arnold, 12 June 1943. Notes on 98th Meeting, CCS; R&R, AFAEP to CG AAF, 12 June 1943, in Plans III-2-R Bk. 1.

86. Memo "for discussion with Gen. Arnold" from Lt. Col. P. C. Crowen, in AAG Bulk file, AAFAC correspondence since 1 April 1943, I.

87. Memo AC/S, OPD for CG AAF, 10 July 1943, in Dissolution of the Antisubmarine Command /Dissolution/, Annex A-2, in AAFAC files.

88. Memo for Marshall from King, 14 June 1943 in Dissolution, Annex A-1.

89. Ltr, Stimson to McNarney, 25 June 1943, in Plans III-R-2 Bk. 2.

90. Ibid.

91. R&R, Chief of Air Staff to AFABI, 1 July 1943, in AAFAC file 001.1. General Stratemeyer ordered that the attached memo from General Marshall be "incorporated in our historical record."

92. Memo for King from Marshall, 28 June 1943, copy in App. 1.

92a. See Dissolution for details regarding this transaction.

93. Memo for Col. Gross from Lt. Col. Reynolds, AFRDB, in Plans III-R Bk. 4.

94. Dissolution, Annex A-13.

95. Memo for all AC/AS from AFREQ, 27 Oct. 1943, in AAG 384.7-B.

96. See papers filed for October 1943 in AAG 384.7-B; Dissolution, 19 ff.

CHAPTER III

1. Memo for King from Marshall, 19 June 1942, in Bowles Report, Tab XII A.

2. Memo for Marshall and McNarney, 3 March 1943, attached to Bowles Report.

3. Ibid. The higher figures come from report entitled "The Strategic Aerial Bombardment of Europe" /Strategic Bombardment/, AFABI, 10 Sep. 1943, in AFIHI files, 1641-2. There figures were originally taken from tabulations made by the Office of Strategic Services.

4. Monthly Intelligence Report, /MIR/ AAFAC, Aug. 1943, 6 and 10.

5. Strategic Bombardment, 10 Dec. 1943.

6. Ibid.

7. Ibid., 10 Sep. 1943; MIR, Aug. 1943, 20.

8. Strategic Bombardment, 10 Dec. 1943.

9. Ibid., MIR, July 1943.

10. Some put the number of U-boats having to cross the transit area as high as 120. MIR Aug. 1943, 13.

11. About 70 per cent of the total Atlantic fleet was estimated to be operating at one time, each cruise lasting about 2 months. Paper, Air Offensive against the U-boats in Transit, filed under 10 March 1943 in AAFAC file 597.1.

12. MIR, June 1943, 20; Air Offensive against the U-boats in Transit.

13. MIR, June 1943, 20.

14. Air Offensive against the U-boats in Transit.

15. Ibid.

16. Ibid. The following statistics, complete to the end of June 1943, give some idea of the persuasiveness of the argument in favor of the Bay offensive.

Month	Approx. Flying Hours	U-boats sighted	U-boats attacked	Flying Hours per sighting	% of Transit U-boats Attacked.
March	4100	42	24	97	20
April	3300	52	28	69	23

Month	Approx. Flying Hours	U-boats sighted	U-boats attacked	Flying Hours per sighting	% of Transit U-boats Attacked.
May	4600	99	65	46	54
June (27-1/3 days)	4700	62	25	76	23
	17000	255	142	67	30

There is a sharp contrast between this rate of sighting U-boats and the number of hours of flying which experience showed were required to obtain a sighting in other operational areas.

Area	Hours per sighting Jan. - Apr. 1943
Newfoundland and Nova Scotia	763
San Juan Sector	790
Trinidad Sector	2175
Guantanamo Sector	12194
Eastern Sea Frontier	20663
Gulf Sea Frontier	59216

It must, of course, be remembered that many of the planes used in these areas would not have been suitable for such operations as those in the Bay. MHR, June 1943, 20-21.

17. These two squadrons were diverted from the western Atlantic in the first instance for the purpose of protecting TORCH shipping. Rad., NCXF (1) to Admiralty, 12 Feb. 1942, in Historical Documents of the 480th Antisubmarine Group (Annex to History of the 480th Antisubmarine Group /History, 480th Gp./) in AAFAC files.

18. Memo for Maj. W. H. Jackson, AAF from Air Chief Marshal Sir John Slessor, Comdr., RAF Coastal Command, 11 Oct. 1943, quoted in extenso in Three Essays, II, 16. Outer Gondola lay between $45\frac{1}{2}°$ and $50°$ N and from $15°$ to $22°$ W. Inner Gondola lay between $45°$ and $48\frac{1}{2}°$ N, and from $7°$ to $10°$ W.

19. Ibid.

20. See History, 480th Gp., for data on movement of units.

21. Letters of Col. Jack Roberts /Roberts ltrs./, Tabs 1 and 2, in AAFAC files. See also History, 480th Gp., Tab 2, 7-8.

22. History, 480th Gp., Tab 2, 2. The unit, on 1 March 1943, became known as the 2037th Wing (Prov.), under direct control of the AAFAC.

On 21 June 1943 it was again redesignated as the 480th Antisubmarine Group (Separate Special). Throughout the present study it will be referred to as the 480th Group.

23. *Ibid.*, 8.

24. *Ibid.*

25. *Ibid.*

26. *Ibid.*, 10. When all remaining combat crews arrived, Colonel Roberts estimated he would have in the 1st Squadron only 42 officers and 152 men, including 2 officers and 63 men attached from VIII Bomber Command. This amounted only to 50 per cent of the T/O personnel strength. Roberts Ltrs., Tab 2, 6.

27. History, 480th Gp., 10.

28. *Ibid.*, 11.

29. Roberts Ltrs., Tabs 1, 2, 10.

30. History, 480th Gp., 14.

31. *Ibid.*, 14-15. See also Roberts Ltrs., Tabs. 1, 2, and 4; memo for Larson from Dr. Morse, 5 Jan. 1943, in AAFAC files 591 and 001.1.

32. *Ibid.*, 12.

33. *Ibid.*, 13. See also Standish Report, Annex 3.

34. Ltr., Hq. 8th AF to CG ETOUSA, 25 March 1943, in AAG 284.7A.

35. History, 480th Gp., 11; Roberts Ltrs., Tab 2, 8.

36. Roberts Ltrs., Tab 2, 5.

37. *Ibid.*, Tab 4.

38. *Ibid.*, Tab 9.

39. History, 480th Gp., 16. Cf. n. 41 below.

40. See n. 16 above.

41. History, 480th Gp., 15 ff. See also Evaluations in App. 2, this study. Only one of the three attacks thwarted by mechanical failure is included in the appendix. In this attack the U-boat was, however, effectively strafed.

42. Ibid., 20.

43. Ibid., 22.

44. Coastal Command Review Feb. 1943, 1 and 3. This source only lists the five attacks for February in which the bombs did not "hang up."

45. See ibid., March to June, for running story of Coastal Command operations in the Bay.

46. Report of Naval Attache in London, Serial 1071, 17 March 1943, in AAFAC file 597.1., CCS 189/4, 22 April 1943, memo from Representatives of the British Chiefs of Staff.

47. Memo for AC/S, OPD from AFAEP, 12 April 1943, in AAFAC file 597.1. Although the Navy had, by 1 April 1943, received 111 B-24 aircraft from the Army, it was stated that none of them had on that date been employed in Atlantic antisubmarine operations.

48. Ibid. The proposal of the British, as originally stated, was disposed of officially in CCS 189/6, 29 April 1943.

49. Report of Naval Attache in London, 17 March 1943. In 53d Meeting, CPS, 6 May 1943, Air Commodore Strafford urged that, if ASV equipped VLR planes could not be made available, those without radar be sent, because in daylight operations, special equipment would not be essential.

50. Memo for DC/S from AC/S OPD, 7 June 1943, in AAFAC file 584.

51. History of the 479th Antisubmarine Group, /History, 479th Gp./, 5, in AAFAC files.

52. "Musketry" was bounded on the north by 47° 30' N, on the east by 09° 30' W, on the south by 43° 30' N, and on the west by 11° 30' W. "Seaslug" was bounded on the north by 47° 30' N, on the east by 13° 00' W, on the south by 44° by 00' N, and on the west by 15° 00' W. These areas became effective 14 June 1943. For these and other dates on the Bay operations, see Monthly Antisubmarine Report, issued by the Admiralty, July 1943, page 15 and September 1943, page 15, in AFIHI files.

53. Ltr., Col. Howard Moore, CO 479th Gp. to CG AAFAC, 18 July 1943, in AAFAC file 583.

54. Ibid. See also History 479th Gp., I, 56.

55. Ibid., I, 52-54.

56. Ibid., I, 9.

57. Rad., Slessor to Larson, 29 July 1943, in AAFAC file 583.

58. Standish Report, Annex II, 3. Cf. revised COMINCH assessments, App. 2, this study.

59. See chart of attacks by 479th Group on enemy submarines, App. 2, this study.

60. See chart of encounters with enemy aircraft, App. 3, this study.

61. Standish Report, Annex II, 4.

62. See MIR, Aug. 1943, 15, for general discussion. Standish Report, Annex II, 4; Monthly Antisubmarine Reports, July to Sep. 1943.

63. Standish Report, Annex II, 4.

64. During these operations, Support Groups spent 576 "ship days" in the Bay, and Coastal Command aircraft flew 3,981 sorties. These figures do not include help received from the Moroccan Sea Frontier and from Gibraltar. Monthly Antisubmarine Report, Sep. 1943, 15.

65. For discussion of this subject see report entitled, "Analysis of Anti-Submarine Warfare Operations in the Moroccan Sea Frontier Area" /Analysis/, ASWORG, 22 July 1943, in Three Essays, Tab III D; ltr., H. Lardner, RAF Operations Research Section, to Capt. T.H. Solberg, American Embassy, London, 6 Sep. 1943 in ibid., Tab III E; History, 480th Gp., 35 ff.

66. Ltr., Lardner to American Embassy.

67. Analysis, ASWORG. This source estimates 25 enemy submarines to have been in the given area. Mr. Lardner, in letter referred to above, believed that no more than eight were ever deployed in the area at any one time.

68. History, 480th Gp., 37-38. Figures quoted are based on COMINCH assessments.

69. See chart of attacks by 480th Group on enemy submarines, App. 2, this study. See also History 480th Gp., 39.

70. The advance air echelon arrived 11 March. The ground echelon arrived at the end of the month, having been delayed in Algiers, waiting transportation. History 480th Gp., 23. The status of the organization as of 26 March 1943 was as follows: 16 planes, 96 officers, 381 enlisted men in the flight echelon; 11 officers and 529 enlisted men in the ground echelon. Roberts Ltrs., Tab 16.

71. Ibid., Tab 20.

72. Ibid., Tabs 20 and 21.

73. Ibid., Tab 21.

74. Ibid., Tab 30.

75. Ibid., Tab 22.

76. Rad., Naval Commander, Northwest African Waters to COMINCH, 15 April 1943, in Three Essays, Tab III F. See also discussion of status of Port Lyautey in Roberts Ltrs., Tab 17.

77. Roberts Ltrs., Tab 26. The Term "Wing" refers to the temporary organization of the 480th Group as the 2037th Antisubmarine Wing (Prov.)

78. Ibid.

79. Ibid., Tab 28, 1.

80. Ibid., 3.

81. Ibid., Tabs 16, 19, and 23.

82. Ibid., passim.

83. Ibid., Tab 30.

84. Ibid., Tab 16.

85. Ibid., Tab 28.

86. Ibid., Tab 20.

87. Report for Brig. Gen. H. M. McClelland from Dr. J. R. Pellam, about 5 Sep. 1943 /Pellam Report/, in Three Essays, Tab III D, 9-10.

88. Roberts Ltrs., Tab 32, et passim.

89. For more figures on British action see Three Essays, Tab III E. For additional information regarding the Navy planes, see Analysis ASWORG, 4.

90. Ibid.

91. Ltr., Dr. Pellam to ASWORG, 10 June 1943, in Three Essays, Tab III D. The tendency for submarines to move outward, in direct proportion

to the range of effective air patrol, is evident from the following table of estimated average U-boat density in the area according to zone distances from the North African and Gibraltar bases.

Date	0-200 Miles	200-400 Miles	400-600 Miles	600-800 Miles	800- Miles	Total
NOV.	8.3	7.7	3.4	1.3	0.7	21.4
DEC.	2.9	4.2	5.6	4.0	2.8	19.5
JAN.	1.6	0.7	3.1	5.1	4.7	15.2
FEB.	1.2	2.8	5.2	5.7	5.0	19.9
MAR.	1.5	2.7	2.1	2.6	3.3	12.2
APR.	1.1	1.5	3.1	2.3	1.8	9.8
MAY	0.7	1.4	2.0	1.9	1.0	7.0
JUNE	0.5	0.7	1.6	1.9	3.8	8.5
JULY	1.0	2.9	3.6	5.3	8.3	21.1
AUG.	0.3	0.6	1.9	4.3	5.8	12.9

Figures adapted from Analysis, ASWORG, 12 Aug. 1943, and History 480th Gp.

92. Roberts Ltrs., Tab 16.

93. Ibid., Tab 20, 4.

94. See Map of activity in the Moroccan Sea Frontier, following p. 123.

95. Pellam Report, 3-4.

96. The Admiralty estimated that 80 per cent of the enemy craft rated "probably sunk" never reach port.

97. History, 480th Gp., 29. Cf. App. 2, which lists nine ineffective attacks.

98. Analysis, ASWORG, 12 Aug. 1943.

99. Ibid.

100. Pellam Report.

101. Ibid.

102. See App. 3. Cf. figures given in History, 480th Gp., 31-33, which are apparently the result of confusing operations in Africa with those in both England and Africa.

103. History, 480th Gp., 29. Cf. Analysis, ASWORG, 22 July 1943, 13.

104. Ibid., 7.

105. Ibid., 9.

106. Ibid., 7.

107. Ibid., Tables 1 and 3.

108. Ibid., 16-19.

109. Ibid., 16, Table 3.

110. MIR, Aug. 1943, 16.

111. See tables, Order of Battle, A/S Forces, in App. 7, this study. During the July activity, three planes of the 480th Group based at Agadir were recalled to Port Lyautey. Coastal Command aircraft sank one submarine and attacked five others in the Gibraltar area, late June to 31 July 1943. MIR, July 1943, 13.

112. Ibid., 5-6.

113. Telephone conversation, Col. McHenry to McNerney in AAFAC files (unnumbered). Roberts Ltrs, Tab 19.

114. Ibid., Tab 22.

115. Notes on 92d Meeting, COS, 22 May 1943, ref. COS 241/1, 22 May 1943.

116. History, 15th Antisubmarine Squadron, 10, in AAFAC file E-214. See maps of squadron locations, following p. 40.

117. MIR, March 1943, 7.

118. The above data, and that following, unless given more specific reference, is taken from MIR.

119. Ibid., May 1943, 7.

120. See Table, North American Theater, App. 2, this study.

121. See Chapter IV, this study, for discussion of the training program.

122. MIR, Feb. 1943, 7; March 1943, 7.

123. See Action Status Reports, AAFAC, for given dates, in AAFAC file 241.1.

124. Annex #3 to Movement Order #1, 26th AMIG, 27 Feb. 1943; Annex #1 to Movement Order #4, 26th AMIG, 5 April 1943; both in AAFAC file "Operations Cuba" (unnumbered). See also paper entitled "History of Enemy Action" in "Preliminary Study of the Carribean Area," in AAFAC files (unnumbered).

125. Copy in AAFAC file 774.

126. See movement orders in AAFAC files 774, 771, 773.

127. Movement Order #1, 26th AWIG, 27 Feb. 1943, in AAFAC file "Operations, Cuba" (unnumbered).

128. See MIR monthly accounts of activity in this area.

129. Interview with Maj. S. D. McElroy, CO 4th Antisubmarine Sq., 12 Feb. 1944, in AAFAC file 572.

130. Ltr., Maj. L. E. Holstead, CO, 7th A/S Sq. to CO 26th AWIG, 25 May 1943, in AAFAC file "Operations, Trinidad" (unnumbered), MIR July 1943.

131. Paper entitled "9th in Trinidad," 5, in AAFAC file 763.2.

132. Ibid., 3. See also notes by Lt. Dattilio in "Preliminary Study of the Caribbean Area."

133. For data on the command situation, see organizational charts in Preliminary Study, ltr., Hq. AAFAC to CG AAF, 8 May 1943, in AAFAC file "Operations, Trinidad"; History 7th A/S Sq., in AAFAC file E-206.

134. Ltr., Hq., Antilles Air Task Force, to CO 26th AWIG, 23 March 1943 in AAFAC file 761.

135. Ltr., Lt. O. W. Havens to Maj. Gomez, 6 Dec. 1942, in AAFAC file 763; History, 7th A/S Sq., 152; ltr., Maj. Gen. L. J. House, CG AATF to Col. H. A. Halverson, CO 26th AWIG, 23 March 1943, in "Operations Trinidad,"; Weekly Report, CO 23rd A/S Sq. to CO 26th AWIG, 22 Aug. 1943, in same file.

136. MIR, Jan. 1943, 5.

137. Ltr., CO 9th A/S Sq., to CO 26th AWIG, 29 Dec. 1942, in AAFAC file 763.

138. MIR, Jan. 1943, 5.

139. Ltr., CO 9th A/S Sq. to CO 26th AWIG, 29 Dec. 1942, in AAFAC file 763.

140. MIR, March 1943. See Table, Latin American Theater, App. 2, this study.

141. Ltr., Hq. AAFAC to CG AAF, 4 March 1943, in AAFAC file 763.

142. Movement order #2, 26th AWIG, 13 March 1943, in AAFAC file 761.

143. History, 7th A/S Sq., 154. See Status Reports, AAFAC, in file 241.1. An extra B-18 was sent out, and 8 were equipped with MAD.

144. MIR, monthly reports on operations in the area.

145. History, 7th A/S Sq., 155.

146. MIR, July 1943, 13.

147. Ibid., 26, and Aug. 1943, 16. The normal strength of the 8th Squadron was 16 B-24D, radar-equipped planes. Status Reports, in AAFAC file 240.1.

148. MIR, Aug. 1943. The Navy wished to keep this unit in the area until the equipment could be thoroughly tested. Memo for all AC/AS from AFRBQ, 27 Oct. 1943, in AAG 334.7-B.

149. See Chap. II, n. 7.

150. See documents in "Preliminary Study of the Caribbean Area."

151. Ltr., Hq. AAFAC to CG AAF, 24 April 1943, in AAFAC file 781.

152. Memo for AFCOR from AFACP, 4 May 1943, in Plans III-B-2, Ek 1.

153. Ltr, Lt. Col. M. S. Becks to Col. H. A. Halverson, CO 25th AWIG, 2 June 1943, in AAFAC file, Operations, Ascension Island, (unnumbered).

154. Joint Directive, JCS to Comdr. S. Atlantic Force and CG S. Atlantic, 4 June 1943, in AAFAC file, Operations, Ascension Island.

155. Ltr., Lt. Col. Becks to CO 26th AWIG, 27 June 1943, in AAFAC file, Operations, Ascension Island.

156. Report, Lt. Col. Becks to CO 26th AWIG, 9 Aug. 1943 in AAFAC file, Operations, Ascension Island.

157. Ltr., President to C/S and COMINCH, 18 March 1943, in AAFAC files 001.1 and Operations, Newfoundland (unnumbered).

158. Corrected draft of memo for the President from C/S and COMINCH, n.d. (external evidence established 19 March 1943) in AAFAC file 001.1. See also below, n. 159.

159. Memo for AC/S OPD from AC/AS A-3, 20 March 1943, in AAFAC file 001.1.

160. Ltr., Air Member, Canadian Joint Staff to Arnold, 5 Jan. 1943, in AAFAC file 575.

161. R&R, comment 1, AFRDB to AC/AS, A-3, 12 Jan. 1943, basic ltr. in preceding note. It was reported that there was in Canada "a noticeable undertone of disappointment" that the AAFAC did not take over the task before the RAF. Ltr., Maj. J. P. Healy, Liaison Officer to RCAF, to CG EDC, 22 Jan. 1943, in AAFAC file 575.

162. AC/S.

163. R&R, comment 3, AC/AS, MM&D to Bomb. Br., AFHQ, 30 March 1943, in AAFAC file 001.1.

164. Ltr., Bomb. Br., AFRQ to CG AAFAC, 2 April 1943, in AAFAC file 001.1.

165. R&R, comment 4, AFRDB, to AC/AS A-3, 12 Feb. 1943, in AAFAC file, Operations, Newfoundland. At the request of COMINCH, 12 B-17's were ordered to Newfoundland, 28 January 1943, to reinforce this squadron which was in turn to reinforce the coverage normally provided by Catalinas when convoys were attacked. Ltr., AFRDB to CG AAFAC, 23 Jan. 1943, in same file.

166. Ltr., AFRDB to CG AAFAC, 25 Jan. 1943, in AAFAC file, Operations, Newfoundland.

167. Report entitled "Survey of Greenland as an Operating Base for Antisubmarine Operations," 27 Feb. 1943, in AAFAC file 577.

168. Ibid., 3.

169. Above data taken from Review of Antisubmarine Intelligence, Detachment, 25th AWG, April 1943 in AAFAC file 576.23; and History, 479th Gp., iv-v.

170. Memo, Hq. AAFAC to all concerned, 25 June 1943, in AAFAC file, Operations, Newfoundland.

171. Review of A/S Intel., April 1943, 1.

172. Memo for CG AAF from AC/S, 23 April 1943, in AAG 324. 7-A.

173. RCAF Eastern Air Command Monthly Antisubmarine Reports, in AAFAC file 50-F (2). The RCAF maintained about 11 squadrons in the Nova Scotia-Newfoundland area, with 2 to 3 regularly on duty from Gander and Torbay. See also Rad., Larson to AFABI, 30 April 1943 in AAFAC file, Operations, Newfoundland.

174. Rad., Larson to CO DetaRsub, and CO 6th A/S Sq., 24 June 1943, in AAFAC file Operations, Newfoundland.

175. See diagram of U-boat disposition in North Atlantic Antisubmarine Intelligence, May 1943, in AAFAC file 576.23.

176. Review of A/S Intel., April 1943.

177. MIR, April 1943, 4-6. The figures given here are not final.

178. N. Atlantic A/S Intel., May 1943, 8.

179. Memo for OPS, (no signature) 15 Jan. 1943, in AAFAC file 577.

180. See report on these investigations in AAFAC file 577.

181. Ltr., Col. H. Moore to CO 25th AWIG, 19 May 1943, in AAFAC file, Operations, Newfoundland.

182. Colonel Moore conducted an experimental flight to Greenland and Iceland during which he dropped off two officers at BW-1 to set up a control room there. The rest of the control personnel arrived later. Ltr., Col. Moore to CO 25th AWIG, 4 May 1944, in AAFAC file, Operations, Newfoundland.

183. Except where otherwise specified, the following tactical procedures are taken from Antisubmarine Manual, SOP III-1, AAFAC, 29 July 1943, in AAFAC file 231.1.

184. Air Tactics in Antisubmarine Warfare, Bureau of Aeronautics, USN, 20 July 1943, 14, in AAFAC file, Tactical Policies (unnumbered).

185. See typical chart of a day's operations off Africa, following p. 157.

186. For pattern, see SOP III-2, 2 June 1943, in AAFAC file 231.1.

187. Colors varied according to the theater. See discussion in Monthly Reports of the Research Coordinator, AAFAC, in AAFAC file 400.1; correspondence in AAFAC file 402.

188. Air Tactics in Antisubmarine Warfare, 15.

189. MIR., June 1943, 40-41.

190. Ibid., Jan. 1943, 20.

191. Ibid., March 1943, 24-27.

192. Ibid., Feb. 1943, 15-16.

193. Ibid., 18-19.

194. Ibid., April 1943, 29.

195. Ibid., May 1943, 23.

196. *Ibid.*, June 1943, 47.

197. *Ibid.*, 49.

198. *Ibid.*, 50.

199. *Ibid.*, 51.

200. *Ibid.*, 55.

201. *Ibid.*, 57.

202. *Ibid.*, Aug. 1943, 30-1.

203. *Ibid.*, July 1943, 32-3.

204. *Ibid.*, Aug. 1943, 31-2.

205. *Ibid.*, 35.

206. See above, Chap. II.

207. Ltr., AAC to Larson, 28 Dec. 1942, in AAFAC file 001.1.

208. Standish Report, Conclusion, 17, figures quoted from A-3 Report, I Bomber Comd. 11 Oct. 1943.

209. Report, I Bomber Comd. to CG AAF, 18 Oct. 1943, in AAFAC file 100.02.

210. Standish Report, Conclusion 18. Attacks and assessment are from COMINCH and are corrected to date according to U. S. Fleet Anti-submarine Bulletin. Operational data from AAFAC and I Bomber Comd. reports to AAF, 19 April and 18 Oct. 1943.

211. This analysis, and the remarks following are taken from *Ibid*. 19-20.

212. *Ibid.*, 26.

213. *Ibid.*, 27. Figures from A-3, I Bomber Comd. They include all operations prior to the withdrawal of the two groups in November 1943.

214. Data corrected to 5 Sep. 1943. U. S. Fleet Antisubmarine Bulletin, Sep. 1943, 13, in AAFAC file 334.

215. Ltr., Hq. AAFAC to CG AAF, n.d., in Plans III-B-2, Bk 1; 1st ind., same ltr., Hq. AAF to CG AAFAC, 21 June 1943 which vetoes the plan contained in basic communication.

216. Report, I Bomber Comd. to CG AAF, 18 Oct. 1943.

217. Status Report, 25 Aug. 1943, App. 4, this study.

218. *Ibid.*

219. HIR, Aug. 1943, 19, figures taken originally from USN and RAF Coastal Command data.

CHAPTER IV

1. Ltr., Hq. AAFAC to all units, AAFAC, 21 April 1943; ltr., Hq. AAFAC to CG AAF, 22 April 1943; ltr., AC/AS, MM&D to CG ASC, 15 May 1943; all in AAFAC file 349.01.

2. Historical Report of Supply and Logistics Subsec., A-4, Hq. AAFAC, n.d., in AAFAC file 913.3.

3. Ltr., Hq. AAFAC to CG AAF, 18 Nov. 1942, in AAFAC file 347.02.

4. Historical Report of Ordnance Sec. Hq. AAFAC, n.d., 3-4 in AAFAC file 246.1.

5. <u>Ibid</u>., 3.

6. Cf. ltr., Hq. AAFAC to CG AAF, 18 Nov. 1942 and 1st ind., Hq. AAF to CG AAFAC, 2 Dec. 1942, in AAFAC file 347.02.

7. Report, Supply and Logistics Subsec. 2-3.

8. Except where otherwise specified, this account of communications is taken from Historical Report, Signal Sec., AAFAC, in AAFAC file 919.

9. This system was adopted, substantially, by the Navy. <u>Ibid</u>. 2.

10. See correspondence in AAFAC file 919.

11. See below, n. 27.

12. For T/O 1-1017, see AAFAC file 919. This squadron on 30 August 1943 consisted of 18 officers, 1 warrant officer, and 209 enlisted men. Report in <u>ibid</u>.

13. Memo for Giles from AFRBQ, n.d., in AAFAC file Operations, Newfoundland.

14. Interview with Maj. McElroy, 12 Feb. 1944.

15. Ltr., Lt. Col. D. E. Muehleisen, AC/S A-3, Hq. 25th AWG to CG AAFAC, 8 May 1943, in AAFAC file 370.3.

16. Memo for Giles from AFRBQ. See n. 8, Chap. III.

17. <u>Ibid</u>.

18. See above, Chap. III.

19. See above, Chap. II.

20. Ltr., Hq. AAFAC to CG AAF, 5 April 1943, in AAFAC file 560.1.

21. Memo for Giles from AFRBQ. See n. 8, Chap. III.

22. R&R, comment 1, 13 April 1943, Bomb. Br., AFRBQ to Allocations and Programs Div., AFOCR, and comment 2, Allocations and Program Div. to Bomb. Branch, AFRBQ, in AAFAC file 241.8.

23. As shipping losses continued to increase in the spring of 1942, Dr. Edward L. Bowles, technical advisor to the Assistant Secretary of War for Air, urged that every effort be made to develop radar as the most promising of the new antisubmarine weapons. Memo for S/W from Dr. Bowles 20 May 1942, in AAFAC files 113.3. General Arnold, on 30 May 1942, ordered the Director of Technical Services to establish the SADU with headquarters at Langley Field. Its mission was declared (1) to be the development of tactics and technique of antisubmarine warfare, using all special devices available or under development, (2) to act as an experimental group, (3) to participate in search and attack, and (4) to train crews in the use of antisubmarine devices and techniques. It was placed under the command of the Commanding General, AAF, with operational control vested in the Commanding General, First Air Force. Ltr., Maj. Gen. M. F. Harmon, C/AS, to AFDTS, 30 May 1942, in AAFAC files 113.3; Maj. Gen. Eisenhower, AC/S to CG AAF, 3 June 1942, in AAFAC file 400.2. The unit was established on 8 June 1942. Constitution Orders, 8 June 1942, AG 320-3 (6-6-42) MR-M-AF; GO #24, 16 June 1942, AAB Langley Field, in AAFAC file 400.2. Although radar provided the principal challenge to research the new organization attacked a large number of technical problems. On 27 January 1943, Col. W. C. Dolan, commanding officer of the unit, reported 58 projects of which 34 had already been completed, mostly dealing with improvements in locating instruments, in aids to navigation and communication, and in lethal agents. SADU maintained liaison with the several research agencies, working on related projects for both Army and Navy. See History, 1st Sea-Search Attack Group, in AFHI files 1878-21.

24. Historical Report by Col. E. R. Casey, Research Coordinator, AAFAC, Aug. 1943, in AAFAC file 400.

25. Ibid., 2.

26. Ibid.

27. Historical Report of Col. R. C. Kugel, officer in charge of training, Hq. AAFAC, n.d., 20, in AAFAC files.

28. Historical Report by Research Coordinator, 6. See also Reports of the Research Coordinator, 20 Jan. 1943, 3 March 1943, 5 May 1943, 3 June 1943 for all technical developments, in AAFAC file 400.1.

29. Historical Report, Signal Sec., AAFAC, n.d., 7-8, in AAFAC file 919.

30. *Antisubmarine Monthly Summary*, Dec. 1942, 18; Reports of Research Coordinator, 5 May 1943, 3-4, 30 Jan. 1943, 4, 11 June 1943, 4.

31. Historical Report by Research Coordinator, 7. MAD was used effectively by the 1st Sea-Search Attack Group, 32 of its total of 43 sightings having been obtained by this equipment. Being an experimental unit, this group received and tested devices long before they were approved for use by the AAFAC or tested fully under overseas conditions. History, 1st Sea-Search Attack Group, 21 and Ex. II, in AFIHI files, 1878-21.

32. *Ibid.*, 6.

33. *Ibid.*

34. Report of Research Coordinator, 11 June 1943.

35. *Ibid.*, 10 July 1943.

36. Historical Report by Research Coordinator, 7.

37. *Ibid.* Correspondence on these projects is contained in AAFAC files 404, Marine Markers; 408, Air-Sea Rescue; and 402, Camouflage.

38. Standish Report, Conclusion, 12.

39. For data on the B-24 modification, see Historical Report by Research Coordinator; Report of Capt. McGuffin on the Modified B-24, n.d. in AAFAC file 241.42; MIR, June 1943, 37; correspondence in AAFAC file 241.42.

40. Historical Report by Research Coordinator, 7-8. Cf. R&R, AFAEP to AO/AS Training, 5 June 1943, in AAFAC file 001.1.

41. *Ibid.*, 4.

42. MIR, Aug. 1943, 38.

43. Historical Report of Research Coordinator, 4-5.

44. *Ibid.*, 9.

45. The following account of training problems deals only with that aspect of the subject under the direct supervision of Headquarters, AAFAC. Special training problems encountered in overseas operations are dealt with in Chapter III in connection with the respective campaigns. The account here presented, unless otherwise specified, is taken from the Historical Report, Training (see above, n. 27). See also Monthly Antisubmarine Summary, Dec. 1942, 27-28.

46. The 516th, 517th, 518th, 519th, 520th, 521st, and 522d Observation Sqs., formerly of the I Air Support Command, equipped with O-46, O-52, and O-47 type aircraft.

47. Report of A-3, I Bomber Cond., 11 Oct. 1943, quoted in Standish Report.

48. Ltr., AFRDB to CG AAFAC, 10 March 1943, in AAFAC file 241.8.

49. This account of radar training is based on a historical report on the subject submitted by the Signal Section, AAFAC, in AAFAC file 919.

BIBLIOGRAPHICAL STATEMENT

The basic sources for this study were collected by the historian of the Antisubmarine Command and left in the custody of the Historical Division. In addition to this file, several other War Department repositories have provided vital information. A glance at the footnote citations will determine in detail the sources used.

Appendix 1 - Memorandum for Admiral King from General Marshall.

By R&R of 1 July 1943, Maj. Gen. George E. Stratemeyer, Chief of Air Staff, forwarded this memorandum to Assistant Chief of Air Staff Intelligence, with the following comment:

"I consider this memorandum one of the strongest and most important documents which has been signed by the Chief of Staff thus far during the war. It will be incorporated in our historical record."

June 28, 1943.

MEMORANDUM FOR ADMIRAL KING:

The question of responsibility for offensive operations against submarines and that of responsibility for long-range air striking forces are so closely related that a proper solution of one, in my opinion, involves consideration of the other. The tentative Arnold-McNarney-McCain agreement appeared to offer an acceptable solution to both of these issues and solely on that basis I stated to you in my memorandum of June 15 that your proposal to take over anti-submarine air operations appeared to offer a practical solution to a vexing problem which has adversely affected the efficiency of our aerial war effort.

I should state here that in all of these Army and Navy air discussions I have tried very carefully to hold myself to a position from which I could consider the problems from a somewhat detached and I hope, purely logical basis. As I remarked in the meeting of the Joint Chiefs of Staff the other day I feel that the present state of procedure between the Army and Navy is neither economical nor highly efficient and would inevitably meet with public condemnation were all the facts known. I have been hopeful that during the actual war effort we could manage our business in such a manner as to be spared the destructive effects of reorganizational procedure. But I am becoming more and more convinced that we must put our own house in order, and quickly, in order to justify our obligation to the country. I feel this very strongly because it is plain to me, however it may appear to others, that our present procedure is not at all what it should be.

Feeling as I do that the two questions involved are part and parcel of the same problem I believe that the Committee on Missions of the Army and Navy should be given both questions in their entirety for appropriate recommendation, or that we should formalize the entire Arnold-McNarney-McCain agreement. The latter procedure promises earlier, and I believe, more satisfactory results as it appears rather likely that the Committee may reach an impasse in the matter as the result of past strong prejudices and bitter discussions.

There is a further and most important consideration involved. The Secretary of War has declared himself emphatically in a letter to General McNarney that unless the entire Arnold-McNarney-McCain agreement is accepted by the Navy he is unwilling to consent to the transfer of Army anti-submarine airplanes to the Navy and that if the matter is taken to the President he desires to be heard by him on the subject.

Under the circumstances I propose that you and I endeavor to reach an agreement along the following lines (which I believe represent the substance of the Arnold-McNarney-McCain agreement), to be made available to the Committee:

<u>a</u>. The Army is prepared to withdraw Army air forces from antisubmarine operations at such time as the Navy is ready to take over those duties completely.

<u>b</u>. Army anti-submarine airplanes would be continued in that service as long as the Navy has need for them.

<u>c</u>. Army anti-submarine B-24 airplanes would be turned over to the Navy in such numbers as they could be replaced by Navy combat B-24s.

<u>d</u>. The Navy is requested to submit a schedule on which the Army can turn over their planes to the Navy and draw Navy replacement B-24s.

<u>e</u>. The Fleet Air Wings which the Navy proposes to station along the Atlantic and Pacific Coasts will contain no striking forces but will be restricted to airplanes capable of undertaking such off-shore patrol as is necessary, in addition to pure anti-submarine operations.

<u>f</u>. The Navy agrees that all long-range striking forces for the defense of the Western Hemisphere and for active operations in other theaters will be assigned as an Army responsibility.

<u>g</u>. Long-range patrol planes assigned to Fleet Air Wings are for the primary purpose of conducting off-shore patrol, relieving the Army strategic striking forces from this duty.

This agreement to the transfer of long-range aircraft for anti-submarine operations makes it clear that such transfer does not establish a basis for the duplication of the long-range air striking force now in being in the Army. Such duplication, if permitted, would be patently uneconomical and would result in an unavoidable drain on our resources.

Meanwhile the Army Anti-Submarine Command will continue to function as at present, insuring that no detriment to the war effort will occur as a result of any delay which may accrue while this matter is being properly settled.

In all of this matter I am inclined to the belief that it bears a marked similarity to the Army problem of divisional organization. A divisional commander knows, for example, that he can handle the artillery and engineers more efficiently if they are all organic parts of the division and do not include elements attached for a particular operation. Practically every division commander therefore presses for a larger artillery and engineer permanent complement and resists the policy of providing reinforcements for particular operations from Army Corps and Army troop pools. We recognize the division commander's point of view as to efficiency, but we also must recognize that such an arrangement is wasteful in the extreme because it involves the immobilization, as it were, of large bodies of troops in order that each division commander may have all of the units that he may require on a particular occasion, always under his control.

The same applies to anti-aircraft and to anti-tank guns, and considerable feeling is constantly displayed regarding these units by the interested commanders. But it requires only a little arithmetical calculation to determine that such a procedure would be so wasteful of manpower and also would so increase the burden of logistical requirements that the gain in divisional efficiency would be heavily offset by the losses in other directions. This has been a continuing problem in the Army since 1917 but I think the Navy has had little of it to contend with until this question of air striking forces has arisen and virtually another Army, in the shape of Marines, is in process of being established. Naval commanders will feel that they can work more efficiently if they have Naval, Air and Marine units, as a homogeneous force, and undoubtedly they can. But on the other hand if this argument is carried to its ultimate conclusion it means the consolidation of the Army and Navy.

(Sgd) G. C. MARSHALL

Chief of Staff.

Appendix 2 - Attacks on enemy submarines by aircraft of the Antisubmarine Command.

The following tables, prepared by the Antisubmarine Command, have been checked with COMINCH lists, as published in U. S. Fleet Antisubmarine Bulletin, monthly to date, with variations noted as follows:

Attacks on U-boats by aircraft of the 479th Group:

   #3, 20 Jul 43, COMINCH assessment, D
   #4, 28 Jul 43,   "   "   F
   #5, 28 Jul 43,   "   "   A

   Recapitulation: Known sunk 3
                    Probably sunk 0
                    Probably severely damaged 1
                    Insufficient evidence of damage 2

Attacks on U-boats by aircraft of the 480th Group:

   #5, 9 Feb 43, COMINCH assessment, G
   #7, 10 Feb 43,   "   "   G
   #9, 2 Mar 43,   "   "   F
   #12, 7 Apr 43,   "   "   G

   Recapitulation: No damage   8
                    Inconclusive 1

ATTACKS ON U-BOATS BY PLANES OF THE 479TH ANTISUBMARINE GROUP IN EUROPEAN THEATER OF OPERATIONS

NOTES:
1. A – Sunk; B – Probably Sunk; C – Probably severely damaged to the extent that sub will not reach port; D – Probably severely damaged; F – Insufficient evidence of damage; G – No damage; J – Insufficient data for analysis, or inconclusive.
2. UBAT – Coastal Command Form UBAT; IBM – Coxdech International Business Machine Anti-Submarine Attack Assessment Reports; U/B Assess. Pm. – Coastal Command U-Boat Attack Assessment Form; CC – Coastal Command, PIR – Periodic Intelligence Report, 479th Antisub. Gp., PIR – Daily Intelligence Report, 479th Antisub. Gp.
3. The four principal ocean-going combat types of U-Boat are: 517-ton, 740-ton, home operational; 1200-ton, cruiser; and 1600-ton, mine-laying and supply (milch cow).
4. All attacks on U/B by this Group were in the Bay of Biscay area, and all missions are antisubmarine patrol missions.
5. S/E – Special Equipment.

					U-BOAT						ASSESSMENT			
No.	DATE	PILOT	SQDN.	TYPE CONTACT	POSITION	TYPE	CAMOUFLAGE	POSTURE	NO. OF DC'S RELEASED	AA FIRE	DAMAGE TO A/C	REMARKS	COMINCH	ADMIRALTY	SUPPORTING DOCUMENTS
1	18 Jul 43	1st Lt. W. R Young	4	S/E-20 mi.	4647N 1121W	Unknown	Unknown	Surfaced	8	None	None	A/C homed on U/B, sighting wake. Pilot released 4 DC's, on each of two runs, attacking from starboard quarter and bow at 200 mph. DC's estimated to have straddled U/B track on first attack. Extreme speed, in fear of losing U/B, resulted in bombing inaccuracy. Good use of radar and cloud cover on approach.	F	None	UBAT, STK/182, 18 Jul 43; PIR #1; IBM, 9 Sep 43
2	20 Jul 43	1st Lt. C. F. Callaher	19	S/E-13 mi.	4510N 0943W	517-ton	Grey	Surfaced	7	Yes	Hits on port fuselage, port inner engine cut – could not be feathered	Sighted two 740-ton surfaced U/B's, after S/E contact at 24 mi. Two RAF A/C also present. Encountered AA on approach, but lost U/B's in intervening rain squall. A/C later homed on 517-tonner, approaching from port quarter. DC's exploded close to U/B. Engine troubles prevented second attack. RAF Halifax relieved A/C and straddled stricken U/B, hastening end. Prisoners later rescued.	A	A	IBM, 9 Sep 43; Ltr, CC, 15 Aug 43; U/B Assess. Pm. #201, 20 Jul 43
3	20 Jul 43	1st Lt. H. E. Dyment	19	Unknown	Unknown	Unknown	Unknown	Surfaced	Unknown	Yes	Lost	A/C failed to return from mission – probably shot down by U/B. British Admiralty believes damage forced U/B to return to base at once.	A	D	IBM, 9 Sep 43; Ltr, CC, 2 Sep 43; PIR #1
4	28 Jul 43	Major S D McElroy	4	S/E-9 mi.	4605N 0933W	740-ton	Grey	Decks awash	8	Yes	Fuse box, radio, and instruments on No. 2 & 3 engines damaged.	On first attack, A/C made run from port quarter, but DC's hung up – interlocker failure – and U/B crash dived. S/E rendered unserviceable during dive. 4 hrs. later, U/B resurfaced and visual sighting reestablished. A/C attacked directly down U/B track from ahead, straining 6 depth charges across U/B under 5 secs, when DC's released. Explosions on U/B track, last DC obliterating swirl. Results – large oil patch and solid debris.	D	F	IBM, 9 Sep 43; Ltr, CC, 2 Sep 43; UBAT, 28 Jul 43
5	28 Jul 43	1st Lt. A. J. Hamer	4	Visual – 5 mi.	4653N 0225W	740-ton	Grey-Green-brown	Surfaced	12	Yes	No. 1 engine put out of action; hits on fuselage.	A/C attacked out of sun from port beam, as U/B began evasive action. 8 DC's released, straddling C/T. Heavy AA silenced by A/C guns. Two men seen to fall in sea from U/B. Second run, 4 DC's dropped, w/6 jammed and U/B flak again intense. RAF Liberator joined in kill, after damage to A/C U/B submerged, then first – two large oil patches and air bubbles seen. Excellent attack in face of heavy enemy fire.	B	A	IBM, 9 Sep 43; Ltr, CC, 21 Aug 43; U/B Assess. Pm. #211, 4 Aug 43; PIR #4

260

ATTACKS ON U-BOATS BY PLANES OF THE 479TH ANTISUBMARINE GROUP IN EUROPEAN THEATER OF OPERATIONS

DATE	PILOT	SQDN.	TYPE CONTACT	POSITION	U-BOAT TYPE	CAMOUFLAGE	POSTURE	NO. OF DC'S RELEASED	AA FIRE	DAMAGE TO A/C	ASSESSMENT COMINCH	ASSESSMENT ADMIRALTY	REMARKS	SUPPORTING DOCUMENTS
30 Jul 43	1st Lt. A. L. Leal	19	Visual	4510N 1030W	Unknown	Unknown	Surfaced	None	Yes	Hits on port bomb bay, severing wires between bombardier's panel and release gear, salvo rods hit, rendering salvo system useless.	G	None	A/C joined two RAF planes in multiple attack on three U/B's traveling in formation, after intercepting sighting report. Each plane selected specific U/B target, as A/C attacked, flak caused damage, making further action impossible. Both British and British sloop carried out destruction of remaining U/B. All three subs were sunk.	PIR #1
2 Aug 43	Capt. J. L. Hamilton	4	S/E-20 mi.	4620N 0955W	740-ton	Dark grey	Surfaced	12	Yes	Hit on left wheel.	A	A	A/C attacked out of sun hoping to effect surprise. Light flak encountered on approach and A/C spent 725 rds. to rake U/B on decks. All DC's released at once accidentally, and U/B was completely straddled. Sub lifted out of water, then settled quickly by the stern, sank 10 secs. later. 15 men seen in water, together with wood debris and oil patch. Dingy dropped to survivors - 5 mm climbed aboard. Two British A/C arrived at scene later.	U/B Assess. Ph. #531, 13 Aug 43; IR, CC, 2 Sep 43; USAT, STW/107, 2 Aug 43; IEM, 9 Sep 43
7 Sep 43	1st Lt. J. O. Bolin	19	Visual - 15 mi.	4514N 1013W	Unknown	Unknown	Decks awash	5	None	None	None	None	A/C noted three Beaufighters in vicinity of U/B, preparing to attack, and own A/C attacked sub 75 secs. after submergence. 2 hrs. later, A/C sighted supposed periscope wake and dropped DC's, which straddled. Testimony of crew and photos later revealed wake to be smoke or flame floats rather than sub. Local evaluation - J.	DIR #33

RECAPITULATION

NUMBER OF U-BOATS ATTACKED   8

    S/E Contacts   4
    Visual Contacts   3
    Unknown   1

NUMBER OF ATTACKS IN WHICH AA FIRE ENCOUNTERED   6

RESULTS TO ENEMY U-BOATS*

    Known Sunk   2
    Probably Sunk   2
    Probably Severely Damaged   2
    Insufficient Evidence of Damage   1
    No Damage   1
    Inconclusive   1

* Cominch Assessments are adopted, except in the case of 1st Lt. H. K. Dyment.

ATTACKS ON U-BOATS BY PLANES OF THE 480TH ANTISUBMARINE GROUP

NOTES:
1. A – Sunk; B – Probably Sunk; C – Probably severely damaged to the extent that sub will not reach port; D – Probably severely damaged; E – Probably slightly damaged; F – Insufficient evidence of damage; G – No damage; J – Insufficient data for analysis, or inconclusive.
2. USAF – Coastal Command Form USAF; IBM – Comtnch International Business Machine Anti-Submarine Attack Assessment Reports; U/B Assess Fm. – Coastal Command U-Boat Attack Assessment forms; CC – Coastal Command Form Précis – British Admiralty Précis of Anti-Submarine Attack; ASW-6 – USN Report of Anti-Submarine Action by Aircraft.
3. The four principal ocean-going combat types of U-Boat are: 517-ton, home operational 740-ton, overseas ocean-going 1200-ton, cruiser; and 1600-ton, mine-laying and supply ("milch cow").
4. S/E – Special Equipment S/C – Set Courses; C/T – Conning Tower.
5. Departure of aircraft from scene of a sighting or unsuccessful attack and later return in effort to surprise re-surfacing U-boat is known as gambit or baiting tactics.
6. All attacks made by this Group were either southwest of Ireland, from a base in England, or off the Spanish, Portuguese, and African coasts from a base in French Morocco.

DATE	PILOT	ADS.	MISSION	TYPE CONTACT	POSITION	AREA	U-BOAT TYPE	U-BOAT CAMOUFLAGE	U-BOAT POSTURE	NO. OF DC'S RELEASED	AA FIRE	DAMAGE TO A/C	ASSESSMENT COMINCH	ASSESSMENT ADMIRALTY	REMARKS	SUPPORTING DOCUMENTS
29 Dec 42	F/Lt. D. C. Northrup	1	A/S Patrol	Visual – 2 mi.	5212N 2400W	SW of Ireland	Unknown	Unknown	Surfacing	12	None	None	F	F	A/C obtained S/E contact after sighting green slipper-shaped swirl. C/T observed breaking surface, but dived immediately, disappearing in 20-25 secs. before A/C reached from port's quarter. First two D/C's pinwheeled swirl. Alert lookout and good attack, considering limited time U/B visible. Sub probably severely shaken.	USAF, STR/35, 29 Dec 42; U/B Assess Fm. #396, 20 Jan 43; Ltr. Cominch #00428, 28 Apr 43
31 Dec 42	1st Lt. W. L. Thorne	1	A/S Patrol	S/E – 8 mi.	5120N 2050W	SW of Ireland	750-ton	Dark grey	Surfaced	9		None	C	C	A/C homed on contact, sighted U/B at 5 mi. in very rough sea, no wake. A/C attacked about starboard beam as U/B began to C/T. After straddle about C/T, A/C circled, 300 ft. diameter oil patch and bubbles seen. A/C adopted gambit tactics, returning after 50 mins., but could not locate oil patch. Well planned and executed attack – serious damage to sub. S/E very efficient to pick up contact in prevailing sea conditions.	USAF, STR/84, 31 Dec 42; U/B Assess Fm. #33; Pr. #35, 8 Jan 43; Ltr. Cominch #00428, 28 Apr 43
6 Feb 43	1st Lt. W. E. Sands	1	A/S Patrol	Visual – 2½ mi.	4612N 1715W	SW of Ireland	517-ton	Grey	Surfaced	8		None	G	G	A/C dived out of sun to attack from starboard quarter. 6 DC's released, seen to overshoot, only two exploded. Second attack from port beam. A/C attempted to release 6 more DC's – four hung up, others dude. No hits on U/B hull. Well executed attack modified by failure in armament and release.	USAF, STR/69, 6 Feb 43; U/B Assess Fm. #433; Précis, 15 Feb 43; 8/1 USAAF, 6 Feb 43; Ltr. Cominch #00428
9 Feb 43	1st Lt. E. O. Butto	1	A/S Patrol	Visual – 3½ mi.	4840N 2035W	SW of Ireland	Unknown	Unknown	Surfaced	6		None	F	F	C/T sighted, no wake apparent in rough sea. A/C attacked immediately. A/C attacked with DC's from 8 secs. after U/B submerged. Explosions slightly ahead of swirl. Oil patch seen, presumably DC residue. Probably minor damage to U/B.	USAF, STR/90, 9 Feb 43; U/B Assess, Fm. #433; Précis, 9 Feb 43; Fm. #433, 22 Feb 43; Ltr. Cominch #00428, 28 Apr 43

ATTACKS ON U-BOATS BY PLANES OF THE 480TH ANTISUBMARINE GROUP

NO	DATE	PILOT	SQDN.	MISSION	TYPE CONTACT	POSITION	AREA	U-BOAT TYPE	CAMOUFLAGE	POSTURE	NO. OF DC'S RELEASED	AA FIRE	DAMAGE TO A/C	ASSESSMENT COMINCH	ASSESSMENT ADMIRALTY	REMARKS	SUPPORTING DOCUMENTS
5	9 Feb 43	Capt. L. F. Jarmazin	2	A/S Patrol	Visual – 4 mi.	4743N 1753W	SW of Ireland	Unknown	Unknown	Diving	4	None	None		G	After spotting wake and C/T, A/C had S/E contact at 3 mi. in very rough sea. DC's released from U/B starboard quarter 40 sec. after submergence. Explosions seen along track of U/B, last plume at spot of swirl. Two patches of oily scum noted. A/C resumed patrol, later spotted periscope and feather at 4 mi. in 4721N 2068W. Periscope dipped at 2-2½ mi., and although attack was attempted, 35 sec. later, all DC's hung up.	U/B Assess. Pw. #441, 9 Feb 43; Précis, 9 Feb 43; U/2 USAAF, 9 Feb 43; UBAT, STF/93, 9 Feb 43
6	9 Feb 43	1st Lt. W. L. Sanford	2	A/S Patrol	S/E – 4 mi.	4705N 1834W	SW of Ireland	517-ton	Dark	Surfaced	12	None	None	B	B	A/C homed on contact, sighted surfaced 517-ton, grey U/B. C/T had disappeared over 1 min. as A/C reached attack position. No attack; W/G waved, 17 min later, visual contact at 4 mi., almost simultaneous with w/B, on a collar U/B. As A/C attacked with 6 DC's from port bow, U/B stern was completely exposed, stick over-shot, but lifted U/B out of water. C/T again visible. Second attack with 3 DC's and W/? straddled U/B. On third run, sub had starboard list. Before 3 DC's were released, water churned, and U/B disappeared on even keel – no swirl. Two explosions seen. Circular patch of foam fluid, not DC residue, with diameter greater than U/B length noted.	Précis, 7/2 USAAF, 10 Feb 43; U/B Assess. Pw. #440, UBAT, STF/92, 10 Feb 43; Pw. #450, Lt. Cominch #06328, 28 Apr 43
7	10 Feb 43	1st Lt. J. B. Kraybill	2	A/S Patrol	Visual 2 mi.	4725N 1450W	SW of Ireland	712-ton	Unknown	Surfaced	None	Yes	None	None	None	Two attacks on U/B from starboard and port quarters respectively. DC's hung up in both cases, and A/C strafed U/B deck silencing AA cannon. On initial approach, U/B fired 2 red star recognition signals. A/C tried third run, but U/B crash-dived. Baiting tactics employed. U/B negative. High explosive and heroism displayed in attempting three attacks in face of enemy fire, after failure of DC release	Précis, P/2 USAAF, 10 Feb 43; UBAT, STF/91, U/B Assess. Pw. #450, 10 Feb 43
8	20 Feb 43	1st Lt. W. S. Johnson	1	A/S Patrol	Visual 3 mi.	4930N 2155W	SW of Ireland	500-ton	Dark green	Surfaced	6	None	None	D	D	A/C dived to attack through cloud from port quarter. DC's released while U/B fully surfaced, straddled fore of U/B. C/T disappeared 15 sec. after explosions in no noticeable foamy motion. Bluish-grey oil patch, 300-400' long together with small bubbles rising in center observed 1 min. later. Baiting tactics used – negative results. No S/E contact, possible due to rough sea.	UBAT, STF/940, 20 Feb 43; Précis, U/1 USAAF, 20 Feb 43; U/B Assess. Pw. #450, TWI, USAAF, London, 4 Mar 43; Pw. #452, 20 Feb 43; HEM, 15 Jul 43

ATTACKS ON U-BOATS BY PLANES OF THE 480TH ANTISUBMARINE GROUP

NO.	DATE	PILOT	SQDN.	MISSION	TYPE CONTACT	POSITION	AREA	U-BOAT TYPE	CAMOUFLAGE	POSTURE	NO. OF DC'S RELEASED	AA FIRE	DAMAGE TO A/C	ASSESSMENT CONTACT	ASSESSMENT ADMIRALTY	REMARKS	SUPPORTING DOCUMENTS
9	2 Mar 43	Capt. K. L. Lucke	1	A/S Patrol	Visual - 2½ mi.	4710N 2123W	SW of Ireland	740-ton	Black C/T	Surfaced	8	None	None		F	A/C dived to attack from U/B port beam. DC's dropped 12 sec. after submergence. Explosions straddled track 2 swirl-lengths ahead of swirl. DC residue only evidence of attack. Gambit tactics used to no avail. U/B probably severely shaken by near miss ahead. S/E temporarily inoperative at time of sighting.	USAT, STG/66, 2 Mar 43, Prélim. F/1 USAAF, 2 Mar 43
10	22 Mar 43	1st Lt. A L Sanford	2	A/S Sweep	Visual - 5 mi.	3015N 1813W	Off Africa	740-ton	White	Surfaced	4	None	None	A	F	A/C, using cloud cover, attacked from starboard beam. Three explosions fell short, 110', 70', and 10' respectively, while a fourth was 50' long. U/B did not use evasive tactics, nor make attempt to dive. Explosion aft of C/T caused U/B to settle stern first at 45° angle, sinking out of sight 55 sec. after explosion. Large cylindrical object, debris, several survivors and oil patch seen. Positive kill, the result of well executed attack	ASW-6 #1, 22 Mar 43, 2037 ANUG, 1Eb, 15 Jul 43
11	7 Apr 43	1st Lt. W. E. Torre	1	A/C Sweep	S/E - 30 mi.	3435N 2456W	Off Africa	740-ton	Cream colored	Surfaced	6	Yes	None	None	None	Contact homed A/C on to U/B, 12 mi. ahead. During approach, U/B put up accurate AA barrage driving A/C off despite W/O fire from planes. A/C requested assistance and B-24 arrived 25 min. later. Each plane stopped to draw U/B fire, while other A/C went in, but U/B continually evaded attack with "S" turns and AA fire. First A/C dropped DC's—3 duds, others struck ahead on track, having reached heading in SW direction. New AA tactics unfamiliar to crew, who were never under fire before, shook fliers to great bone, Extensive use of S/E contact worthy of note.	ASW-6 #2, 6 Apr 43, 1st Area
12	7 Apr 43	2nd Lt. H. G. Easterling	1	A/S Sweep	Visual - 5 mi.	3435N 2456W	Off Africa	740-ton	Cream colored	Surfaced	6	Yes	Hits - negligible	None	None	A/C "P" received sighting report from "T", spotted U/B firing all AA guns, it it maneuvered in circles and "S" turns. Planes decided on coordinated plan of attack, involving feint runs, making definite U/B fire, while constant firing. "E" made run up U/B track, but prior to release of DC's, sub made hard turn to right, and A/C turned with it. 4 DC's struck water 600' short, other two 150' ahead, all on U/B track. 1050 rds. fired during attack. U/B seen on surface headed northwest	ASW-6 #2, 7 Apr 43, 1st Area

ATTACKS ON U-BOATS BY PLANES OF THE 480TH ANTISUBMARINE GROUP

DATE	PILOT	SER.	MISSION	TYPE CONTACT	POSITION	AREA	TYPE	CAM'FLAGE	POSTURE	No. DC'S RELEASED	AA FIRE	DAMAGE TO A/C	CONNCH	ADMIRALTY	REMARKS	SUPPORTING DOCUMENTS
	Northrup	2	S/V cover	Visual 4 mi.	41°28'N 18°W	West of Portugal	Unknown	Unknown	Surfaced	4	None	None	F	None	A/C flying 20 mi ahead-and-astern search pattern, when U/B sighted. A/C dived to attack from starboard quarter, but U/B already under when run was made. 3 DC explosions observed, one disturbed U/B track. 75' diameter patch seen as A/C circled area for 1 hr., later rejoined C/V.	TBM, 12 Aug 43, A=M=5 #5, 7 May 43, 2nd Area
		2	cover	Visual 6 mi.	41°03'N 16°W	West of Portugal	Unknown	Unknown	Surfaced	4	None	None	F	None	C/T disappeared 25 sec. then point of release reached. A/C made run from dead ahead, DC's dropped in train - fourth exploded at forward edge of swirl. No surface indications left by U/B. A/C resumed G/V cover after 15 min. Probable that U/B was below lethal range of DC's.	TBM, 12 Aug 43, A=M=5 #6, 7 May 43, 2nd Area
		2	Sweep	Visual	41°08'N 11°W	Off Africa	Type 1	Dark brown	Surfaced	4	None	None	E	None	C/T disappeared 15 sec. before release point reached, stern still visible at 4-5°° angle when run was made.D/C attacked from port storm, making. U/B forward motion had slowed appreciably. 3 DC explosions, one directly over C/T, two straddle 1 V/L. Stern disappeared, b.t. DC's lifted out of water again, forcing bow down. Large bubble and oil slick, 200' long, 8' wide appeared. A/C circled scene for 30 min, then S/C for base.	TBM, P Aug 43, A=M=5 #7, 15 May 43, 2nd Area
		1	Sweep	S/E 2 mi.	13°54' 21°10'W	Off Africa	740-ton	Olive drab	Surfaced	3	Yes	None	F	None	A/C homed on contact, ascended to use cloud cover, and sighted U/B at 1-2 mi. First attack 90° to port, tried to release 6 DC's - only one fell. Made reverse attack from star'card, DC's hung up. U/B used violent evasive tactics. A/C circled, tripped one DC manually for test. On third run from 90° to port, 2 DC's dropped. Ex-plosion 30' and 60' short of track. DC residue and phosphorescent U/B wake seen after attack. A/C used cloud cover to check DC hang up and M/G jam.	TBM, 12 Aug 43, A=M=5 #8, 3 Jun 43, 1st Area
		2	Sweep	S/E 7 mi.	35°34' 18°W	Off Africa	517-ton	Unknown	Decks awash	9	Yes	None	E	None	Initial S/E contact at 22 mi., disappeared when A/C lat down to 100'. Second contact proved to be U/B, spotted at 1 mi. U/B opened fire immediately with M/G and cannon. A/C started dead ahead run, firing M/G on run from starboard beam at 80° flt., 4 DC's released, explosions 10-20' ahead of U/B stern and straddling. U/B disappeared bow first, no swirl, no churning - possibly indicating damage to screws. Flame float dropped to guide attack of other DC's. Large oil slick and pieces of debris seen.	TBM, 12 Aug 43, A=M=5 #9, 19 Jun 43, 2nd Area

274

ATTACKS ON U-BOATS BY PLANES OF THE 480TH ANTISUBMARINE GROUP

							U-BOAT			NO. OF DC'S RELEASED	AA FIRE	DAMAGE TO A/C	ASSESSMENT		REMARKS	SUPPORTING DOCUMENTS
DATE	PILOT	SQDN.	MISSION	TYPE CONTACT	POSITION	AREA	TYPE	CAMOUFLAGE	POSTURE				COMINCH	ADMIRALTY		
6 Jul 43	2nd Lt. J. W. Adams	2	C/V Cover	Visual – 8 mi.	3928N 1426W	West of Portugal	517-ton	Light grey	Decks awash	4	None	None	G	None	First run in at 100', U/B dived and C/T was under 8 sec. when release point reached. U/B silhouette still visible at 15' depth. A/C attempted to release 6 DC's – all hung up. Second run from port, only one explosion at leading edge of swirl. Large brown patch seen – nothing further.	IBM, 9 Sep 43, A-A-5 #11, 6 Jul 43, 2nd Avon
7 Jul 43	1st Lt. T. H. Isley	1	A/S Sweep	S/E – 15 mi.	3750N 1430W	Off Africa	517-ton	Light grey	Surfaced	6	None	None	D	None	A/C homed contact, spotted U/B at 8 mi. Run in from 200', 10 sec. after C/T disappeared. DC explosions straddled U/B track 200' ahead of apex of swirl. Large oil bubbles and DC residue rose 15 sec. after attack, eruptions continued 5 min. Immediate brown stain 40 min. – nothing further. Skillfully executed attack.	IBM, 9 Sep 43, A-A-5 #12, 7 Jul 43, 1st Avon
7 Jul 43	1st Lt. W. S. McConnell	1	A/S Sweep	S/E – 7 mi.	3740N 1530W	Off Africa	517-ton	Slate grey	Surfaced	7	Yes	Hit on nose, hydraulic system, radio compass, instruments unserviceable.	B	None	Visual sighting almost instantaneous with contact. A/C dived to attack from 90° port. DC's straddled U/B, which appeared to break in two, aft of C/T. Later section rose 10-12' out of water, settled with no forward motion. Fire from U/B and 3 of crew slightly A/C also strafed sub's deck. Excellent attack, brought damaged A/C safely to base.	IBM, 9 Sep 43, A-A-5 #13, 7 Jul 43, 1st Avon
8 Jul 43	1st Lt. J. H. Darden	2	A/S Sweep	S/E – 16 mi.	4037N 1314W	West of Portugal	517-ton	Dark grey	Surfaced	6	Yes	Hits on nose, fuselage, wings, and props. Bomb bay damaged	B	None	A/C homed on contact, using cloud cover, for approach out of sun. A/C sighted U/B 8 mi. away, dived and passed over bow at 50', releasing 4 DC's. Explosions straddled bow and C/T. AA from U/B hit nose A/C and stopped on run. Sub was circling, out of control in tight turns, trailing stream of brown oil and losing headway. A/C made second run at 50', but AA fire hit bomb bay, preventing release of DC's. Third run, as U/B pushed, settled, and slipped under stern first. DC's released manually. Entire area literally covered with oil. LNG received minor wounds.	
9 Jul 43	1st Lt. G. J. Demann	2	A/S Sweep	Visual – 12 mi.	3828N 1336W	West of Portugal	517-ton	Grey	Decks awash	4	None	None	B	None	A/C at 150', attacked after U/B submerged 17 sec. First DC exploded 200' ahead of swirl, last seen to detonate at starboard edge of swirl. Third DC remained in very dark color. Large oil slick spread over area. Perfect timing, and good lead.	IBM, 9 Sep 43, A-A-5 #15, 9 Jul 43, 2nd Avon

275

ATTACKS ON U-BOATS BY PLANES OF THE 480TH ANTISUBMARINE GROUP

276

NO.	DATE	PILOT	SQDN.	MISSION	TYPE CONTACT	POSITION	AREA	U-BOAT TYPE	CAMOUFLAGE	POSTURE	NO OF DC'S RELEASED	AA FIRE	DAMAGE TO A/C	A.S.W. ASSESSMENT CONCUR ADMIRALTY		REMARKS	OPERATING AUTHORITY
23	9 Jul 43	1st Lt. T. E. Kuenning	1	A/S Sweep	Visual – 4–5 mi.	3920N 1300W	West of Portugal	517-ton	Slate grey	Surfacing	8	None	None	B	None	First run at 50', 6 DC's dropped across U/B bow. Explosions seen aft of C/T, one short and five over. Other DC's released on second run, detonated aft of C/T along port side. Bow of U/B rose at 45° angle, 15' out of watr, sub then fell back on track, stern first. Both attacks completed 2 min. from time of sighting. Black oil patch seen later.	ltr, Cominch, #03747, 1 Nov 43 AZM-6 #17, 9 Jul 43, 1st Arvn
24	9 Jul 43	1st Lt. W. W. Pomeroy	1	A/S Sweep	Visual – 10 mi.	4015N 1405W	West of Portugal	300-ton	Brown	Surfaced	6	Yes	None	C	None	U/B remained surfaced, firing, from C/T, until strafing silenced AA, as U/C made first run. DC's not released as bomb bay door. required shut. Second attack after C/T disappeared 6 sec. Four explosions, one short, three straddling, U/B track, seen by crew. No visible evidence of damage. Baiting tactics used – black object rising out of short wake seen at 3838N 1422W, disappeared from A/C.	ltr, #03747, AZM-6 #19, 9 Jul 43, 1st Arvn
25	10 Jul 43	Capt. L. L. Jarnagin	2	A/S Sweep	Visual – 6 mi.	3917N 1332W	West of Portugal	517-ton	Light grey	Surfaced	8	None	None	C	None	A/C came in from 10', released 6 DC's which straddled 50-10' ahead of track. U/B turned sharply to starboard, making no attempt to dive or fire AA, although 4 of crew on deck. A/C made second run from port, releasing DC's 25 sec. after U/B submerged. Explosions straddled U/B track. Large bubbles and oil slick appeared.	ltr, Cominch, #03747, 1 Nov 43 AZM-6 #24, 10 Jul 43, 2nd Arvn
26	11 Jul 43	1st Lt. W. S. McDowell	1	A/S Sweep	S/E – 14 mi.	4124N 1500W	West of Portugal	517-ton	Grey	Surfaced	10	Yes	Hole in right stabilizer.	?	None	A/C sighted U/B at 5 mi., with number of crew in C/T and 1 man running from aft to reach C/T. First run in from 90° port at 100'. 7 DC's dropped all short. U/B AA fire damaged stabilizer on run, but was silenced by M/G. Second attack from 75', 50° to starboard, 30 sec. after U/B went under. DC's straddled track. Visible results – Dull grey geyser and black object after explosions; later, two brownish-black oil slicks, 1. 200' in diameter.	ltr, #03747, AZM-6 #21, 11 Jul 43, 1st Arvn
27	12 Jul 43	2nd Lt. L. Gain	1	A/S Sweep	S/E – 23 mi.	4230N 1630W	West of Spain	740-ton	Light grey	Surfaced	7	None	None	A	None	U/B sighted in rough sea, part of crew on deck, speed 12 knots. A/C descended through overcast, from 5600' to 250' before breaking out, made practicable by use of absolute altimeter. Attack from 35' at 90° from starboard. 5C explosions straddled U/B aft of C/T. Stern blown out of water, disappeared before bow. A/C circled for second run, but spotted 15 survivors in groups in water. Eruption of large oil bubbles and debris also seen. A/C dropped dingy and tried to lay ring of smoke bombs. U/B survivors rescued three days later by HMS Hurricane.	ltr, #03747, 2 Sep 43, AZM-6 #22, 12 Jul 43, 1st Arvn

--- ATTACKS ON U-BOATS BY PLANES OF THE 480TH ANTISUBMARINE GROUP ---

DATE	PILOT	SQDN.	MISSION	TYPE CONTACT	POSITION	AREA	U-BOAT TYPE	CAMOUFLAGE	POSTURE	NO. OF DC'S RELEASED	AA FIRE	DAMAGE TO A/C	ASSESSMENT COMINCH	ASSESSMENT ADMIRALTY	REMARKS	SUPPORTING DOCUMENTS
13 Jul 43	1st Lt. M. S. Cantrell	2	C/V Cover	S/E - 12 mi.	3904N 2008W	East of Portugal	Unknown	Unknown	Surfaced	4	None	None	F	None	A/C sighted wake of U/B at 9 mi. Sub crash dived at 4 mi. at steep angle and stern momentarily protruded at 30°. Sub under 5 sec. when A/C dropped DC's. Explosions straddled 50' ahead of swirl. Series of bubbles and oil patch merging with DC residue, only visible results. Well executed attack, extent of damage depends on amount of forward motion lost in U/B abnormal dive.	Ltr, Cominch, FOIG7, 1 Nov 43; ASW-6 #23, 13 Jul 43, 2nd Area
14 Jul 43	1st Lt. J. M. Pennoyer	2	A/S Sweep	S/E - 19 mi.	4003N 1157W	West of Portugal	517-ton	White	Surfaced	7	Yes	Hits on bomb bay, fuselage, No. 1 engine, hydraulic system, S/E, winging in rear racks shot out.	M	None	A/C homed on contact through cloud cover to make approach out of sun. Spotted U/B 12 mi. away, attacked from port beam at 50°. AA fire from U/B commenced at 3/4 mi. distance. M/G from A/C scored hits on C/T and deck, hitting one gunner in C/T. 6 DC's released on first run, only 1 did damage due to damage sustained. U/B submerged 19 sec. as A/C made second run, with one engine out. DC's selected from undamaged front racks, straddled track ahead of forward swirl. Bubbles and oil slick seen later. 4 - 5 of U/B crew observed in water, believed to have been swept off C/T.	Ltr, 9 Sep 43; ASW-6 #24, 14 Jul 43, 2nd Area

RECAPITULATION

NUMBER OF U-BOATS ATTACKED   29
   S/E Contacts   12
   Visual Contacts   17

NUMBER OF ATTACKS IN WHICH AA FIRE ENCOUNTERED   8

RESULTS TO ENEMY U-BOATS:*

   Known Sunk   2
   Probably Sunk   4
   Probably Damaged to extent that sub
     will not reach port.   1
   Probably Severely Damaged   5
   Probably Slightly Damaged   6
   Insufficient Evidence of Damage   6
   No Damage   3
   Inconclusive

* Cominch assessments are adopted whenever available.

ATTACKS ON U-BOATS BY AAF ANTISUBMARINE COMMAND PLANES IN LATIN AMERICAN THEATER OF OPERATIONS

> NOTES:
> 1. E - Probably slightly damaged; F - Insufficient evidence of damage; O - No damage.
> 2. IBM - Costruch International Business Machine Anti-Submarine Attack Assessment Reports; ASW-6 - UFM Report of Anti-Submarine Action by Aircraft; ANAL - USN Analysis of Anti-Submarine Action by Aircraft; NOB - Naval Operating Base; DIR - Daily Intelligence Report; ATG - Antisubmarine Wing.
> 3. The four principal ocean-going combat types of U-Boat are: 517-ton, home operational; 740-ton, overseas ocean-going; 1200-ton, cruiser; and 1600-ton, mine-laying and supply ("milch cows").
> 4. S/E - Special Equipment; C/T - Conning Tower.
> 5. Attacks by the 8th Antisubmarine Squadron were made from Zandery Field, Surinam, with B-24 aircraft, while those of the 9th Antisubmarine Squadron were from Trinidad, British West Indies, employing B-18 aircraft.

D.	DATE	PILOT	SQDN	MISSION	TYPE CONTACT	POSITION	AREA	U-BOAT TYPE	U-BOAT CAMOUFLAGE	U-BOAT POSTURE	NO. OF DC'S RELEASED	AA FIRE	DAMAGE TO A/C	COMDCH ASSESSMENT	REMARKS	SUPPORTING DOCUMENTS
1	2 Mar 43	1st Lt. R. Wilson, Jr.	9	A/S Sweep	S/E-17 mi.	10°59N 62°05W	NW of Trinidad	740-ton	White	Surfaced	4	None	None	E	B-18C homed on contact, spotted wake at 3/4 mi. Positively identified as U/B, when directly overhead - high C/T noted. Approach and attack from port bow at 100', DC's exploded in direct line, 50' ahead of swirl, shook A/C crew. U/B visible as bombs released, later diwd. Sub did not sight A/C before pass was made. WOB, Trinidad 25th Mar Op. estimate heavy damage to U/B.	IBM, 15 Jul 43, ASW-6 #13, 2 Mar 43, DIR #26, 2 Mar 43, 9th AvOn
2	3 Mar 43	1st Lt. L. J. Cormier	9	Killer hunt	S/E-8 mi.	11°02N 61°55W	NW of Trinidad	740-ton	White	Surfaced	4	Yes	None	E	B-18B, flying on dark night, had contact in position of previous attack by another plane 2 hrs. earlier. Visually spotted U/B at 3/4 mi., turned landing lights on - met by AA tracers. Lights extinguished, and second pass made, but U/B disappeared, after 2 hr. square search, 4 more contacts obtained, DC's released on visual sighting on fourth run, stimulated U/B, at least two explosions within lethal range. Sub dived after attack. No visible results due to poor visibility.	ASW-6 #14, 3 Mar 43, 9th AvOn DIR #27, 3 Mar 43, 9th AvOn ANAL #0230, 14 Apr 43
3	19 Jul 43	2nd Lt. W. F. Destiche	8	A/S Patrol	S/E-25 mi.	05°56N 48°40W	NE of French Guiana	Unknown	Unknown	Surfaced	5	Yes	Hits on tail and prop	F	B-24 spotted U/B at range of 5/E contact, attacked from port at 100', DC's exploded 50' short and on U/B course small oil slick resulted. U/B fired cannon and M/G, slightly wounding two of A/C crew, and forcing A/C to return to base after 30 min. Later information indicates U/B sunk by USN Catalina on 21 Jul 43 in 03°56N 48°45W, approximately 72 mi. from position of damaging attack by Army A/C.	IBM, 9 Sep 43, DIR, 19 Jul 43, 8th AvOn 8th AvOn DIR #243, 22 Jul 43, 26th AFHD DIR #258, 6 Aug 43, 26th AFHD DIR #262, 10 Aug 43, 26th AFHD

874

ATTACKS ON U-BOATS BY AAF ANTISUBMARINE COMMAND PLANES IN LATIN AMERICAN THEATER OF OPERATIONS

DATE	PILOT	SQDN.	MISSION	TYPE CONTACT	POSITION	AREA	U-BOAT TYPE	U-BOAT CAMOUFLAGE	U-BOAT POSTURE	NO. OF DC'S RELEASED	AA FIRE	DAMAGE TO A/C	COMINCH ASSESSMENT	REMARKS	SUPPORTING DOCUMENTS
24 Jul 43	1st Lt. G. M. Richmond	8	A/S Patrol	Visual – 3-5 mi.	07°14′N 50°05′W	NE of French Guiana	Unknown	Unknown	Surfaced	5	Yes	Hits on left elevator, bomb bay, and No. 3 engine, tail skid shot away.	0	A/C dived to attack from 75', left waist gunner covering approach. At 2 mi., U/B fired with 37 mm AA and .50 cal. M/G. 4 DC's prematurely released, when bullet pierced bomb release panel. Two explosions 50 yds. astern of U/B. Other DC manually dropped 3½ min. after submergence, exploded 200 yds. ahead of swirl. U/B evaded by turning broadside to A/C, causing attack to be made at 90°. Two of crew slightly wounded	IRM, 15 Jul 43; DIR #247, 26 Jul 43 26th ANTS
3 Aug 43	1st Lt. J. W. Roberts	8	A/S Patrol	S/E	13°07′N 68°27′W	Off Venezuela	Unknown	Unknown	Surfaced	None	Yes	None	0	A/C, in running fight with U/B during darkness, lost contact; obtained S/E on same sub 4 hrs. later. U/B fired AA M/G, and star shells. A/C returned with thorn fire from waist, nose, and tail guns. U/B eluded further action by crash dive. Sub too far left for DC attack in both cases.	DIR #257, 5 Aug 43; 26th ANTS; IRM, 9 Sep 43

RECAPITULATION:

NUMBER OF U-BOATS ATTACKED   5

    S/E Contacts   4
    Visual Contacts   1

NUMBER OF ATTACKS IN WHICH AA FIRE ENCOUNTERED   4

RESULTS TO ENEMY U-BOATS:

    Probably Slightly Damaged   2
    Insufficient Evidence of Damage   1
    No Damage   2

ATTACKS ON U-BOATS BY AAF ANTISUBMARINE COMMAND PLANES IN NORTH AMERICAN THEATER OF OPERATIONS

NOTES:
1. B - Probably severely damaged; E - Probably slightly damaged; H - Insufficient evidence of presence of sub; J - Inconclusive data for analysis.
2. IBM - Comlnch International Business Machine Anti-Submarine Attack Assessment Reports; ASW-6 - USN Report of Anti-Submarine Action by Aircraft; ANAL - USN Analysis of Anti-Submarine Action by Aircraft; DIR - Daily Intelligence Report; AWD - Antisubmarine Wing; ANAFSUB - AAF Antisub. Coml. Analysis of Anti-Submarine Action by Aircraft; MIKE - Mission Report.
3. S/E - Special Equipment; s/c - Set Course; DD - Destroyer; C/T - Conning Tower; ASW - Anti-Submarine Warfare; C/V - Convoy.
4. The four principal ocean-going combat types of U-boat are: 517-ton, home operational; 740-ton, overseas ocean-going; 1170-ton, cruiser; and 1600-ton, minelaying and supply (Milch cow).
5. Squadrons carried out the attacks listed below from the following bases: 40th Bomb. Sqdn. (redesignated 4th Antisub. Sqdn. 29 Nov 42) - Mitchel Field, N. Y.; 45th Bomb. Sqdn. (redesignated 2nd Antisub. Sqdn. 5 Mar 43) - Cherry Point, N. C.; 6th, 19th, and 20th Antisub. Sqdns. - Gander Field, Newfoundland; 17th Antisub. Sqdn. - Boca Chica, Key West, Fla.; 18th Antisub. Sqdn. - Langley Field, Va., and 25th Antisub. Sqdn. - Jacksonville, Fla.

NO.	DATE	PILOT	SQDN.	MISSION	TYPE CONTACT	POSITION	AREA	U-BOAT TYPE	U-BOAT CAMOUFLAGE	U-BOAT POSTURE	NO. OF DC'S RELEASED	AA FIRE	DAMAGE TO A/C	COMINCH ASSESSMENT	REMARKS	SUPPORTING DOCUMENTS
1	20 Oct 42	1st Lt. R. A. St. Clair	46	A/S Patrol	Visual - 200 yds.	3357N 7708W	Off Cape Fear	Unknown	Unknown	Submerged	3	None	None	H	A-29 sighted shadow and swirl of U/B, attacked from 100', 2 DC's exploded 100' and 150' ahead of swirl, third DC a dud. Concentric oil slick observed, probably DC residue. A/C remained in vicinity 30 min, then, due to base, S/C for base. Insufficient evidence of U/B, possibly large whale or fish.	MIKE #297, 20 Oct 42, 46th Bomron; ASW-6 #1, 22 Oct 42, 46th Bomron; ANAFSUB, 20 Oct 42
2	23 Nov 42	1st Lt. A. L. Majure	40	A/S Patrol	Visual	3703N 7008W	Off Cape Henry	Unknown	Unknown	Submerged	4	None	None	None	B-18 circled, while DD and corvette laid DC pattern on S/B contact. U/B sighted visually, but contact reestablished when A/C directed ships to oil slick. A/C attacked from 300' on instructions from DD - no visible result. S/C for base after 1 hr., leaving 3 Navy A/C and 2 vessels in area.	MIKE #14, 23 Nov 42, 40th Bomron
3	14 Mar 43	Major C. H. Norman	20	A/S Patrol	Visual	5126N 4820W	Off Newfoundland	Unknown	Unknown	Surfaced	1	None	None	None	B-17 had four sightings in close proximity within 3 hrs, and 45 min., two of which resulted in attacks. DC released during first attack — no claim. Setting tactics used, U/B reloaded in 5159N 4808W, bomb bay doors failed on raid. U/B crash dived at 45°-60° angle, no forward speed. Other sightings in vicinity of 5126N 4820W.	TWX, Halifax fl., 16 Mar 43
4	14 Mar 43	1st Lt. D. H. Busley	20	A/S Patrol	Visual	5117N 4708W	Off Newfoundland	Unknown	Unknown	Submerged	1	None	None	None	B-17 released DC in dive attack - alight oil slick resulted. A/C troubled with failure of bomb bay doors, accounting for use of only one DC. Additional sighting - uneventful. RCAF believes there were 4 U/B's operating, with two duplicate sightings. (See No. 3 above)	TWX, Halifax fl., 16 Mar 43
5	14 Apr 43	1st Lt. S. M. Grider	19	A/S Patrol	Visual - 3/4 mi.	4522N 4115W	SE of Newfoundland	500-ton	Unknown	Deck awash	1	None	None	None	B-17 attacked from 50' with c/t still visible. DC detonated 50'-151' off port quarter - 3 DC's hung up. A/C strafed c/t with 90 rds. from W/G. No visible evidence of damage to U/B.	DIR #129, 15 Apr 43, 25th ANTS

280

ATTACKS ON U-BOATS BY AAF ANTISUBMARINE COMMAND PLANES IN NORTH AMERICAN THEATER OF OPERATIONS

No.	DATE	PILOT	SQDN.	MISSION	TYPE CONTACT	POSITION	AREA	TYPE	U-BOAT CAMOUFLAGE	POSTURE	NO. OF DC'S RELEASED	AA FIRE	DAMAGE TO A/C	COMINCH ASSESSMENT	REMARKS	SUPPORTING DOCUMENTS
6	19 Apr 43	1st Lt. E. J. Dudek	6	A/S Patrol	Visual - 1/2 mi.	5053N 4114W	Off New-foundland	750-ton	Dirty grey	C/T visible	6	None	None	D	B-24 spotted U/B in haze. Picked up attack from 75°, re-leasing DC's 5 sec. after C/T disappeared; U/B stern still visible. Fresh yellow-green oil slick, 30' in diameter, and air bubbles resulted as two DC's straddled diving U/B. Gambit tactics used for 1 hr. 15 min. after attack—nega-tive. Plane S/O for base due to poor weather.	ANAL #262, 19 Apr 43, 6th Arsq ASW-6 F1, 20 Apr 43, 6th Arsq Ltr #001599, 10 Aug 43, Cominch
7	24 Apr 43	Unknown	17	A/S Patrol	Visual - 11 mi.	2340N 8305W	Off Havana, Cuba	Unknown	Grey white	Surfaced	4	None	None	None	B-25 spotted object 300' long, which disappeared after 30 sec., leaving slight disturbance - no avail. Two DC's detonated in area of disturbance. Evalua-tion of Gulf Sea Frontier - possible sub.	DIR #154, 24 Apr 43, 25th AvSq
8	2 May 43	Capt. H. J. Larson	19	C/V Cover	S/E - 15 mi.	5132N 4510W	Off New-foundland	750-ton	Black	Decks awash	4	Yes	None	D	B-17 homed contact and spotted U/B at 3 mi. Attacked from 50°, releasing DC's astride C/T - was still visible - third DC esti-mated direct hit. Results: C/T rose about 3', then settled under; oil slick 400'-500' diameter noted. Gambit tactics adopted, and two 550-bombers one rust color, other black, sighted in 5053N 4503W at half hour interval. W/O used as DC's all expended. In last at-tack, AA encountered, but U/B crew all leaving from men on deck. S/E highly effective in all three attacks.	ASW-6 #2, 3 May 43, 19th Arsq DIR #147, 3 May 43 25th ANSq Ltr #001599, 10 Aug 43, Cominch ANAL #272, 31 Jul 43, 19th Arsq
9	28 May 43	1st Lt. J. N. Vivian	18	Killer hunt	S/E - 35 mi.	3440N 7122W	Off Cape Hatteras, Va.	517-ton	Black	Surfaced	4	None	None	E	U/B spotted at 3 mi, crash dived in 30 sec. B-24 attacked from 100', releasing DC's 15 sec. after C/T disappeared. Explosions 150'-300' ahead of swirl, huge spreading oil slick rose 200' from swirl center. A/C forced to return to base by weather trouble - to 30 min. Jubilant attack-crew only had one week's train-ing in ASW.	ASW-6 #43-7, 28 May 43, 18th Arsq IBM, 12 Aug 43
10	26 Aug 43	1st Lt. G. S. Luketz	25	C/V cover	Visual - 10 mi.	3110N 7845W	Off Savannah, Ga.	750-ton	White, grey C/T	Surfaced	4	Yes	None	J	B-25 unable to identity U/B till 1 mi. away. Sub, on course to intercept C/V, fired AA at ½ mi. DC on first run, in fear of overshooting - explosion 25' from U/B side. Other DC's, re-leased on second run, U/B made radical 700-900 turn in crash-diving. DC's detonated at spot, 50' ahead, and 100' ahead of swirl. No visible results. Another A/C later reported new oil slick in area.	DIR #26A, 28 Aug 43, 25th ANSq IBM, 9 Sep 43

331

ATTACKS ON U-BOATS BY AAF ANTISUBMARINE COMMAND PLANES IN NORTH AMERICAN THEATER OF OPERATIONS

RECAPITULATION

NUMBER OF U-BOATS ATTACKED	10
S/E Contacts	2
Visual Contacts	8
NUMBER OF ATTACKS IN WHICH AA FIRE ENCOUNTERED	2
RESULTS TO ENEMY U-BOATS:	
Probably Severely Damaged	2
Probably Slightly Damaged	1
Insufficient Evidence of Presence of Subs	1
Inconclusive Data for Analysis	1
No Assessment	5

* Assessed by A-2, AAF Antisubmarine Command

Appendix 3 - Encounters with enemy aircraft by planes of the Antisubmarine Command.

The following tables were prepared by the Antisubmarine Command.

ENCOUNTERS WITH ENEMY AIRCRAFT BY PLANES OF THE 480TH ANTISUBMARINE GROUP

RECAPITULATION

TOTAL ENCOUNTERS	19
S/E Contacts	3
Visual Contacts	13
Unknown	3
TOTAL NUMBER OF E/A ENCOUNTERED	55
AVERAGE NUMBER OF E/A PER ENCOUNTER	2.9
RESULTS TO E/A:	
Destroyed	8
Probably Destroyed	1
Damaged	6
RESULTS TO OUR A/C:	
Destroyed	4
Damaged	6

ENCOUNTERS WITH ENEMY AIRCRAFT BY PLANES OF THE 479TH ANTISUBMARINE GROUP IN EUROPEAN THEATER OF OPERATIONS

NOTES:
1. D - Destroyed; H - Damaged; N - No claim; P before a symbol - Probable.
2. TG - Tail Gunner; TTG - Top Turret Gunner; FNG - Right Waist Gunner; CNG - Center Nose Gunner; RNG - Right Nose Gunner; LNG - Left Nose Gunner.
3. FIR - Periodic Intelligence Report; L79th Antisub. Op.; IIR - Daily Intelligence Report; L79th Antisub. Op.; "B - Coastal Command Combat Report.
4. S.E. - Special Equipment.
5. All encounters with E/A by this Group were in the Bay of Biscay area, and all at times are antisubmarine patrol missions.

| | | | | | E/A | | | | | | 479th A.C. | | |
DATE	PILOT	SQN.	TYPE A/CRAFT	POSITION	ENG. NUMBERS	CAMOUFLAGE	DURATION OF COMBAT	FIRE F/W A/F A.C	RESULTS TO E/A	FIRE FROM E/A	DAMAGE SUSTAINED	CASUALTIES	REMARKS
26 Jul 43	1st Lt. S. K. Grider	19	Visual	4745N 0735W	9 Ju 88's	Unknown	Unknown	T: 125 rds. DW: 40 rds. RNG: 15 rds. LNG: 12 rds. TTG: 50 rds.	H	Cannon and machine gun	None	None	Cloud cover used in evading E.A.
8 Aug 43	Capt. W. L. Thomas, Jr.	"	Unknown	Unknown	Unknown	Unknown	24 min.	Unknown	H	Unknown	Lost	10	Messages in tracer F & A tails.
8 Aug 43	Capt. C. R. Werz	19	S.E.	4530N 0523W	1 Ju 88	Dirty white	4 min.	N3 - 6 rds.	H	Nose cannon 20 rds.	None	None	
15 Aug 43	2nd Lt. J. Bertus	19	Visual	4313.0737	26 FW 200's	Top – green grey.	Unknown	None	H	None	None	None	E.A. in staggered formation, lost a base.
16 Aug 43	1st Lt. H. A. Barnett, Jr.	19	Visual	4412N 0725W	1 Ju 88	Top – green; Bottom – grey-green.	2 min.	LWG - 100 rds. TG - 40 rds. FWG - 30 rds. TG - 80 rds. LWG - 30 rds. RNG - 20 rds.	H	None	None	None	E/A encountered F/W causing him to circle close. E.A. tried to evade. AC-10 per meter. A/C seen losing alt. and sagging as it started.
19 Aug 43	1st Lt. H. Hilliker	19	"	4445N 1033W	8 Ju 88's	Top – dark green; Bottom – light green.	22 min.	LWG - 40 rds.	P	None	None	None	7 E.A. reported to attack. A/C Group led. A/C from 7.5 used cloud cover evasion.
19 Aug 43	1st Lt. W. Grider	19	Visual	4509N 1125W	11 Ju 88's	Dark green.	27 min.	LWG - 150 rds. TG - 400 rds. FWG - 150 rds. TG - 50 rds. LWG - 30 rds. RNG - 30 rds.	-	Cannon - time fused.	Lost	4	A/C used cloud cover evasion but forced to come.
19 Aug 43	1st Lt. A. L. Leal	19	S/E	4550N 0942W	4 Ju 88's	Unknown	Unknown	LWG - 230 rds. TG - 230 rds. FWG - 200 rds. TG - 250 rds.	2 PH	Cannon and machine gun.	Damage to starboard lower aileron, engines, hydraulic system, controls, nose, fuselage.	None	
23 Aug 43	1st Lt. K. E. Dustin	"	S.E.	4453N 0948W	10 Ju 88's	Dark green.	1 hr., 47 min.	LWG - 240 rds. TG - 600 rds. FWG - 160 rds. TG - 100 rds. RNG - 150 rds. CNG - 60 rds.	D 2d	Cannon and 7.9 machine gun.	Hits on pilot and radar compartments, No. 1 engine, and bomb bay.	3 w.a. ed.	All E.A. attacks aggressive and evasive. A/C used evasive tactics in circles. Bombardier and waist G never opened bomb bay with an to jettison'g.

234

ENCOUNTERS WITH ENEMY AIRCRAFT BY PLANES OF THE 479TH ANTISUBMARINE GROUP IN EUROPEAN THEATER OF OPERATIONS

NO.	DATE	PILOT	SQDN.	TYPE CONTACT	POSITION	E/A ENCOUNTERED	CAMOUFLAGE	DURATION OF COMBAT	FIRE FROM AAF A/C	RESULTS TO E/A	FIRE FROM E/A	DAMAGE SUSTAINED 479th A/C	CASUALTIES	REMARKS	SUPPORTING DOCUMENTS
10	23 Aug 43	1st Lt. E. T. Flensburgh	4	Visual	4727N 0855W	9 JU 88's	Unknown	1 hr. 5 min.	None	X	None	None	None	A/C investigating dinghy with 3 men when E/A appeared. A/C climbed into sun and headed for cloud cover.	LtR #15
11	25 Aug 43	1st Lt. J. O. Bolin	19	Visual	4626N 0930W	1 JU 88	White	3 min.	TTG - 100 rds. RWG - 10 rds. TG - 100 rds.	X	Cannon and machine gun.	Hits on both port engines, inner caught fire.	None	After examining 2 yawls, A/C attacked by E/A. Damaged port engines feathered several times enroute to base.	DfR #20
12	25 Aug 43	1st Lt. J. R. Irvin	4	Visual	4542N 0913W	14 JU 88's	Unknown	Unknown	None	X	None	None	None	A/C jettisoned DC's; evaded E/A by crossing Spanish coast in cloud cover at Cape Ortegal. Warned 2 naval escort groups which fired on E/A—no details.	LtR #21
13	2 Sep 43	2nd Lt. J. S. Chiasato	19	S/S	4908N 1003W	3 DO 217's	Unknown	Unknown	None	X	None	None	None	Contact obtained at 17 mi. after evading E/A. A/C fired on by 40 mm Spanish AA guns while investigating Spanish vessel.	LtR #28
14	7 Sep 43	1st Lt. W. R. Young	4	Visual	4501N 1104W	4 JU 88's	Top - dark gray; Bottom and sides - white-gray.	18 min.	TTG - 200 rds. RWG - 1400 rds. RWG - 50 rds. LWG - 275 rds. TG - 250 rds.	2 PH	Time fused cannon.	Hits on right and left flaps and possibly gas tank.	None	E/A, using cloud cover, fire parallel; track to make line attack from starboard. E/A leader approached, rest hesitant. 10'x2' black object fell from 1 E/A, ballooned out, descended slowly.	LtR #33
15	8 Sep 43	1st Lt. E. T. Flensburgh	4	Visual	4820N 1052W	8 JU 88's	Unknown	46 min.	Unknown	2D H	Cannon and machine gun.	Radio, No. 1 engine, rudder, trim tabs, and top turret shot out of commission. A/C forced to ditch --broke in two at radar compartment. Hits on fuselage and pilot's compartment. Dingy shot away, while ditching--A/C sank, 1½ min.	7	E/A attacked steadily, alternating from starboard to port. Explosion in cockpit. A/C forced to ditch --broke in two at radar compartment. Flares attracted 2 RAF A/C to scene. Rescue by British sloop 11 Sep 43, position 4827N 1327W.	LtR #53
16	9 Sep 43	Capt. E. R. Owen	19	Visual	4640N 0951W	1 JU 88	Unknown	Unknown	RWG - 20 rds. LWG - 20 rds. TG - 20 rds.	X	None	None	None	A/C evaded E/A in cloud patches. Landed at Gibraltar as radio intercepts indicated additional E/A between position and base.	LtR #36
17	15 Sep 43	1st Lt. W. L. Stapel	22	Visual	4650N 1108W	8 JU 88's	Unknown	Unknown	None	X	None	None	None	E/A closed in from port in loose stepped-up formation, firing in twos. A/C gained cloud cover before E/A could attack.	DfR #41
18	18 Sep 43	1st Lt. H. R. Van Zyl	22	Visual	4235N 0840W	8 JU 88's	Unknown	Unknown	MG - 150 rds. LWG - 200 rds. RWG - 350 rds. TTG - 150 rds.	FW 2X	20 mm fused cannon and machine gun.	Rudder controls, fuselage, rear nose wheel, plexi-glass on top turret.	None	3 E/A attacks in formation from above and port rear. Lead E/A caused only damage. A/C evaded further attack in clouds.	DfR #44

235

——ENCOUNTERS WITH ENEMY AIRCRAFT BY PLANES OF THE 479TH ANTISUBMARINE GROUP IN EUROPEAN THEATER OF OPERATIONS ——

NO.	DATE	PILOT	SQDN.	TYPE CONTACT	POSITION	E/A ENCOUNTERED	E/A CAMOUFLAGE	DURATION OF COMBAT	FIRE FROM ANY A/C	RESULTS TO E/A	FIRE FROM E/A	479th A/C DAMAGE SUSTAINED	479th A/C CASUALTIES	REMARKS	SUPP RPTS DOCUMENT
19	18 Sep 43	2nd Lt. R. D. Purdue	19	Visual	46°01N 09°55W	3 JU 88's	Unknown	17 min.	None	N	None	None	None	A/C climbed for overcast and E/A closely followed on parallel course. During attack, E/E picked up E/A at 5 and 11 mi.	LR #24
20	27 Sep 43	1st Lt. C. H. Cummings	22	Visual	46°24N 07°55W	5 ME 110's 1 ME 109	Top third dark grey, sides and bottom white.	1 min.	20 mm cannon and machine gun.	N	None	Hits on left wing, No. 2 engine, No. 1 engine and wing cowling, right flap, rudder, and 41 hit tips.	None	A/C completed investigation, smoke float when F/A attacked from port quarter and fire E/A jettisoned and own A/C returned to base safely through clouds.	LR #73
21	4 Oct 43	Major ... Rush	22	Visual	46°50N 05°52W	12 JU 88's	Unknown	Unknown	None	N	None	None	None	A/C immediately headed for cloud cover.	LR #..
22	7 Oct 43	1st Lt. L. M. Schroeder	22	Visual	4.53N 10°22W	5 JU 88's	Unknown	Unknown	None	N	None	None	None	Closed in E/A-crated in clouds later sim at F/A which made a pass at A/C-no later evasive action taken.	LR #3
23	7 Oct 43	1st Lt. R. L. Siegel	22	Visual	4°52N 08°58W	4 JU 88's	Unknown	Unknown	TT1 - 20 rds.	N	None	None	None	F/A crossed in front of F/C at approximately same altitude. Did not observe F/A as they were heading into sun.	LR #3
24	9 Oct 43	2nd Lt. F. S. Funk	4	Visual	4°22N 10°04W	1 JU 88 4 ME 110's	Unknown	Unknown	None	N	None	None	None	E/A with white bands on aft fuselage, were not eager to carry out attack. A/C jettisoned DC's and evaded through overcast.	LR #..
25	17 Oct 43	Capt. J. A. Estes	22	Visual	47°11N 08°15W	12 JU 88's	Top - drab; Btm - white.	17 min.	1275 rds.	PD PH	20 mm cannon and machine gun	No. 4 engine disabled, right wing damaged, antenna shot away, right tire shot flat.	One	F A tiled up on starboard and port wings, led rocket signalled be firing of attack. A/C evaded remainder of E.A.after initial contacts, in cloud cover.	LR #73; C.P. ML 11, 17 Oct 43

RECAPITULATION

TOTAL ENCOUNTERS		25
S/E Contacts	5	
Visual Contacts	19	
Unknown	1	
TOTAL NUMBER OF E/A ENCOUNTERED		165
AVERAGE NUMBER OF E/A PER ENCOUNTER		6.6
RESULTS TO E/A:		
Destroyed	3	
Probably Destroyed	1	
Damaged	40	
Probably Damaged		
RESULTS TO OUR A/C:		
Destroyed	3	
Damaged	7	

ENCOUNTERS WITH ENEMY AIRCRAFT BY PLANES OF THE 480TH ANTISUBMARINE GROUP

NOTES:
1. D - Destroyed; H - Damaged; N - No claim; P before a symbol - Probable.
2. TG - Tail Gunner; TTG - Top Turret Gunner; RWG - Right Waist Gunner; LWG - Left Waist Gunner; CWG - Center Nose Gunner; CNG - Center Nose Gunner; LNG - Left Nose Gunner.
3. DIS - Daily Intelligence Summary; L50th Intsub. Rp-; WIS - Weekly Intelligence Summary; L50th Antisub. Op.; MCAFS - U. S. Aircraft - Action with Enemy Report;
   CCR - Coastal Command Combat Report; CCIS - Coastal Command Intelligence Summary; CCAFCR - Coastal Command Form CRASH.
4. S/E - Special Equipment; C/T - Convoy; J/C - Set Course; E/V - Escort Vessel; PLE - Prudent Limit of Endurance.
5. All encounters with E/A by this Group occurred while it was based in Southern England, French Morocco, or Tunisia.

No.	DATE	PILOT	SQDN.	MISSION	TIME CONTACT	POSITION	AREA	E/A ENCOUNTERED	CAMOUFLAGE	DURATION OF COMBAT	FIRE FROM ALP A/C	RESULTS TO E/A	FIRE FRM E/A	DAMAGE SUSTAINED 480th A/C	CASUALTIES	REMARKS	SUPPORTING DOCUMENTS
1	3 Dec 42	Capt. K. L. Locke	1	A/S Patrol	Visual - 1 mi.	51:15N 10:00W	NW of Ireland	1 JU 88	Black markings	25 min.	50 rds.	N	None	None	None	E/A approached on starboard bow, parallel to A/C, which immediately took evasive action consisting of 90° turns to port and starboard and flying in and out of clouds. E/A then made crossover to port and A/C not in several bursts. Enemy plane last seen entering clouds. S/E unserviceable; MG's not jettisoned during attack.	CCR; STF/2017, 3 Dec 42; CCIS #1P, 6 Dec 42
2	26 Jan 43	1st Lt. W. S. Johnson	2	A/S Patrol	Visual - 3 mi.	47:14N 07:15W	Bay of Biscay	1 JU 88	Mottled green	7 min.	TG- 24 rds. TTG-100 rds. LWG- 75 rds. LNG- 22 rds.	N	Nose gun	None	None	E/A dived to attack out of sun, both planes opened fire at 600/800 yds. A/C scored hits on E/A starboard engine, wing root, wing, and fuselage. E/A lost in haze, low-ing height, with white smoke issuing between starboard engine and fuselage. Poorly executed attack by JU 88; failed to conceal self in the sun and was wide open to fire from A/C.	CCR; STF/2016, 26 Jan 43; CCIS #18P, 31 Jan 43
3	29 Jan 43	1st Lt. W. S. Johnson	1	A/S Patrol	Visual - 1 mi.	45:00N 12:00W	NW of Spain	2 JU 88's	Mottled brownish-green. Top of wings - like British A/C.	3 min.	TG- 30 rds. TTG-150 rds. RWG- 30 rds. LWG-150 rds. NG- 30 rds.	1H 1H	Nose gun	Holes in leading edge of port wing, rear star-board fuselage, port side.	None	E/A, flying staggered formation, attacked from starboard quarter, opened fire at 1000 yds., A/C at 800 rds. Then A/C travers hit E/A, fire ceased. E/A last seen billowing black smoke. Other E/A pulled off astern, more damping attack. A/C evaded in clouds. Lack of aggressiveness on part of E/A pilots, main cause of their failure.	CCR; STF/2012, 29 Jan 43; CCIS #18P, 31 Jan 43
4	13 Feb 43	1st Lt. W. S. Johnson	1	A/S Patrol	Visual - 1 mi.	49:15N 07:25W	SW of England	2 E/A	Unknown	5 min.	None	N	Machine gun	None	None	Shortly after take off, engine trouble developed. A/C continued, attacked by high port and starboard ahead. A/C dived to 300'. E/A unidentified due to darkness. Motor trouble continued and A/C R/B for base.	WIS #6, 14 Feb 43; Activities of 480th A/S Sqn., Item 21.

ENCOUNTERS WITH ENEMY AIRCRAFT BY PLANES OF THE 480TH ANTISUBMARINE GROUP

DATE	PILOT	SQDN.	MISSION	TYPE CONTACT	POSITION	AREA	E/A ENCOUNTERED	CAMOUFLAGE	DURATION OF COMBAT	FIRE FROM OWN A/C	RESULTS TO E/A	FIRE FROM E/A	DAMAGE SUSTAINED	LOSSES A/C CASUALTIES	REMARKS	SUPPORTING DOCUMENTS
13 Aug 43	1st Lt. F. W. Heffernan, Jr.	1	C/V Cover	Visual – 10 mi.	4200N 1610W	West of Portugal	1 FW 200	Dark grey. Top of fuselage - dark grey and dark green.	22 rds.	TG-330 rds. TTG-640 rds. BG-170 rds. LBG-160 rds. TG-140 rds.	B	20 mm cannon and machine gun	None	None	A/C spotted flares and AA fire from V/T, noted E/A coming directly for head-on attack. E/A fired full short, A/C moved kite on beam, hatches and part ring. E/A closed in climbing return to C/V, out 2 km. After 6 bands broke to underside lower cannonade. A/C put up heavy AA through which E/A closed. E/A finally climbed V/A and smoke was seen to come from No. 3 engine. E/A climbed up, had difficulty in climbing, disappeared in cloud. Three killed during combat. Plane crashed at El Farrol, Spain, killing remainder of crew.	USAAF, 13 Aug 43, 1st Army HQ FO/1, 15 Aug 43, WX FO/1, 22 Aug 43
17 Aug 43	Capt. E. D. Mannell, Jr.	1	C/V Cover	S/V 12 - 15 mi.	3912N 1400W	West of Portugal	2 FW 200	Dark black	Unknown	TG-100 rds. TTG-400 rds. BG- 25 rds. NG-150 rds.	D	20 mm cannon	No. 3 and 4 engines shot out, large hole in both wings, wing right, sling by after 8 drills, lines severed, top turret plane shot out, Left A/C after ditching.	3	A/C bored in cautious, spotted E/A at 1 mi. making parallel bearing run from C/V. A/C closed in and at 1/2 mi. opened fire. 1-2s. Initial burst caused heavy damage to both planes and one E/A was later destroyed. Second E/A continued to attack, A/C scored damaging fire, but out of control, was forced to ditch. 3/2 crew, to get out. E/A diverted course in 15 min. Downed V/A seen to crash into water by C/V seamen.	USAAF, 17 Aug 43, WX FO/1, 22 Aug 43, WX FO/1, 29 Aug 43
25 Aug 43	2nd Lt. F. A. Graham	2	A/S Sweep	Visual	4310N 0925W	Off Spain	5 ME 110 8 & 4 JU 88	Olive drab Grey fuselage	Unknown	None	M	None	None	None	E/A circled overhead preparing to peel off. A/C dove to attack less ME-110 with an circling small Spanish boat. E/A turned to position boat and head for the Spanish coast. Other 12 E/A made no effort to attack A/C, which S/C for best bearing course at 50', Failure of E/A to follow A/C possibly due to lack of fuel.	WX FO/1, 29 Aug 43, WX FO/1, 25 Aug 43 (TWI, ALSOS)
27 Aug 43	Capt. L. E. Jarmagin	2	A/S Patrol	Visual	4344N 0920W	Off Spain	13 ME 111 & DO 217	Unknown	Unknown	None	M	None	None	None	V/A started to peel off and A/C immediately took cloud cover.	WX FO/1, 27 Aug 43, (TWI, ALSOS) WX FO/1, 29 Aug 43
27 Aug 43	1st Lt. E. E. Dunning	1	A/S Sweep	Visual – 1000 yds.	4312N 0920W	Off Spain	1 FW 200	Unknown	10 min.	345 rds.	M	20 mm cannon	None	None	A/C attacked E/A slightly above and astern from 1500', Many hits registered on V/A fuselage and No. 1 and 2 engines. During these moments attacks, V/A attempted cloud cover several times but each time they successfully eluded A/C.	USAAF, 27 Aug 43, 1st Army HQ FO/1, 29 Aug 43

ENCOUNTERS WITH ENEMY AIRCRAFT BY PLANES OF THE 480TH ANTISUBMARINE GROUP

DATE	PILOT	SQDN.	MISSION	TYPE CONTACT	POSITION	AREA	E/A ENCOUNTERED	CAMOUFLAGE	DURATION OF COMBAT	FIRE FROM A/C	RESULTS TO E/A	FIRE FROM E/A	480th A/C DAMAGE SUFFERED	CASUALTIES	REMARKS	REPORTING DOCUMENTS
26 Feb 43	1st Lt. C. A. Tomlinson	2	Anti-shipping patrol	Unknown	Unknown	N of France	Unknown	Unknown	Unknown	Unknown	M	Unknown	Lost	10	A/C message indicated E/A attack. Other data reveal A/C downed by fighters; rammed by fighter or fired at from Brest. Crew of 7 all A/C known dead, and it is hoped, subsequently raised by enemy surface craft and interned as prisoners of war.	Ltr. 20 Dec 43, 3 Sqr Hq., 2nd Airway AG-35400
24 Jun 43	1st Lt. E. S. Kimball	1	C/V Cover	Visual – 5 mi.	4115N 1500W	off Portugal	1 FW 200	Unknown	Unknown	None	M	None	None	None	A/C requested to investigate unidentified plane headed for C/V. Before A/C could gain altitude for attack, C/V opened fire with AA and turned off E/A, which disappeared from A/C returned to base.	WAR /21/ 27 Jun 43
18 Jul 43	Capt. H. D. Maxwell, Jr	1	C/V Cover	Visual – 4 mi.	3840N 1400W	off Portugal	1 FW 200	Unknown	5 min.	70- 50 cal. rds. 70-375 rds. WR-15 rds. WR-170 rds.	M	7.9 mm cannon and machine gun	Propeller hit	None	A/C spotted E/A which dived in clouds. Later sighted on port side of C/V while breaking run from 1500'. A/C attacked and No. 4 engine of E/A was smoking. E/A forced to close cover to replace in ammunition and repair gun jam. When A/C had closed clear, E/A had disappeared.	WAR 18 Jul 43 1st Army WD /24/ 25 Jul 43
25 Jul 43	1st Lt. E. W. Hyde	1	C/V Cover	Visual – 20 mi.	4222N 1600W	West of Portugal	1 FW 200	Blackish-green	22 min.	1600 rds.	D	Cannon and machine gun	Hits on wings, props, no. 1, 3, 4 engines. Upper turret shot off.	1	A/C sighted screen of E/A, identified E/A as enemy E/W. E/A dived to attack and fire was exchanged at 25 – 50 yds off water. E/A hit on wings, 2 props, and fuselage; black smoke coming from Nos. 1, 3, and 4 engines, of E/A hit wing first. Two of A/C killed instantly by shell. Following combat, A/C jettisoned DC's. Continued on 2 engines, 3/4 low base, everal lights shot out by GG. A/C reached port safely. All rescued next day.	WAR 26 Jul 43 1st Army WD /25/ 1 Aug 43
31 Jul 43	Capt. G. L. Hosier	2	A/S Sweep	S/E – 7 mi.	4422N 1538W	West of Portugal	1 FW 200	Olive drab	11 min.	650 rds.	D	20 mm cannon and 7.9 mm machine gun	Hits on leading edge of port wing, top starboard rudder, port side of fuselage. Gyro Flight instruments inoperative.	None	A/C homed on s/E contact and surprised E/A at 600 yds. with sighting burst. E/A underwent violent evasive action, but A/C maintained slight altitude advantage throughout attack. E/A hit in two engines, started to burn, burst into flames, and crashed after jettison of bombs. Final burst of A/C hit E/A in wing root.	WAR 31 Jul 43 2nd Army WD /31/ 1 Aug 43

223

ENCOUNTERS WITH ENEMY AIRCRAFT BY PLANES OF THE 480TH ANTISUBMARINE GROUP

DATE	PILOT	SQDN.	MISSION	TYPE CONTACT	POSITION	AREA	E/A ENCOUNTERED	CAMOUFLAGE	DURATION OF COMBAT	FIRE FROM A&P A/C	RESULTS TO E/A	FIRE FROM E/A	DAMAGE SUSTAINED 480th A/C	CASUALTIES 480th A/C	REMARKS	SUPPORTING DOCUMENTS
28 Aug 43	1st Lt. F. W. McKinnon, Jr.	1	A/S Sweep	Unknown	4000N 0900W	Off Spain	1 E/A	Unknown	8 min.	Unknown	N	Unknown	Lost	1	A/C engaged -- On being attacked by E/A... later -500'. The B-24's on parallel course diverted to area, 9 survivors rescued by small boat, navigator killed in ditching. Crew returned to base 12 Sep 43. 3 in hospital in neutral country.	MIS #67, 29 Aug 43 USAM, 28 Aug 43 1st Army MIS #13, 29 Aug 43 (TWX, 6776)
10 Sep 43	Capt. H. McKeown	1	A/S Sweep	S/E - 18 mi.	4150N 0550E	West of Corsica	2 DO 24 1 DO 26	Grey	33 min.	4400 rds.	3D	20 mm cannons and top turret	2 hits	None	A/C based on contact to eight three templanes at 3 mi. A/C was believed over, as A/C was bolstered to be FW's or one-bottle Italian A/C. A few minutes away, B-24 spotted 200 survivors in life vests, decided to investigate these planes. On approaching, A/C identified as E/A preparing to land for take off. A/C dropped to 50', making 1/4 turn to attack all 3 E/A during run, firing all E/A. Went sideways and burned.	MIS #62, 12 Sep 43 Sep. to MIS #62-24, 25 Sep 43 GRACE, 13th Wing, 1st Army 10 Sep 43
18 Sep 43	Major L. E. Jarnagin	2	A/S Patrol	Unknown	4250N 1100W	West of Spain	1 E/A	Unknown	Unknown	Unknown	M	Unknown	Lost	10	B-24 reduced -- "Am engaging aircraft", nothing further heard. Extensive search - negative.	MIS #75, 26 Sep 43 TWX, Sep 43 19 Sep 43 ISH, LAGA Q.
7 Oct 43	Capt. G. L. Hester	2	A/S Sweep	Visual - 2 mi.	4630N 1100W	NW of Spain	5 JU 88	Top - dull green; bottom - silver-grey	35 min.	1650 rds.	1FD 2M	20 mm cannon and machine gun	11 hits - negligible	None	A/C spotted three E/A, strung out, coming up in formation. Under-fire and navigator canned with guns due to absence of two of crew DU's jettisoned in 11 attacks--7 from port bow and nose, remainder from starboard quarter and bow. E/A split up to gain time, returned to low altitude, one first attacks. 1 E/A machine-gunned again, 2 E/A also seen smoking, one going down.	USAM, 7 Oct 43 2nd Army MIS #87, 10 Oct 43
23 Oct 43	1st Lt. W. S. McDowell	1	C/V Cover	Visual - 20 mi.	3920N 1050W	West of Portugal	1 FW 200	Unknown	Unknown	None	M	None	None	None	E/A spotted heading toward C/V at 3200'. A/C climbed above E/A, made tight turn, and closed to 800 yds. from rear. Enl plane evaded in clouds - not seen again. A/C returned to C/V, of having strafed FLK, w/c for base. Visibility poor.	MIS #90, 31 Oct 43

Appendix 4 - Action Status of the Antisubmarine Command, 23 March, and 26 August 1943.*

ACTION STATUS of ANTISUBMARINE COMMAND
23 March 1943

1 A/S Sq. — Report of March 17 shows 10/B24s of air echelon at Port Lyautey. Balance of air echelon and ground echelons in process of moving. Two of replacement crews and planes had arrived and were closely followed by two more. Total for squadrons— 19 B24s. Three replacement aircraft have been allocated but no replacement crews will be made available until after April 30th. Roberts requests 6 extra copilots, 2 navigators and 2 bombardiers. Replacement crews will be trained from other squadrons for future shipment. Action has been taken to carry his provisional wing personnel in 25th Wing to relieve acute promotion problem in these squadrons pending organization of a recommended 27th A. S. Wing with appropriate manning table.

2 A/S Sq. — Same as the one above (1 A/S Sq.)

3 A/S Sq. — Fort Dix - 12 B25s - no special equipment
Operational

4 A/S Sq. — Mitchel Field
2 B24s in sub depot
9 B18 B's
6 B24 crews trained and 6 now at school. Training B24s from 6 A/S Sq. to be turned over to this sq upon receipt of operational B24s by 6 A/S Sq.

5 A/S Sq. — Westover Field
9 B25's—no special equipment. 3B25s in sub depot. Three B24 crews at school.
Operational

6 A/S Sq. — Westover Field
6 B24's for training and limited operations
2 Winterized B24's just received to be followed by additional 10 from Warner Robbins. Scheduled to move north by May 1. Orders requested for movement to be made upon receipt and calibration of equipment. 4 crews will have completed Wing training schedule by April 1 and 8 crews

* Action Status Report, prepared by the Antisubmarine Command, and preserved in AAFAC file 241.1.

by April 15. As operational B24's are received training B24's will be made available to 4 AS/Sq. and 8 AS/Sq.

7 AS/Sq. - Jacksonville
4 B34s, scheduled for transfer
10 B18Bs - 3 of these and portion of flight echelon ground crew enroute to Trinidad - 7 additional will be sent to Trinidad to relieve flight echelon of 9 AS/Sq. upon completion of transition and training. 2 additional Bs can be made available to this squadron provided 26 Wg can furnish crews.

8 AS/Sq. - 36th St Miami
9 B34s due for transfer
3 B24s two with radar
6 B24 crews trained and 6 at school until April 1.
Additional B24s will be made available in April from 6 AS/Sq.

9 AS/Sq. - Trinidad
10 B18B's. Six aircraft enroute to Miami to be followed by remaining 4 when replaced by 7 AS/Sq. 12 crews of this squadron scheduled to attend April class at school.

10 AS/Sq. - Galveston
7 B34s which are to be transferred squadron is operational at present but due for transition to B25's. Two crews for B24s completing school March 30.

11 AS/Sq. - Fort Dix
Transition to B25's underway O52's to B34s to B25s.
Limited operations. Lack of navigators serious.

12 AS/Sq. - Langley Field
Transition 047 to B18 completed.
Some pilots still limited. Lack of navigators serious.
Limited operations. 12 B18Bs.

13 AS/Sq. - Grenier Field
12 B25s. Transition 047-B34-B25.
Limited operations. Only one navigator.

14 AS/Sq. - Otis Field
Transition 047 to B25s completed.
Only one navigator-Operational with the exception of navigators.

15 AS/Sq. - Jacksonville.
Has 12 B 34s having just about completed transition from O 47s. Is on a _limited_ operation status. Loss of B 34s in the immediate future will necessitate transition B 25s and B 24s. Shortage of navigators.

16 AS/Sq. - Charleston.
   Transition from O 47s to B 34s completed and squadron has been operation with 8 B 34s for past month. Loss of B 34s will require additional transition period to B 25s and 24s. Instrument lacking. No link trainer has been available. One enroute to base, one navigator.

17 AS/Sq. - Boca Chica
   Transition from O 47s to B 34s just completed and squadron on limited operation status. Shortage of personnel still exists. Transition to B 25s beginning as soon as airplanes can be made available.

18 AS/Sq. - Langley Field.
   School Squadron. All training of B 24 crews and ground personnel carried on here. 12 B 24s with various categories of equipment are used. Present class is 20 air and ground crews. 24 crews scheduled for April. The present 30 day course may have to be increased in time as the experience level of the crews being trained decreases. Priority in training of heavy crews has been given to squadrons having the most medium experience.

19 AS/Sq. - Langley Field
   Air echelon enroute to Gander.
   12 B17s. Ground echelon to be moved by personnel orders as transportation is available. Only organization equipment short in 20th AS/Sq. to be taken. One B17 delayed due to mechanical trouble and special mission.

20th AS/Sq.-Gander
   4 B 17s with Mark 2 radar. Squadron just assigned this command and still has substantial detachments on other duty. Air echelon of 19th will be attached on arrival at Gander. Detachment at Argentia being moved to Gander.

21st AS/Sq.-New Orleans.
   12 O 47s. An observation squadron redesignated March. Action to have this squadron transferred to the command several months ago was initiated due to the experience of personnel in antisubmarine missions while attached for operations. Plan the immediate move of squadron to Gulfport to begin transition to B 25s. Present field not suitable for transition and operation of medium equipment.

22nd AS/Sq.- Cherry Point, N.C. (Marine Base)
   10 A 29s. This squadron assigned to the command March ____ and redesignated. Is qualified as operational with A 29s. Due to the experience of pilots it is planned to give

squadron a high priority in transition and assignment of
B 24s. 12 crews scheduled for April class at Ly.

23rd AS/Sq.-San Antonio de los Banos.
12 A 29s. This squadron assigned to the command March ___ and
redesignated. Consists of an air echelon only as the ground
echelon was absorbed by 4th A.F. The air echelon was
moved to present location duty to tactical situation and
it is planned to return it to Drew Field where ground
echelon will be formed from a cadre and filler personnel.
Air echelon is operational with present equipment but
will be reequipped and trained on B 24s on a high priority.

ACTION STATUS OF ANTISUBMARINE COMMAND
26 August 1943

1st A/S Sq. — Port Lyautey, Africa.
and
2nd A/S Sq.
    22 B-24s — Operational (VLR(E) 517 RADAR)
    2 B-24s — Operational (VLR 517 RADAR)
    Remarks — One replacement crew now en route in a VLR(E) B-24 517 RADAR aircraft; aircraft included in above figures. One B-24 VLR(E) 717 modified nose turret replacement aircraft not included in above figures scheduled to depart from Langley Field 27 August 1943. Orders have been requested for an additional replacement aircraft.

479th A/S Op- St. Eval, Great Britain
(4th, 6th,
19th & 22nd
A/S Sqdns.)
    57 B-24s — Operational (VLR(E) 717 RADAR)
    Remarks — 15 of above now en route.
    Orders received rescinding movement of the ground echelon of the 6th and 22nd Antisubmarine Squadrons to Great Britain. 2 acft with crews to depart Langley 27 August 1943.

3rd A/S Sq. — Fort Dix, New Jersey.
    10 B-24s — Operational (VLR(E) no RADAR)
    1 B-24 — Operational (VLR(E) 717 RADAR)
    2 B-24s — In depot (VLR 517 RADAR)
    4 B-25s — Operational
    Crews — 11 Trained B-24 crews.

5th A/S Sq. — Westover Field, Mass.
    2 B-24s — Operational (VLR(E) 717 RADAR)
    4 B-24s — Operational (VLR(E) No RADAR)
    1 B-24 — Operational (VLR 517 RADAR)
    2 B-24s — In depot (VLR (E) 717 RADAR)
    1 B-24 — In depot (VLR 521 RADAR)
    5 B-25s — Operational
    1 B-25 — In depot
    Crews — 13 trained B-24 crews.

7th A/S Sq. — Jacksonville, Florida.
    No aircraft assigned
    Remarks — Squadron scheduled to complete OTU training 4 Sept. 1943.

8th A/S Sq. — Trinidad, B.W.I.
    12 B-24s — Operational (VLR(E) 717 RADAR)
    Remarks — 4 of the above aircraft now at Miami awaiting transfer.
    Crews. — 12 trained B-24 crews.

9th A/S Sq. — 36th Street Airport, Miami, Florida.
    9 B-24s — Operational (VLR(E) No RADAR)
    1 B-25 — In depot
    Crews — 12 trained B-24 crews.

10th A/S Sq. — Galveston, Texas.
    9 B-24s — Operational (VLR(E) No RADAR)
    2 B-24s — Operational (VLR 517 RADAR)
    3 B-24s — In depot (517 RADAR)
    1 B-34 — Operational (RADAR and tow reel)
    1 B-25 — In depot
    Crews — 12 trained B-24 crews.

11th A/S Sq. — Fort Dix, New Jersey.
    5 B-24s — Operational (VLR(E) No RADAR)
    1 B-24 — Operational (VLR 521 RADAR)
    4 B-25s — Operational
    1 B-25 — In depot
    3 B-34s — Operational (RADAR and tow reel)
    Crews — 12 trained B-24 crews.

12th A/S Sq. — Langley Field, Virginia.
    4 B-24s — Operational (VLR(E) No RADAR)
    1 B-24 — In depot (VLR(E) No RADAR)
    6 B-25s — Operational
    2 B-25s — In depot
    Remarks — 12 trained B-24 crews.

13th A/S Sq. — Grenier Field, N. H.
    5 B-24s — Operational (VLR(E) No RADAR)
    3 B-24s — In depot (VLR(E) No RADAR)
    5 B-25s — Operational
    4 B-25s — In depot.
    Crews — 12 trained B-24 crews.

14th A/S Sq. — Otis Field, Mass.
    6 B-24s — Operational (VLR(E) No RADAR)
    4 B-25s — Operational
    4 B-25s — In depot
    Crews — 12 trained B-24 crews.

15th A/S Sq. — Batista Field, Cuba.
    9 B-24s — Operational (VLR(E) No RADAR — 1 of which is
        at Miami awaiting transfer)
    2 B-24s — Operational (VLR 521 RADAR)
    9 B-25s — Operational
    2 B-34s — Operational (RADAR and tow reel)
    Crews — 12 trained B-24 crews.

16th A/S Sq. - Charleston, S. C.
    7 B-25s - In depot
    1 B-34 - In depot (RADAR and tow reel)
    Remarks - Squadron scheduled to complete OTU training
              28 Aug 43.

17th A/S Sq. - 36th Street Airport, Miami, Florida.
    1 B-34 - In depot (RADAR and tow reel)
    Remarks- Squadron entered OTU training 23 August 1943.

18th A/S Sq. - Langley Field, Virginia - Operational Training Squadron.
    8 B-24s - Operational (VLR(E) 717 RADAR - 5 of which
              are replacements)
    3 B-24s - Operational (VLR(E) 517 RADAR)
    1 B-24 - Operational (VLR 521 RADAR)
    5 B-24s - Operational (VLR 517 RADAR)
    7 B-24s - Operational (VLR No RADAR)
    1 B-24 - In depot (VLR(E) 717 RADAR)
    1 B-24 - In depot (VLR(E) 517 RADAR)
    1 B-24 - In depot (VLR 517 RADAR)
    1 B-24 - In depot (VLR No RADAR)

20th A/S Sq. - Mitchel Field
    12 B-17s - Operational (VLR RADAR)
    3 B-17s - In depot (VLR RADAR)
    1 B-34 - Operational (RADAR and tow reel)

21st A/S Sq. - Gulfport, Miss.
    5 B-25s - Operational
    1 B-25 - In depot
    Remarks - 4 crews on DS at Trinidad with 12 crews of
              the 23rd Antisubmarine Squadron.

23rd A/S Sq. - Drew Field, Tampa, Florida.
    16 B-25Gs- Operational
    Remarks - 12 crews augmented by 4 crews of the 21st
              Antisubmarine Squadron on DS at Trinidad.

24th A/S Sq. - Westover Field, Mass.
    11 B-25s - Operational

25th A/S Sq. - Jacksonville, Florida.
    11 B-25s - Operational
    1 B-25 - In depot.

    NOTE: - 9 B-24 VLR(E) 717 RADAR aircraft are at Middletown Air
              Depot for nose turret modification and are not reflected
              in preceding figures.

```
Hq & Hq Sq.    - Mitchel Field, N. Y.
  Anti-Sub       1 A-17   - Operational
   Comd.         1 B-18   - Operational
                 1 BT-14  - Operational
                 1 RB-25A - Operational
                 1 C-60   - Operational
                 3 UC-78s - Operational

Hq Sq. 25th    - Mitchel Field, N. Y.
  A/S Wing.      3 UC-78s - Operational
                 1 RB-25  - Operational
                 1 A-29   - In depot

Hq Sq. 26th    - 36th Street Airport, Miami, Florida.
  A/S Wing.      2 B-25s  - Operational
                 4 UC-78s - Operational
                 1 B-18   - Operational
```

Summary of Aircraft

TACTICAL

	B-24 VLR(E)	B-24 VLR	B-25	B-17	B-24
Operational	166	21	80	12	7
In depot	17	8	24	3	2

NON TACTICAL

	A-17A	A-29	B-18	BT-14	B-25	C-60	UC-78
Operational	1	-	2	1	4	1	10
In depot	-	1	-	-	-	-	-

Appendix 5 - Station Lists, Antisubmarine Command, 23 October 1942 and 31 July 1943.*

HEADQUARTERS
ARMY AIR FORCES ANTI-SUBMARINE COMMAND
90 Church Street
New York City

STATION LIST)
                :
NUMBER   1)   October 23, 1942.

The following is a list of units presently assigned and attached to this headquarters.

ORGANIZATION	STATION
Headquarters, AAF Anti-Submarine Command	90 Church Street, New York City
Hq & Hq Sq, AAF Anti-Submarine Command	Mitchel Field, New York
2d Bombardment Group (H)	Langley Field, Virginia
20th Bombardment Squadron (H)	Langley Field, Virginia
49th Bombardment Squadron (H)	Langley Field, Virginia
96th Bombardment Squadron (H)	Langley Field, Virginia
46th Bombardment Squadron (M) (Atchd)	Cherry Point, North Carolina
13th Bombardment Group (M)	Westover Field, Mass.
39th Bombardment Squadron (M)	Dover, Delaware
40th Bombardment Squadron (M)	Mitchel Field, New York
41st Bombardment Squadron (M)	Westover Field, Mass.
393rd Bombardment Squadron (M)	Westover Field, Mass.
45th Bombardment Group (M)	Miami, Florida
78th Bombardment Squadron (M)	Jacksonville, Florida
79th Bombardment Squadron (M)	Miami, Florida
80th Bombardment Squadron (M)	Miami, Florida
433rd Bombardment Squadron (M)	Galveston, Texas
76th Bombardment Squadron (M) (Atchd)	Drew Field, Tampa, Florida

* AAFAC File 212.3

ORGANIZATION	STATION
377th Bombardment Group (H)	Fort Dix, New Jersey
516th Bombardment Squadron (H)	Fort Dix, New Jersey
517th Bombardment Squadron (H)	Atlantic City, New Jersey
518th Bombardment Squadron (H)	Grenier Field, New Hampshire
519th Bombardment Squadron (H)	Otis Field, Mass.
378th Bombardment Group (H)	Langley Field, Virginia
520th Bombardment Squadron (H)	Jacksonville, Florida
521st Bombardment Squadron (H)	Charleston, S. C.
522nd Bombardment Squadron (H)	Lantana, Florida
523rd Bombardment Squadron (H)	Langley Field, Virginia
124th Observation Squadron (Atchd) (Operational Control Only)	New Orleans, La.
128th Observation Squadron (Atchd) (Operational Control Only)	New Orleans, La.
I Patrol Force Hq (Provisional)	Mitchel Field, New York
Gulf Task Force (part of AAF ASC)	Miami, Florida
413th Signal Company, (Avn)	Mitchel Field, New York
303rd Signal Company, Wing	Miami, Florida

By command of Brigadier General LARSON:

/s/ Julius Sossen
/t/ JULIUS SOSSEN,
1st Lt., Air Corps,
Actg. Adjutant.

HEADQUARTERS
ARMY AIR FORCES ANTISUBMARINE COMMAND
Office of the Commanding General
90 Church Street
New York 7, N.Y.

STATION LIST

Number 13   31 July 1943

The following is a list of the units of this command as of this date:

ORGANIZATION   STATION

Hq AAF Antisubmarine Comd   90 Church St NYC NY
Hq Sq AAF Antisubmarine Comd   Mitchel Fld NY
6th Antisubmarine Sq (Hv)   APO 865 c/o Postmaster NY
18th Antisubmarine Sq (Hv)   Langley Fld Va
20th Antisubmarine Communications Sq   Mitchel Fld NY
413th Signal Co. (Avn)   Mitchel Fld NY

Hq 25th Antisubmarine Wing   90 Church St NYC NY
   Hq Sq 25th Antisubmarine Wing   65 University Place NYC
   2rd Antisubmarine Sq (Hv)   Fort Dix NJ
   5th Antisubmarine Sq (Hv)   Westover Fld Mass
   11th Antisubmarine Sq (Hv)   Fort Dix, NJ
   12th Antisubmarine Sq (Hv)   Langley Fld Va
   13th Antisubmarine Sq (Hv)   Grenier Fld NH
   14th Antisubmarine Sq (Hv)   Otis Fld Mass
   16th Antisubmarine Sq (Hv)   Charleston SC
   20th Antisubmarine Sq (Hv)   Mitchel Fld NY
   22nd Antisubmarine Sq (Hv)   Bluethenthal Fld NC
   24th Antisubmarine Sq (Hv)   Westover Fld Mass
   338th Signal Co (Wing)   Mitchel Fld NY

Hq 26th Antisubmarine Wing   DuPont Bldg, Miami, Fla
   Hq Sq 26th Antisubmarine Wing   36th St Airport, Miami Fla
   7th Antisubmarine Sq (Hv)   Jacksonville, Fla
     (Grd Echelon)
   8th Antisubmarine Sq (Hv)   36th St Airport, Miami Fla
     (Grd Echelon)
   8th Antisubmarine Sq (Hv)   APO 687, c/o Postmaster NY
     (Air Echelon)
   9th Antisubmarine Sq (Hv)   36th St Airport Miami Fla
   10th Antisubmarine Sq (Hv)   Galveston, Texas
   15th Antisubmarine Sq (Hv)   Jacksonville, Fla
     (Grd Echelon)
   15th Antisubmarine Sq (Hv)   APO 632, c/o Postmaster,
     (Air Echelon)   Miami, Fla.

17th Antisubmarine Sq (Hv) (Grd Echelon)	36th St Airport, Miami Fla
17th Antisubmarine Sq (Hv) (Air Echelon)	APO 632, Miami Fla
21st Antisubmarine Sq (Hv)	Gulfport, Miss
23rd Antisubmarine Sq (Hv)	Drew Fld Fla
25th Antisubmarine Sq (Hv)	Jacksonville Fla
333rd Signal Co (Wing)	Miami Fla
479th Antisubmarine Group (Separate Special)	APO 641 c/o Postmaster NYC NY
4th Antisubmarine Sq (Hv)	APO 641 c/o Postmaster NYC NY
19th Antisubmarine Sq (Hv)	APO 641 c/o Postmaster NYC NY
480th Antisubmarine Group (Separate Special)	APO 762 c/o Postmaster NYC NY
1st Antisubmarine Sq (Hv)	APO 762 c/o Postmaster NYC NY
2nd Antisubmarine Sq (Hv)	APO 762 c/o Postmaster NYC NY

Liaison Offices

AAF Antisubmarine Command Liaison Office	Room 3D-981 Pentagon, Washington, DC., Phone Republic 6700 Ext 71451 or 6575
AAF Antisubmarine Command Liaison Officer with Navy	Office of the Commander in Chief US Fleet, Room 3809 Navy Bldg, Washington, D.C., Phone: Republic 6700 Ext 76250

By command of Brigadier General LARSON:

/s/ Frederick Bauer Jr.,
/t/ FREDERICK BAUER JR.,
Lt Col, A.G.D.,
Adjutant General

Appendix 6 — Key personnel, Headquarters, AAFAC, 1 May 1943.*

<u>Commanding General</u>	Brig. Gen. W. T. Larson
<u>Chief of Staff</u>	Col. G. A. McHenry
<u>Deputy Chief of Staff</u>	Col. F. L. Fair
<u>Adjutant General's Office</u>	
Adjutant General	Lt. Col. F. Bauer, Jr.
Asst. Adjutant General	Maj. F. R. Bertero
<u>Asst. Chief of Staff - A-1</u>	
A-1	Lt. Col. B. J. Nesbitt
Asst. A-1	Maj. W. L. Jenkins
<u>Asst. Chief of Staff, A-2</u>	
A-2	Lt. Col. C. A. Burrows
Asst. A-2	Lt. Col. J. E. Condron
Tactical	Capt. H. B. Ingersoll
Strategic	Maj. A. Standish
<u>Asst. Chief of Staff, A-3</u>	
A-3	Col. J. G. Fowler
Asst. A-3	Lt. Col. C. T. Goldenberg
Plans & Training	Lt. Col. R. C. Kugel
Operations & Control	Lt. Col. C. J. Cochrane
Weather	Lt. Col. L. A. Walker
Research Coordinator	Maj. D. R. Casey
<u>Asst. Chief of Staff, A-4</u>	
A-4	Lt. Col. D. O. Smith
Technical	Lt. Col. F. H. Matthews
Procurement & Construction	Lt. Col. E. O. Keller
Supply	Maj. F. H. Waring
<u>Inspector General</u>	
Air Inspector & Inspector General	Col. L. E. Boutwell
Asst. Air Inspector	Lt. Col. A. L. Edson
<u>Signal Section</u>	
Signal Officer	Lt. Col. G. A. Westphal
Engineering (Radio)	Maj. J. E. Morton
Radio	Capt. W. W. Werner
Radar	Maj. L. S. Hermelin

* AAFAC Directory, 1 May 1943, in AAFAC file 418.1.

Quartermaster	Col. W. H. Roberts
Ordnance Officer	Lt. Col. H. C. Thayer
Chemical Officer	Lt. Col. T. P. Gahan
Surgeon	Lt. Col. D. H. Summers
Judge Advocate General	Lt. Col. C. L. Fisher, Jr.
Finance Officer	Maj. E. S. Carland
Engineer	Lt. Col. A. H. Kemp
Chaplain	Maj. O. H. Urban
Special Services	Maj. O. Tjader

Appendix 7 - Order of Battle, Antisubmarine Aircraft, for final
week of August, 1943.*

	TYPE AND NUMBER				
	VLR	LR	MR	SR	LTA
ICELAND					
U.S.N.	0	10	0	0	0
R.A.A.	14	0	19	0	0
GREENLAND					
U.S.A.A.F.	0	0	8	0	0
U.S.N.	0	6	0	0	0
NEWFOUNDLAND & NOVA SCOTIA					
U.S.A.A.F.	12	0	0	0	0
U.S.N.	7	0	0	0	0
R.C.A.F.	14	103	39	0	0
EASTERN SEA FRONTIER					
U.S.A.A.F.	20	0	34	0	0
U.S.N.	0	17	20	158	28
GULF SEA FRONTIER					
U.S.A.A.F.	19	0	15	0	0
U.S.N.	0	50	0	101	18
PANAMA SEA FRONTIER					
U.S.N.	0	11	0	32	0
GUANTANAMO SECTOR					
U.S.N.	0	36	0	14	2
PUERTO RICO SECTOR					
U.S.A.A.F.	0	0	6	0	0
U.S.N.	0	1	8	28	0
TRINIDAD SECTOR					
U.S.A.A.F.	5	0	21	6	0
U.S.N.	0	24	4	14	4
CURACAO-ARUBA SECTOR					
U.S.A.A.F.	4	0	6	25	0
U.S.N.	0	4	0	14	0
BERMUDA					
U.S.N.	10	8	0	15	0

* Compiled by Antisubmarine Command from U.S. Navy and British Coastal
Command data, and printed in ASWR43.

	VLR	LR	MR	SR	LTA
4th FLEET					
U.S.N.	13	59	0	0	0
ASCENSION ISLAND					
U.S.A.A.F.	1	0	6	14	0
MOROCCAN SEA FRONTIER AND GIBRALTAR					
U.S.A.A.F. & R.A.F.	24	23	55	0	0
UNITED KINGDOM					
U.S.A.A.F.	48	0	0	0	0
U.S.N.	0	15	0	0	0
R.A.F.	45	182	173	0	0
TOTAL	236	509	424	421	52

GRAND TOTAL — 1642

INDEX

A

A-20, 237 (n 1)
A-29, 193, 237 (n 1)
AC/AS Intelligence, 50
AC/AS Personnel, 83
Accra, 144
ACV, 146-147, 240 (n 48)
Adjutant General's Department, The, 205
Admiralty, British, 15, 28, 67, 80, 251 (n 96)
Africa, 35, 42, 45, 47, 58, 63, 77, 82, 86-87, 93-93, 97, 115, 117-122, 128, 130, 145-146, 164, 200, 251 (n 91, 102)
Agadir, 119, 122, 252 (n 111)
AGL stations, 198-201
Air Antisubmarine Development Detachment, 206
"Air Antisubmarine Force," 37
Air-Officer-Commanding-in-Chief, 98. See also Slessor.
Air Service Command (ASC), 100, 196-197, 205
   Headquarters, 198
   Overseas Section, Supply Division, 198
Air Transport Command (ATC), 196-198, 203, 205
Alaska, 13
Algiers, 249 (n 70)
Allied Antisubmarine Survey Board, 74
Ammunition Supply Authorities (AMSA), 196-197
Andrews, Adm. Adolphus, 4-5, 84. See also Commander ESF.
Antilles, 45
Antilles Air Task Force, 140
   Trinidad Detachment of, 140
Antisubmarine Monthly Intelligence Report, 214
Antisubmarine Warfare Operations Research Group (ASWORG), 46, 206-207

Army Air Support Command, 5
Army Service Forces (ASF), 205
   Commanding General, 238 (n 17)
Arnold, Gen. H. H., 16-18, 23, 39, 44-45, 60, 63-64, 71, 77, 84, 148-149, 237 (n 6), 238 (n 17), 243 (n 85), 260 (n 23). See also CG AAF.
Arnold-McNarney-McCain agreement, 78, 80-82, 227
Ascension Island, 144-145
Asia, 45
Assistant Secretary of War for Air, 260 (n 23)
ASV equipment, 30, 36, 72, 161, 241 (n 51), 248 (n 49)
ASV-2, 239 (n 23)
ASV-10, 53, 107
Atlantic, Battle of the, 1, 29, 54, 86, 108, 226
Atlantic Convoy Conference, 54-55, 62-63, 90, 108, 148-149, 151, 205, 217
ACC-1, 151
Australia, 193
AYD altimeter, 210
Azores, 92, 114

B

B-17, 7, 147-149, 153, 169-172, 193, 233 (n 41), 237 (n 1), 255 (n 165)
B-17E, 193
B-18, 7, 18, 22, 30, 141, 193, 237 (n 1)
B-18B, 166-168
B-18R, 141
B-24, 15, 41-42, 44, 46, 52, 66, 68, 72, 74-75, 78, 82, 94, 98, 100, 103, 106, 111-112, 115, 123-125, 127-128, 134-135, 145-147, 149, 163-165, 172-173, 178, 181, 184-186, 193-194,

B-24 (contd), 202, 207, 213, 219, 221, 233 (n 40, 41), 237 (n 1), 240 (n 48), 241 (n 51, 57), 248 (n 47), 261 (n 39)
B-24D, 45, 120, 144-145, 161, 168, 172-173, 176, 179-180, 182-187, 254 (n 147)
B-25, 15, 83, 134, 193, 222, 233 (n 40), 237 (n 1)
B-25D, 154
B-25G, 144
B-34, 193, 221-222, 237 (n 1)
Bangor, 6, 18
Bay of Biscay, 42, 47, 50-54, 74-75, 77, 91, 93-97, 105, 107-115, 125, 131, 165, 202-204, 245-246 (n 16), 248 (n 45, 52), 249 (n 64)
Beeks, Lt. Col. H. S., 145
Belem, 144
Bellinger, Adm. P. N. L., 39
Bermuda, 26, 202
Bloody Marsh, 134
Bluie West One, 154-155
BOLERO, 63, 147
Bombardment Branch, 82
Bombardment, Director of, 40, 66, 149
Bombs
  Mark XI, 161, 163, 178-179, 181-182
  Mark XVII, 166-170, 211
  Mark XXIX, 164, 166-167
  Mark 37, 176-177
  Mark 47, 172, 174-175
Bowles, Dr. Edward L., 36-37, 44, 65-67, 69, 88, 241 (n 56), 260 (n 23)
Bradley, Maj. Gen. Follett, 18, 23, 25-26
Brazil, 89, 145
British, 8, 15, 28, 52, 54, 61, 67, 77, 86, 88, 93-98, 100-103, 107-109, 119, 121, 128, 130, 139, 147-148, 153-154, 190, 195, 235 (n 68), 239 (n 23), 248 (n 47), 250 (n 89)
British Chiefs of Staff, 74
British Isles, 42, 86, 88. See also Great Britain.

Bureau of Aeronautics, 73
BW-1, 256 (n 182)

C

Canada, 54, 61, 147-148, 151, 153-154, 198, 239 (n 31), 255 (n 161)
Canadian Joint Staff, 148
Canary Islands, 164
Canning, W/C P.F., RAF, 24
Cape Finisterre, 114, 123, 180
Cape Hatteras, 3, 30, 236 (n 80)
Caribbean, 17, 35, 42, 44, 83, 88, 136-138, 140, 144, 166, 201-202, 208
Caribbean Defense Command, 139
Caribbean Sea Frontier, 32, 89, 138-140
  Commander, 140
Casablanca, 121-123
Catalina, 255 (n 165)
Charleston, S. C., 18
Chief of Staff, U. S. Army, 63 (n 81)
Chiefs of Staff (U. S. Army and U. S. Navy), 146-147
China, 193
Church St., 41
Churchill, Prime Minister, 148
Civil Air Patrol (CAP), 9, 20, 132, 198, 232 (n 24)
Coastal Air Force, 25-26
  Commanding General, 25
  Controller, 25
  Headquarters, 26
Coastal Command, RAF, 15, 17, 24-25, 28, 44, 47, 52, 62, 67, 80, 88, 95-97, 99-103, 106-107, 110, 117, 119-120, 128, 130, 147, 181, 208, 241 (n 56), 248 (n 45), 252 (n 111)
Coastal Frontier, 5
Coast Guard, 1, 3
Combined Chiefs of Staff, 61-63, 240 (n 51)
  Papers
    CCS 189, 240 (n 51)

CCS 189/2, 241 (n 51)
CCS 189/3, 241 (n 51)
CCS 189/6, 248 (n 49)
CCS 203, 61
Combined Staff Planners (CPS), 59, 239 (n 31), 240 (n 51), 248 (n 49)
    Papers
        CPS 49/D, 241 (n 51)
        CPS 56/3, 59
COMINCH, 3-4, 21, 31, 67, 69-71, 174, 242 (n 68), 255 (n 165). See also King.
Commanding General, AAF, 25, 37, 40, 70, 196, 206, 260 (n 23). See also Arnold.
Commanding General, AAFAC, 67, 204-205. See also Larson.
Committee on Missions of the Army and Navy, 81
Congress, 11, 232 (n 27)
Controller
    Army Air Forces, 102
    British, 102
    Coastal Air Force, 25
    Station, 103
Control Room, 119
Cuba, 35, 138, 200
Curacao, 140
Cyclops, 1

D

Dakar, 144
Darden, Lt. J. H., 176
DB-7B, 237 (n 1)
Detachment Headquarters, 154
Devonshire, 82, 110
DF equipment, 60
DO-24, 125, 192
DO-26, 125, 192
Doenitz, Admiral, 137, 146, 155
Dolan, Col. W. C., 260 (n 23)
Dudeck, Lt. E. J., 168-169
Dunkeswell, 82, 110, 128
Durston, Air Marshal, 62
Dutch Guiana, 139

E

8th Air Force, 49-50, 54, 83, 91, 98-99, 107, 110, 238 (n 17)
    Commanding General, 99
8th Antisubmarine Squadron, 138, 144-145, 254 (n 147)
VIII Bomber Command, 99-100, 247 (n 26)
18th Antisubmarine Squadron, 83, 134-135, 218
87th Service Squadron, 110
Eagle boat, 3
East and Gulf Coasts, 26, 30
Eastern Defense Command (EDC), 5, 20, 22, 26, 30, 40, 197
    Commanding General, 5
    Headquarters, 82
Eastern Sea Frontier (ESF), 3, 9, 17, 19-20, 26, 32, 34-35, 40-41, 87, 89, 94, 130-137, 139, 230 (n 4), 246 (n 16)
    Commander, 3-4, 19-20
Edinburgh Field, 141, 167
Eisenhower, Maj. Gen. Dwight D., 22-26, 30, 44
Elizabeth City, 4
England, 42, 44, 52, 58, 63, 94, 96-98, 101, 106, 108, 110, 150, 193, 241 (n 51), 251 (n 102)
English Channel, 86
European Theater (ETO), 52, 77, 102a, 107, 238 (n 17)
    Commanding General, 52
Europe, 52, 65, 86, 88, 102a, 146, 154
Expert Consultant to the Secretary of War, 36. See Bowles.

F

1st Air Force, 5, 18-20, 22, 82-83, 196, 233 (n 35)
    Commanding General, 23, 260 (n 23). See Bradley.
    Headquarters, 198
I Air Support Command, 5-6, 14, 19-20, 232 (n 24)

1st Antisubmarine Army Air Command, 38-39
1st Antisubmarine Group, 99, 103-104
1st Antisubmarine Squadron, 97, 99, 102, 106, 161, 165, 173-174, 184, 247 (n 26)
I Bomber Command, 5-7, 9, 14, 16, 18, 21, 23-26, 30, 32, 34-36, 38-39, 41, 82, 84, 189, 191, 198-199, 206, 211, 215, 225-227, 231 (n 13, 22)
   Commanding General, 23. See also Larson.
1st Naval District, 4
1st Sea-Search Attack Group, 36, 83, 261 (n 31)
4th Antisubmarine Squadron, 108, 111, 135, 138, 150, 180, 182, 202
4th Fleet, 145
   Commander, 145. See Ingram.
4th Naval District, 4
5th Naval District, 4
15th Antisubmarine Squadron, 138
40th Bombardment Squadron, 138
43d Bombardment Squadron, 231 (n 12)
417th Bombardment Squadron, 141
421st Bombardment Squadron, 147, 149
444th Quartermaster Platoon, 110
479th Antisubmarine Group, 82-83, 95, 108-112, 130, 150, 192, 228
480th Antisubmarine Group, 47, 82-83, 95, 105-107, 109-110, 115-117, 120-122, 125-128, 130, 191-192, 228, 247 (n 22), 250 (n 77), 252 (n 111)
516th Observation Squadron, 262 (n 46)
517th Observation Squadron, 262 (n 46)
518th Observation Squadron, 262 (n 46)
519th Observation Squadron, 262 (n 46)
520th Observation Squadron, 262 (n 46)
521st Observation Squadron, 262 (n 46)
522d Observation Squadron, 262 (n 46)
Fedala, 121
Fleet Air Wing 15, 117, 119, 123
Florida, 138
Focke-Wulf 200 (FW-200), 115, 125, 184-186, 191-192
France, 15, 52, 95
Frank, General, 18
Freetown, 89
French Coast, 49
Frocarro, Lt. C. J., 177

G

Galveston, Tex., 18
Gander Lake, 150, 255 (n 173)
Gerhart, Lt., 178
Gettysburg, 134
GHQ Air Force, 13-14
Gibraltar, 93, 109, 115, 117-119, 121-122, 128, 249 (n 64), 251 (n 91), 252 (n 11)
   AOC, 119
   Straits of, 114
"Gondola," 53, 98, 104, 107, 246 (n 18)
Governors Island, 199
Great Britain, 63, 147, 162, 239 (n 31)
Greenland, 52-53, 90, 146-147, 149, 153-155, 170, 208, 240 (n 48), 256 (n 182)
   Base Command, 154
   Patrol Force, 154
Guantanamo, 140, 246 (n 16)
Gulf and Caribbean areas, 17-18, 20, 39
Gulf of Mexico, 20, 30, 35, 44, 138
Gulf Sea Frontier (GSF) 18-20, 30, 32, 34-35, 40-41, 87, 89, 94, 130-131, 133-137, 139, 246 (n 16)
   Commander, 18, 20, 30
Gulf Task Force, 18

H

Haiti, 35
Hale, Maj. Gen. Willis H., 242 (n 70)
Halifax, 170
Halifax, Lord, 235 (n 68)
Hamilton, Lt. J. L., 182
Hammer, Lt. A. J., 180, 182
Hawaii, 45, 242 (n 70)
High Command, 55
HUSKY, 63, 147

I

Iceland, 90, 106, 146-147, 154, 240 (n 48), 256 (n 182)
India, 45, 193
Ingram, Vice Adm. Jonas H., 145
Ireland, 97
Isley, Lt. T. A., 173-174

J

Johnson, Lt. W. S., 165
Joint Action of the Army and Navy 1935 (FTP-155), 12, 14-16, 19, 232 (n 33)
Joint Army and Navy Basic War Plan, Rainbow #5, 232 (n 33)
Joint Chiefs of Staff, (JCS), 18-19, 44-45, 61, 64-65, 68-71, 74, 80-81, 145, 236 (n 87), 237 (n 6), 240 (n 51), 242 (n 68)
   Papers
      JCS 93, 237 (n 6, 7)
      JCS 93/1, 44, 237 (n 6)
      JCS 263/2/D, 69, 71
      JCS 268, 68-70
      JCS 268/1, 69, 71
Joint Command, 140
Joint Committee on New Weapons and Equipment (JCNW), 36, 47, 61
Joint Control and Information Center, 6
Joint Control Room, 198
Joubert, Air Marshal, 28
JU-88, 105-106, 111, 115, 125, 184, 192

K

Key West, 3
Kidd, Group Captain, 110
King, Admiral, 15-17, 30-32, 38-39, 53, 55, 58, 61-62, 64, 69-71, 73-75, 79, 82-83, 108, 131, 204, 236 (n 87). See also COMINCH.
Kuenning, Lt. T. E., 178

L

Lakehurst, 4
Langley Field, Va., 6, 18, 36, 82-83, 120, 134-135, 206, 218, 220, 260 (n 23)
Lardner, Mr., 249 (n 67)
Larson, Brig. Gen. Westside T., 23, 25, 40, 45, 47, 76, 84. See also CG AAFAC.
Larson, Capt. H. J., 170
LB-30, 148
Leahy, Adm., 74
Leigh searchlight, 96, 113
Liberator, 82, 115, 122, 147-148 180-182, 186. See also B-24.
Libles, W/C S. R., 24
Lisbon, 174, 179, 184
Lockheed Aircraft Corporation, 222
Long Island, 1
Loran equipment, 207
LR aircraft, 64, 70-71

M

McCain, Rear Adm., 77
McClelland, Brig. Gen. H. H., 238 (n 13)
McDonnell, Lt. W. S., 175
McNarney, Gen. 20, 30-31, 39, 64, 77
Magnetic airborne detector (MAD), 188, 210, 212, 214, 261 (n 31)
Maine, 3, 5-6
Marines, 73
Marshall, Gen., 31-32, 38-39, 44, 58, 64, 68-71, 73, 80-81, 86, 228, 242 (n 70), 243 (n 85, 91)
Materiel Command, 207
Maxwell, Capt., 184
Mediterranean, 45, 77, 92, 115, 128, 155, 158, 164, 193
Mexico, 198
Miami, 18, 41, 138, 141
Military Requirements, Director of, 40

"Minor Joint Air Exercise No. 1," 233 (n 35)
Mitchel Field, N. Y., 6
Mobile Training Units, 222
Montauk Point, 1
Moore, Col. Howard, 110, 150, 256 (n 182)
Moroccan Sea Frontier, 42, 109, 114-115, 117-118, 120-123, 125-126, 128, 131, 249 (n 64)
Morocco, 106, 129
Morse, Dr. P. M., 46-47, 238 (n 13)
Mozambique, 89
"Musketry," 109, 111, 248 (n 52)

N

9th Antisubmarine Squadron, 135, 141-142, 166
19th Antisubmarine Squadron, 108, 111, 150, 170, 202
19 Group, RAF, 103, 110
96th Bombardment Squadron, 231 (n 12)
Natal, 45, 144-145
National Defense Research Council, 206-207, 222
Naval Operating Base, 141
Navy, 1-85 et passim
    Commander in Chief, 61
Navy Department, 69-71, 82
Navy Task Force 24, 149
Nazi, 86, 148, 185
Newfoundland, 1, 42, 52-53, 63, 75, 90, 108, 131, 146-148, 151, 153-155, 170, 200-204, 240 (n 48), 246 (n 16), 255 (n 165, 173)
Newfoundland Base Command, 149
New Jersey, 1
New York City, 2, 18, 41, 141, 150, 198
NK 538, 134
Noble, Admiral, 55,
Norness, 1-2
North Atlantic Naval Coastal Frontier, 2, 14
    Commander, 3-4
North Carolina, 5

North Sea, 86
Norway, 97-108
Northwest African Coastal Air Force, 117
Nova Scotia, 1, 246 (n 16), 255 (n 173)

O

O-46, 262 (n 46)
O-47, 193, 262 (n 46)
O-52, 193, 262 (n 46)
1177th Military Police Company, 110
1813th Ordnance Service and Maintenance Company, 110
ONS-5, 90, 152-153, 155, 170
Operational Planning, AAFAC, 218
Operational Training Unit (OTU), 83, 120, 134-136, 217-220, 222-223
Operations, Commitments and Requirements, AC/AS, 82, 196
Operations Division, WDGS, 22, 40, 66
Operations Section, AAFAC, 217-218
Overing, Maj. Glendon P., 141

P

Pan Am, 134
Panama [Sea Frontier], 32
PBY, 121-124, 133, 168
PBY-5A, 154
Pearl Harbor, 1-2, 4, 232 (n 24)
PG boat, 3
Plans, AAFAC, 217-218
Portland, 5
Portland Channel, 1
Port Lyautey, 63, 106, 115, 117, 119, 122-123, 128, 172, 191, 200, 252 (n 111)
Port of Spain, 141
Portugal, 114-115, 127
Provost Marshal, 121
Puerto Rico, 35, 87, 140

PV-1, 154
PY boat, 3

R

Radar
  Mark II, 153
  Mark III, 96
  SCR 517, 122, 124, 187
  SCR 517C, 94, 102a
  SCR 717A, 209
Radio Direction Finder (RDF), 117
Radio sonic buoy, 188, 210-211
RAF, 15, 52, 64, 91, 111, 147, 154, 194, 255 (n 161). See also Coastal Command.
RCAF, 64, 150-151, 240 (n 39), 255 (n 173)
Recife, 145
Research Coordinator, 206-208, 212-214
Research Section, 219
Roberts, Lt. Col. Jack, 99, 117-120, 239 (n 35), 247 (n 26)
Roosevelt, President, 63, 66, 80, 146-147, 240 (n 48)
Royal Canadian Navy (RCN), 150-151, 240 (n 39)
Royal Navy, 88, 240 (n 39)
Russell, Brig. Gen. C. W., 48-49
Russia, 35, 45

S

2d Air Force, 83
2d Antisubmarine Squadron, 97, 99, 102, 104, 106, 128, 162, 172, 176, 178
2d Prov. Bombardment Flights, 154
6th Air Force, 139
6th Antisubmarine Squadron, 135, 150, 168, 202
7th Antisubmarine Squadron, 142
17th Antisubmarine Squadron, 138
St. Eval, 99-100, 103, 106, 110
  Station Commander, 103
St. John's, 150-151
St. Nazaire, 162, 182

Salem, 4
Salm, Lt. E., 179-180
Sanford, 1st Lt., W. L., 162-164, 172
San Juan, 246 (n 16)
Sao Salvador, 144
SC boat, 3
Schmidt, Lt. R. C., 182
Scotland, 97
Sea-Search Attack Development Unit, (SADU), 36, 205-206, 213, 260 (n 23)
"Seaslug," 109, 248 (n 52)
Secretary of the Navy, 67
Secretary of War, 65, 67, 232 (n 27). See also Stimson.
Services of Supply, 100
Sicilian campaign, 92, 128
Slessor, Air Vice Marshal, 98, 110, 238 (n 17)
Somervell, Lt. Gen. B. H., 238 (n 17)
South America, 122
South Atlantic Force, 145
  Commander, 145
South Carolina, 18
Southern Defense Command (SDC) 20, 40
Spain, 113-114
Stimson, Secretary, 44, 65-66, 79-80, 84
Strafford, Air Comdr., 241 (n 51), 248 (n 49)
Stratemeyer, Gen., 49, 80, 243 (n 91)
Supply and Logistics, 197
Sweeney, F/O, 181

T

3d Air Force, 18, 20, 196
3d Naval District, 4
10th Bombardment Squadron, 141
10th Fleet, 69-72, 76, 242 (n 68)
  Commander, 70, 242 (n 65)
12th Air Force, 97
20th Antisubmarine Squadron, 148-150, 153
20th Bombardment Squadron,

23d Antisubmarine Squadron, 83, 138, 144
25th Antisubmarine Squadron, 134
25th Antisubmarine Wing, 41, 83, 99, 150, 198-199, 202
25th Bombardment Group, 141
26th Antisubmarine Wing, 41, 83, 138-139, 198-199, 221
  Headquarters, 138, 140
30th Antisubmarine Communications Squadron, 199-200
2037th Antisubmarine Wing, 246 (n 22), 250 (n 77)
"Tactical" antisubmarine air force, 76
Technical Training Command, 221
Technical Services, Director of, 206-207, 214, 260 (n 23)
Texas, 200
Thorne, Capt. W. E., 161
Tidewater Tillie, 162, 164
Torbay, 255 (n 173)
TORCH, 52, 106, 246 (n 17)
Torpex, 103, 161, 163, 178-179, 181-182
Training, AAFAC, 217-218
  Asst. Chief of Air Staff, 217
Trinidad, 35, 43, 131, 136, 138-141, 166
  Area Air Service Command, 140
  Detachment, 140
  Sector, 140, 246 (n 16)

U

United Kingdom, 45, 62, 75, 82-83, 93, 97, 99, 102-106, 108-110, 115, 128, 150-151
United Nations, 59

U. S. Atlantic Fleet, 145, 245 (n 11)
  Air Antisubmarine Development Detachment, 206
  Commander in Chief, 145
U. S. Fleet, 12-14, 70, 76
  Commander in Chief, 57, 63, 145
  Deputy Chief of Staff, 39

V

VLR aircraft, 52, 54-55, 63-64, 68-72, 75, 80, 94, 107-108, 120, 144-145, 147, 149, 193-194, 209, 239 (n 29, 31), 241 (n 51), 248 (n 49)
VP-73, 122
VP-92, 122

W

War Department, 16, 22, 39, 44, 64, 68-69, 75, 77, 82, 203, 236 (n 87)
  General Staff, 22-23, 30, 40, 66
Washington, D. C., 25, 140
Wellington, English, 113
Western Electric, 223
Westover Field, Mass., 6, 18, 202
White House, 80
Williamson, Colonel, 60
Wilmington, 5

Z

Zanderij Field, 139

www.ingramcontent.com/pod-product-compliance
Lightning Source LLC
Chambersburg PA
CBHW082029300426
44117CB00015B/2413